ƒP

The Free Press
New York London Toronto Sydney

Praise for *The City In Mind*

"Kunstler is providing an invaluable service to American culture. Kunstler has given thousands of ordinary Americans a vocabulary for articulating what they love and loathe about their surroundings. Kunstler's literary territory is dazzling, multifarious, frequently infuriating—and quite often exhilarating."

—*The Atlanta Journal-Constitution*

"A connoisseur's romp through cities good and bad . . . Armed with a wicked sense of style and absolute confidence in his worldview, Kunstler adds this collection of short, interlinked essays to his growing series on what makes or breaks an urban space. His critical eye is sharp because he shares with his subjects the will to create an ideal city, where transportation flows easily and people of different classes mingle congenially. That enthusiasm, along with a uniquely acerbic tone, shines through in these pages. A salutary treatise for architects, mayors, and laypeople."

—*Kirkus Reviews*

"Kunstler probes the malignancy with a pathologist's precision and a comedian's irony. And in scathing prose he makes a strong case that the 'drive-in utopias' Americans built over the last eighty years can't work."

—Joseph Dolman, *The New Leader*

Praise for *The Geography of Nowhere*

"A wonderfully entertaining, useful, and provocative account of the ravaging of the American environment by the auto, suburban developers, purblind zoning, and corporate pirates."

—*The Boston Globe*

"Provocative and entertaining. . . . Just how the American landscape got to be this way and what can be done about it are the subjects that Mr. Kunstler tackles with considerable energy and wit in *The Geography of Nowhere*."

—John O. Norquist, Mayor of Milwaukee, in *The Milwaukee Journal*

Praise for *Home From Nowhere*

"Boring is not an issue in *Home from Nowhere,* a deliciously wicked, over-the-top nonfiction romp across the tortured terrain of suburban America."

—*The Philadelphia Inquirer*

"Anyone who feels a sense of being worn down by the ugliness of the American landscape, with its forest of plastic signs for Midas and McDonald's, will be interested in the ideas in this book."

—*The Boston Globe*

"What distinguishes Kunstler's work and what attracts a growing readership is an imaginative, blustery, energetic writing style. No one is writing more clearly and ardently about living in America's human habitats."

—*Detroit Free Press*

This book is for Andres Duany, the restless warrior.

ƒP

THE FREE PRESS
A division of Simon & Schuster, Inc.
1230 Avenue of the Americas
New York, NY 10020

First Free Press trade paperback edition 2003

The Free Press and colophon are trademarks
of Simon & Schuster, Inc.

For information about special discounts for bulk purchases,
please contact Simon & Schuster Special Sales:
1-800-456-6798 or business@simonandschuster.com

Designed by Jeanette Olender
Manufactured in the United States of America

5   7   9   10   8   6   4

Library of Congress Cataloging-in-Publication Data

Kunstler, James Howard.
The city in mind : meditations on the urban condition / James Howard Kunstler.
p.   cm.
Includes bibliographical references (p.   ).
1. Sociology, Urban.   2. Cities and towns—Case studies.
3. Cities and towns—History.   I. Title
HT119 .K86   2002
307.76—dc21
2001040897

ISBN-13: 978-0-684-84591-3
ISBN-10:   0-684-84591-1
ISBN-13: 978-0-7432-2723-0 (Pbk)
ISBN-10:   0-7432-2723-9 (Pbk)

THE CITY

IN MIND

Meditations on the Urban Condition

JAMES HOWARD KUNSTLER

Contents

The second law of thermodynamics tells us that in the real world, disorder always increases. Yet simple observation tells us that, in the real world, life creates order everywhere: the universe is winding up, not down.

KEN WILBER

Preface

This book doesn't pretend to be the last word on cities. There are plenty of good books on the subject, which is as broad as civilization itself. But I wrote this one at a time when my own culture could not be more confused about the nature and meaning of cities and city life. My modest aim here is to redirect what has amounted in recent times to a pretty incoherent national discussion about how we live, to survey how history regards urban living arrangements in some very different periods and settings, and to discern what kinds of choices and predicaments the future may present to us.

America at the turn of the millennium is suffering the woeful consequences, largely unanticipated, of trying to become a drive-in utopia. The attempt took roughly eighty years, from the end of the First World War to the brink of global warming, oil depletion, and other epochal disorders hard upon us. This nation's massive suburban build-out was an orgy of misspent energy and material resources that squandered our national wealth and left us with an infrastructure of daily life that, left as is, has poor prospects in the new century. It is also hard to overstate the cultural destruction that was one of it chief side effects, especially the loss of knowledge, tradition, skill, custom, and vernacular wisdom in the art of city-making that was thrown into the dumpster of history in our effort to fulfill General Motors' *World of Tomorrow.*

The idea that city-making is an art rather than a product of statistical analysis or social service casework is largely the point of my opening chapter on Georges Eugène Haussmann's heroic renovation of Paris in the mid-1800s. Under the emperor Louis-Napoleon (an improved version of the original Bonaparte, his uncle), Haussmann made over Paris from a stinking and decrepitating rat-maze of slums into the epitome of everything we value about city life.

In the second chapter, about Atlanta, I try to demonstrate the folly of Edge City (so-called) as both a design model and a way of living. Edge City, a term coined by the writer Joel Garreau, was supposed to represent everything cutting-edge and ultramodern in the postindustrial evolution of cities. I essay to show how Atlanta took the urban model of car-crazy Los Angeles to its most ludicrous and, in my view, terminal stage. With Atlanta, you can forgo agonizing over the future, because the present doesn't even work there.

The third chapter takes us back roughly five hundred years to a unique event in history: the collision of two very strange but well-developed and dominant cultures so vastly different that they might have come from two separate planets. In 1519, a tiny Spanish expeditionary force under a brilliant rogue commander, Hernán Cortés, made contact with the death-enthralled empire of the Aztecs and conquered their gigantic, beautiful, sinister capital city, Tenochtitlán. The spirit of the Spanish Inquisition meets its match in Huitzilopochtli, voracious eater of still-beating Aztec hearts. I attempt to show how this astonishing chain of incidents resonates still in the culture of contemporary Mexico City, a prototype of hypertrophic "third-world" urbanism, plagued by a failed social contract, lawlessness, economic disorder, and a wrecked ecology.

Next I reflect upon the strange destiny of Berlin, a city whipsawed by the tragic enormities of twentieth-century politics. Above all, Berlin expresses the paradoxes of history: how Europe's best-educated people could succumb to political mania, moral suicide, and mass murder; how an urban organism can survive nearly total destruction and find itself fifty years later in better condition than the cities of its chief destroyer; how the politics of freedom and openness produced an architecture of despotism, and vice versa. And how the result of all these vicissitudes is a search for nothing grander than *normality*.

We turn next to Las Vegas, America's leading boom town at the turn of the millennium, a city built by gangsters for gangsters, based on the tragically foolish idea that it is possible to get something for nothing, and now weirdly mutating into a *family vacation destination*. I discuss the strange physical form of the city, an evolution of the most extreme cultural and technological developments in the past century, and argue that Las Vegas has reached the limits of its hypertrophic growth. Las Vegas may also reflect a condition more and more common throughout America as a whole: that ridicule is the unfortunate destiny of the ridiculous, trumping even the tragic view of history.

Rome is the backdrop for tracing the meaning of classicism as a set of ideas necessary for the continuing project of civilization. This chapter takes a long historical view, tracing the sources of the classical in Greece and Italy, its full flowering in the Roman Empire, the long and gruesome unlearning in the millennium following the fall of Rome, and the rescue of classicism in the Renaissance. Classicism was thrown away once again by the forces of modernism during the nervous breakdown of culture that the twentieth century represented, so the question is posed, can classicism now rescue us?

I chose to write about Boston because I think it has done more to prepare for the twenty-first century than most other American cities, and indeed it may be one of the few habitable cities left in America when the orgy of cheap oil draws to a close and it becomes necessary to conduct normal life and work in walkable neighborhoods connected by decent public transit. Boston had a hard time of it in the twentieth century, and the political legacy of that period still exerts a baneful influence. But the city is in the process of overcoming those other common disasters of the recent urban scene in this country: the tyranny of the automobile and the flight of the prospering classes. In the years ahead, I argue, Boston will demonstrate the value of city life to a culture that all but gave up on the idea.

Finally, I look to London as the origin in Anglo-American culture for the idea that country life is the antidote to the hopelessness of industrial urbanism. This idea, which has reached its fullest expression in contemporary America, begins with the English Landscape movement, and leads directly to the circumstance of London becoming the world's first great industrial city—and therefore the first major world city to suffer the unanticipated consequences of advanced technological progress. In America, where we have inherited so many English ideas about landscape and place, the result in our time has been the notion that city life can be dispensed with altogether for a simulacrum of the rural. The idea culminates in the absurdities of our contemporary battles over "green space" and "open space," while our human ecologies—namely our towns and cities—remain devalued, depopulated, and decivilized.

★ ★ ★

Under the most favorable circumstances, it is apt to take at least a hundred years to clean up the mess we made of our nation, if we can do it at all—and I stick to a point made in my previous book, *Home from Nowhere,* that life is tragic and there are no guaranteed rescues from the great blunders of history.

Don't get me wrong. I hope we do recover. I believe we have the knowledge and the resources to reorganize the physical arrangement of American life from a national automobile slum to a land full of places that are truly worth living in. Therefore, I stick to another central point of my previous book: that a land made up of places not worth caring about will sooner or later become a nation not worth defending (or a way of life not worth carrying on). All this begs the question of whether we have the will to reorganize our everyday environment. Personally, I believe the future will compel us to change our way of life, to give up the fiasco of suburbia and all its revolting accessories and recondense our living and working places into the traditional human habitats called cities, towns, and neighborhoods.

In the past eight years I traveled all over the United States (except Alaska) and got to see almost every city of any consequence in the lower forty-eight states. It was a shock to discover how far gone most of them are. Since I wrote about Detroit in *The Geography of Nowhere* (1993), wildflower meadows have sprouted where miles of slum row houses stood—and I don't mean to say that this is necessarily an improvement, because it only means the hole at the center of Detroit's metropolitan doughnut has gotten larger and emptier instead of redeveloping. St.

Louis is a virtual mummy's tomb between its empty downtown and the West End. Baltimore has become a flyblown carcass. Buffalo looks as if it suffered a prolonged aerial bombardment. A giant vacuum cleaner seems to have sucked the populations out of Memphis, Nashville, and Little Rock. Small towns in the Midwest are perhaps the most heartbreaking to see. I remember a spring afternoon I spent as the sole pedestrian in downtown Appleton, Wisconsin—its commercial activity had all been shifted to an asteroid belt of highway strips and architectural garbage five miles outside town. Ditto Louisville; Dayton; Meridian, Mississippi; Billings, Montana; Macon, Georgia. And so on. The list is long and dreary, and it certainly prompts the casual observer to wonder if our future holds a civilized existence.

The concern about what happens to my own country underlies all the chapters in this book. Will it take an autocrat to repair American cities, as in the case of Napoleon III and Paris? How do culture and history support the social contract? Now that we've created our national automobile slum, what are its possible destinies? Can we find a way to reestablish a meaningful distinction between the urban and the rural? Can we make Beauty (capital B) matter again in our everyday world?

The chief byproduct of all this, for me, and as usual, has been the project of creating a book that will be compelling to read. Most of all, I believe readers want to commune with an intelligence congenial to their own, and if they learn a thing or two, or gain an insight, so much the better. So, apart from the momentous themes presented here, I wish you a ripping good read and even a few laughs as you consider these meditations on the urban condition.

PARIS

The Achievements of Napoleon III and
Georges Eugène Haussmann

There seems to be something about Paris that arouses in foreigners sentiments of regret.

RICHARD SENNETT

It's hard to know for sure that the elusive Mr. Sennett meant it quite this way, but for me being in Paris invokes a powerful sense of regret that my own culture is so hopelessly lame and clueless, in the civic arts especially, as to fail to create anything nearly as spiritually rewarding as the city of Paris in the way of an urban ecology. Rich and spectacular as it is in some ways, even Manhattan, by comparison, is a physically sordid agglomeration of endlessly repeated submediocre typologies and overblown engineering stunts with little history and a dubious future.

Nobody visits Paris because of its geography. Its site is unremarkable. A lot of it is dead flat. The Seine is an unimpressive river. Its best feature is the lovely granite embankment that was not made by nature. The weather isn't even that good. The city is valued because of the excellence of its man-made artifacts, and for the superb interrelation of the buildings and public realm. It was far from always so. At the beginning of the period that concerns us, Paris was the most notoriously vile big city in Europe: dark, unsanitary, foul-smelling, dilapidated, disease-ridden, and impossible to get around in.

For all that, amazing continuities have existed in Paris without which its transformation into modernity would not have been so brilliant. For example, the consensus that supported a severe and rigorous architectural classicism changed hardly at all from the days of Louis XIV through the turmoil of the Revolution and then the era of Napoleon Bonaparte. Social and economic relations were smashed and reconstructed, but the classically proportioned building façade remained as normal as the oxygen content of the air.

It is now roughly one hundred and fifty years since the great modernization took place. The Paris we see today is the brilliance of that transformation shining through a patina of age, of having been brilliant now for a rather long time, a beautifully preserved relic of innovation. What was once breathtakingly state-of-the-art in civic improvement now seems quaint. But the details remain powerful and powerfully instructive. The great ordering systems of the street walls, the balconies, the mansard roofs, the ubiquitous white limestone façades of the buildings, the precision of the tree plantings, all induce a tremendous sense of satisfaction that you are finally in a human habitat that completely makes sense— especially coming from chaotic America where everything is provisional, and most of *that* is worse than mediocre, from our lousy urbanism to the plywood butterflies screwed over a neighbor's garage door down the street. Nobody goes to Paris and complains about an excess of coherence, unity, and excellence. In Paris, even the handwriting on every grocer's chalkboard displays an astounding unanimity of gracefulness. A meditation on Paris must take into account the remarkable devotion to standards of excellence from the grand to the small scale and especially its persistence over time, a quality of culture that resolves the comfortable certainty of *what was* and the anxious uncertainty about *what will be* into a hopeful present.

Much of the physical Paris that is so beloved today derives from the efforts of two remarkable men: Louis-Napoleon Bonaparte (aka the emperor Napoleon III, 1852–71) and Georges Eugène Haussmann, his administrative chief of Paris (official title: prefect of the Department of the Seine). Both men were able and intelligent leaders of complementary temperaments. Ironically, Haussmann was the authoritarian and the emperor far more respectful of others people's views and sensibilities. Haussmann was vain, imperious, at times a bully. The emperor displayed little egotism and regarded his position as a simple matter of fate. Haussmann had no patience for procedural rigmarole, unless he was employing it as a weapon against his many enemies. The emperor had to function within a social framework of other rich and powerful figures, many of whom owed their wealth and power to modern industry, not to the favor of the emperor—bankers, merchants, manufacturers—and he learned to work with them in his empire-building. Of the two men, Louis-Napoleon was clearly a nicer person. But in the task at hand, they required each other. They had this in common: They understood the enormous needs of the city as it struggled to enter the modern, industrial age, and set about briskly with dispatch and competence to take care of those needs. They practically turned Paris inside-out and upside-down in the process but managed to keep the vastly improved civic organism recognizably Paris. The celebrated City of Light is mostly their doing.

The New Napoleon

France had emerged from the consecutive traumas of the Revolution and the romantic military melodrama of Napoleonism in fragile condition, like a fever patient who has gone through several near-death experiences. After Waterloo, the nation had developed an aversion to strong governments, but as a result it suffered through decades of weak, irresolute regimes: Charles X, a Bourbon restored within the framework of a very limiting constitutional monarchy, then Louis-Philippe's "July Monarchy," not much of an improvement.[1] Through those years the city of Paris endured eight major street insurrections.

Yet Waterloo also marked the beginning of an extraordinary period of relative peace between nations in Europe. Canals, steam power, and innovations in farming began to change life dramatically. The population of Paris doubled from a half million to over a million between 1800 and 1850. Many of the newcomers were deracinated country people caught up in the great convulsion of industrialism that was sweeping away traditional ways of life. The luckier ones found work as artisans, skilled craftspeople who made everything from candles to coffins. Most, though, came to Paris as unskilled laborers. The life of this growing urban working class was ordered by the merciless demands of burgeoning industry, and grievance was more or less its perpetual mood.

Industrialism was a social and economic experiment the world had never seen before, and its consequences often came as a shock to the elite classes who benefited most from it. The idea that technological progress might produce widespread misery was also a new, rather shocking thing, not exactly consistent with earlier notions left over from the Enlightenment about the inevitable perfectibility of mankind and the assumed upward arc of progress toward universal happiness. It took the educated classes a while to get the picture, and even then not all of them were sympathetic. Explosive forces underlay these novelties of modern social relations and technology.

But the middle class and economic elites of France were also tired of continual civil disorder and disruption. The revolts of 1848 were the last straw for them—the feckless king Louis-Philippe skulking out of the mob-besieged Tuileries in the February chill disguised in a shabby old coat with his whiskers shaved off, and then months of street fighting between the larval communists and yet another generation of hopeful republicans. (The communists were all shot by the end of summer.) This was the opportunity seized by Louis-Napoleon Bonaparte, nephew of the first emperor.[2]

Unlike many pretenders to lost thrones, Louis-Napoleon was neither a rascal nor an imbecile. He was well-educated, possessed a lively, free-ranging intellect, paid attention to the great innovations of his times, and showed a genuine empathy for those afflicted by the social hardships posed by modernity. Some of his personal ideas, expressed in his own writings before assuming power, were considered socialist. He believed that the state had definite and enlarged responsibilities under industrial modernity to support the public welfare, especially in the physical setting of the city.

Louis-Napoleon had been prepared by his mother and the still-considerable coterie of original Bonapartists for the eventuality of power. His mother settled the family in Switzerland, and Louis was partly schooled in Germany. He showed a dogged determination to achieve power, minus the usual megalomania that accompanies the will-to-power, making two youthful attempts to enter France and present himself as a Bonapartist alternative to Louis-Philippe (1836 and 1840), both fiascoes. The second attempt, at Strasbourg, landed in him in custody of Louis-Philippe for six years. Incarcerated on a fortress on the Somme, he escaped in 1846 to England, always his refuge of choice as an adult.

In 1848, with social unrest sweeping Europe, the July Monarchy overthrown, and Paris convulsed by yet another worker insurrection, Louis-Napoleon came to Paris and secured a seat in the new National Assembly. That was September, as the "notables" of politics attempted to stitch together a Second Republic. Events moved rapidly. In December, a Party of Order put forward Louis-Napoleon as a presidential candidate and, to the great consternation of French Republicans, he won 75 percent of the popular vote over a half dozen rivals.

He was eager to get on with an ambitious agenda of public works, especially as a means to employ the poor. Having spent much time in London, which had gone through the civic improvements of the Regency a generation earlier, Louis-Napoleon was keenly aware of the backwardness of Paris. For three years the prince-president, as they called him, was frustrated by a quarrelsome legislative assembly that could not find the will to act on anything he wanted to do, and he was stuck for four years with the politically dexterous, popular, but hopelessly frugal Jean-Jacques Berger as his prefect of the Seine. Where public works were concerned, the two were locked in a standoff: Louis-Napoleon refused to raise taxes and Berger refused to borrow funds. To complicate matters, the Second Republic had been set up in such a way that the president was limited to a single term. Through 1851, Louis-Napoleon's partisans worked feverishly to keep him in office by enacting a legal repeal of the provision. When the effort failed, the prince-president moved to seize power in a coup d'etat. He chose the anniversary of his uncle's great victory at Austerlitz: December 2. It was a shock to the nation.

Resistance was swiftly repressed. Louis-Napoleon dissolved the National Assembly. In the aftermath, thousands of opponents were arrested, and over nine thousand were deported to Algeria, but there were no executions. Many of those arrested were simply let go. Within a few weeks of the coup, days before Christmas 1851, Louis-Napoleon staged a national referendum on his coup. The result was even more overwhelmingly in his favor than the margin of his presidential victory had been three years earlier. For another year he operated in the limbo of a suspended Republic, still called president but wielding extraordinary powers. On December 2, 1852, he declared the Second Empire.

Throughout Louis-Napoleon's presidency, Haussmann had been of service to the Bonapartist cause. He'd filled the role of prefect in two minor provincial departments, Var, in Provence, and Yonne, a hundred miles southeast of Paris, showing a steely willingness to repress republicanism, which he interchangeably labeled as *"rouge."* To Haussmann, all opponents of centralized power were communist rabble. The day after the coup, Haussmann was appointed prefect of Bordeaux, the Department of the Gironde, a big step up, where he was expected to enforce the regime's consolidation of power. A national consensus soon emerged. Given a choice between Republican demagogues—always associated with horrible memories of the guillotine a half century earlier—or of discredited Orleanists, or of a vigorous new Bonaparte, the country settled for Louis-Napoleon and the prospect of order and stability. Haussmann continued to impress his patron, especially with the pageantry he staged for Louis-Napoleon's visit to Bordeaux in October 1852. It was not until well after the emperor had consolidated his power, in June 1853, that the do-nothing prefect of Paris, Berger, was finally booted out and Haussmann, hardly known in Parisian political circles, was picked to replace him.

Louis-Napoleon and Haussmann were made for each other, the ambitious, sphinxlike emperor and the voluble prefect whose favorite subject was his own accomplishments. Both were good at taking charge in a culture that was ready for action after a long vacuum of leadership. Both possessed different kinds of innate authority. Both could command attention and marshal great resources toward focused, precise ends. Both hungered for real civic achievement. Louis-Napoleon was famously self-possessed, renowned for not wasting words, utterly confident in his sense of purpose. Haussmann was equally confident, physically large and imposing, with determination like one of the new steam locomotives that was to become such a common feature of modern life. He would not be stopped. Describing his own political philosophy in his memoirs, it was characteristic of Haussmann to say without a hint of irony, "The only practical form of democracy is the empire."

Louis-Napoleon was certainly a different Napoleon than the original, his uncle, and perhaps a better one. He was the opposite of impetuous and had little interest in militarism for the sake of glory. But he had a Bonaparte's craving for decisive action as well as a very firm administrative sense of what was necessary to achieve his goals. His goals were the practical improvement of the French people's lives rather than the conquest of Europe.

Out of Darkness

The city that Louis-Napoleon took over as emperor was a rat-maze of poorly connected, narrow, disorienting streets, medieval in character, with a centuries-long accretion of tightly packed buildings falling into decrepitude. It was the miraculous disadvantage of Paris to have escaped a great fire, like the one that cleaned out central London in 1666. The ancient buildings of Paris's east end, the Marais, including the great mansions (*hôtels particulier*) of the old nobility, had been subdivided into working-class tenements at appalling densities, said to exceed the later slums of lower Manhattan. Neither sunlight nor fresh air could penetrate the miserable dwellings. Disease flourished to the extent that recorded deaths far outnumbered baptisms (compensated only by rural immigration). The interior courtyards of the old hotels increasingly filled up with artisans' workshops, shops, and shanties. The degradation of property led to a consistent loss of real estate value in the oldest parts of the city, even while rents rose astronomically.

The slums continued to grow vertically as workers poured in from the hinterlands and extra stories were added to ancient two- and three-story structures. The lower, middle, and professional classes remained mixed in the increasingly squalid old neighborhoods. The bourgeois professionals inhabited the lower floors while the less affluent lived upstairs, higher up in inverse proportion to their income. In effect, the old urban fabric of Paris, including many architecturally distinguished old buildings, was being strip-mined for rents—the future being sold off for the sake of present profit.

It is said that the stench of Paris could be detected from ten miles out of town. Chamber pots were dumped into collection vats in the basements, which were emptied only periodically, or else poured into the streets. Even privies were uncommon because so many Parisian buildings did not have rear yards. Olsen writes, "Paris lacked the luxury even of defective sewers."[3] That is perhaps hyperbole, but the sewers were utterly inadequate and in many cases completely plugged. Buildings were not equipped with running water (another contrast with London, where the houses of the expanding middle classes, at least, received water up to the third story off a system of mains). In all of Paris there were a handful of fountains operated by steam-driven pumps at the Seine, which was also the city's chief sewer. Drinking water was distributed laboriously around town by water carriers, who charged a lot for small quantities, and the water was mostly contaminated. Garbage was not collected but rather tossed into the streets at night. Adding to these difficulties was a substantial horse population. The old cemeteries in the heart of the city remained in use—and they were busy places. Fierce cholera epidemics struck the city in 1832 and again in 1849, killing twenty thousand and then nineteen thousand, respectively. The disease killed people of all classes, but the densest slums with the worst sanitation problems suffered the highest death rates—the congested quarters on the Île de la Cité and the tenements of the Grève around the Hôtel de Ville (city hall). The cause of cholera, the bacillus *Vibrio comma,* and its communication through water polluted by human waste, was unknown at the time. The later modernist schemes of Le Corbusier and his disciples for clearing cities wholesale and replacing them with "towers in a park" were all a legacy of the traumatic urban "congestions" of the nineteenth century.[4]

It was extremely difficult and even dangerous to get around the city. Many streets were not paved. On the Place de la Concorde—former home of the guillotine ("the national razor") during the Reign of Terror—the paving blocks had been dug out for use as missiles in the long sequence of urban uprisings by the growing impoverished proletariat, and in winter it became a vast mud wallow. The narrowness of the streets made freight transport a nightmare for carters and pedestrians alike. Sidewalks didn't exist. Many streets ended in blind alleys. The conduct of ordinary business became increasingly impossible. Some supposedly principal arteries leading into the heart of town, such as the Rue St-Denis, actually got narrower as they reached the city center. The entire system was a claustrophobic labyrinth. The only practical east-west crossing was along the crowded banks of the Seine—the masonry revetments did not yet exist. The meager supply of public open spaces made orientation very difficult, affording few vistas beyond the end of a block. Great public monuments were crammed into the dark immensity of unrelieved slum fabric. The walls of the old Louvre and the adjacent Tuileries Palace were hemmed in by a mass of awful slums. On the Île de la Cité, the medieval heart of Paris, the cathedral of Notre Dame poked up among a rotten clutter of ancient houses on dark, tortured streets.

The population of the outskirts multiplied as rapidly as the city itself, aggravating matters. In the 1840s, Louis-Philippe squandered his very limited funds on an ill-conceived refortification scheme. Rather than improve security, it eventually helped to bring down the July Monarchy. There hadn't been a barrier around the town since the customs gates were torn down during the Revolution.[5] The new fortifications, placed well beyond the then-built-up quarters, were supposed to remain unencroached upon, but despite a ban on construction, a new ring of instant shantytowns or *banlieue* sprouted in the wall's shadow for those new arrivals who could not afford the higher slum rents of the central city. The denizens of these new slums, the *banlieusards,* became some of the most enthusiastic street fighters during the uprising of 1848, and were of great aid in provisioning barricaded parts of the city. In the future, after Louis-Napoleon and Haussmann, these *banlieue* would come to occupy the open land outside the walls, too—a persistent and notorious ring of shacks called simply the Zone that would not be cleared entirely until the 1950s.

Altogether, the city of Paris found itself in an urban crisis when Louis-Napoleon assumed imperial power. It was a political tinderbox, a continuing public health catastrophe, an unfit place for business, an increasingly dubious seat of a modern civilization.

Previous Efforts

Of course, the city had never endured such a massive population explosion before the onset of industrialism, and any discussion of previous efforts must be seen in this light. Until the Revolution, civic improvement projects had taken two forms: first, a few monumental open spaces within the existing city, conceived as real estate development ventures, and second, experiments in the building of monumental streets not necessarily linked to current real estate development.

Of the first type, an early example was Henry IV's Place Royale (now the Place des Vosges), in the Marais, built 1607 to 1612, adjacent to a failed royal silkworks. A speculative enterprise, it incorporated a residence for the king and mansions for sale to court members and aristocratic climbers, all unified behind a common façade. The ten-thousand-square-foot interior plaza, one of the most beautiful, intimate urban "outdoor rooms" in Europe, was used for royal ceremonies and could only be entered by formal portals through the buildings. The ordinary public had no access to it, and it functioned as an aristocratic world apart from the growing canker of regular Paris.

The Place Dauphine on the western tip of the Île de la Cité, at the juncture of the Pont Neuf, was built around the same time, an ensemble of thirty-two uniform multiuse buildings with façades in the manner of Serlio enclosing a small triangular interior plaza, with public access through it.[6] The fashionable project included, shops, restaurants, and lodgings to let for visiting officials and diplomats who needed to be near the royal administrative center and law courts. For all this, the Place Dauphine backed up against some of Paris's worst slums in the Île de le Cité. An ambitious proposal for a Place de France near the present day Place de la République, modeled on Rome's Piazza del' Popolo, came to grief when Henry IV died in 1610. It was to have been composed of what today we call live-work units for artisans. Of the scheme, only the radial streets Rue Charlot and Rue de Turenne were ever built.

Louis XIII accomplished little. His successor, Louis XIV, though preoccupied through his long reign (1643–1715) with developing the astounding counter-city of Versailles (as an antidote to the increasingly noxious capital), still paid attention to Paris as the economic engine of the state. The most significant development project undertaken in his name was the Place Vendôme. Started by the architect-developer Jules Hardouin Mansart in 1686 as a for-profit townhouse scheme, the project got into trouble, and Louis was importuned to rescue it by putting the royal mint and other offices along the site. At first, Mansart had erected only the building façades as a sales gimmick to entice buyers. When the scheme failed, they were torn down and the plaza was redesigned in 1699 to the familiar octagon it is today. The Place des Victoires was a more successful private venture, a 127-foot-diameter circular plaza, also by Mansart, focused on an equestrian statue of the king.

These private projects, which the crown certainly helped to promote, were undertaken earnestly, but in a context of growing urbanistic futility that demoralized rich and poor alike. None of them addressed the fundamental problems of the city: bad streets, terrible sanitation, and awful housing for the majority. The royal treasury could not support the immense construction of Versailles, with its complex hydraulic gardens, and also finance the kind of civic improvements that Paris required to make it livable. The ambivalence and irresolution of the French crown toward the urban problems of the capital would surely add to the ferocity of the Revolution when it came in 1789.

Beginning in 1670, Louis XIV pulled down the old crescent of fortifications of Charles V along the northern perimeter of town, and established the Grand Boulevards in an arc that ran roughly from the Tuileries to the Bastille—itself a remnant bastion of the old wall. The liberated corridor of new boulevards ran an average one hundred meters wide along what had been the ramparts. Development was left strictly to the private sector, and the boulevards would not be lined by buildings for decades to come. They functioned as a kind of broad country road formalized by planted rows of trees and were intended as a pleasure promenade for the affluent classes. The word *boulevard* was itself a mutation of the German *bollwerk*. It turned out, however, that ordinary Parisians used the perimeter boulevards as an east-west transportation corridor, in the absence of a more direct route across the center of town.

In 1671 Louis XIV built the Invalides, an old soldiers home and infirmary housing seven thousand men, in a then-rural quarter on the Left Bank. The purpose of the project was to declare the king's love and care for the brave soldiers who maintained him in power and thus insure the loyalty of the army—a wise application of royal funds. Three new, broad monumental avenues radiated south off the complex into the rural gloaming, but nothing would be built along them for years, either.

The Champs-Élysées was laid out beginning in 1677 by the Sun King's pet landscape architect, Lenôtre, designer of the gardens at Versailles. The Champs-Élysées functioned as a formal entrance to Paris from the west and as a grand approach to the Tuileries Palace (where Louis XIV stayed as infrequently as possible). In its enormous scale and formality, it had little function besides visually announcing that *you are leaving the countryside and approaching the capital city of a most powerful monarch*. At the time of its completion and for a long time afterward, the Champs-Élysées would be essentially a country road of extreme formality and breadth. It was not until after the Revolution that the western end of the city began to develop. If you were alive in the Paris of Louis XIV, the impression of these new boulevards and avenues would be of a tremendous formalizing of nature, rather than of urbanization. The chief device, the parallel rows of trees, was a fairly easy way to achieve stunning monumental effects and perspectives with little actual material and labor. These abstract diagrammatic schemes signified little beside the king's ability to make a rural landscape orderly—something he clearly relished. However, when they finally were developed with buildings decades later, the boulevards and avenues of Louis XIV would become templates for the best of the Second Empire's new street typologies, and they remain models for excellent street sections into our time.

The Place Louis XV was the major achievement of the Sun King's grandson-successor, renamed the Place de le Révolution and finally Place de la Concorde in 1795. As a civic open space, its scale has always been too large and forbidding. In fact, in its original conception, it was to function more as a baroque buffer between the gardens of the Tuileries and the unbuilt formal expanse of the Champs-Élysées. For decades it was an obstacle to the development of the western end of the city. In our time, it has evolved into an overly large automobile traffic rotary, almost impossible to traverse on foot.

The Rational City

There were many attempts to regulate building in Paris over many regimes, for both practical and aesthetic purposes. In 1607 Henry IV mandated the alignment of houses and banned structural overhangs of wood construction, but the edicts were hardly enforced. In any case, the city was facing a permanent shortage of wood for major construction and in the future virtually all new buildings would be some combination of dressed stone, brick, or stucco.

In 1667, the crown attempted to impose a height restriction for all houses in Paris of eight *toises* (15.6 meters or about fifty feet), which might accommodate as many as five stories plus an attic. These were also not strictly enforced. A royal order of 1669 attempted to regularize building façades for the first time. It was limited in this case to a single development on property owned by the church of Saint-Germain-l'Auxerrois, but it established a precedent that would form one of the bases of Haussmann's work later on. Around the same time, the double-pitched roof became a standard device in Paris because it lowered the profile of the roof—keeping it within official restrictions—without diminishing its capacity.

Between 1724 and 1765, the crown had tried unsuccessfully by edict to prevent further development of the city. The idea of urban planning as a discipline began to emerge from the shadow of architecture with the realization that growth could probably not be halted by command but at best only guided toward certain standards. The movement paralleled the Enlightenment. In a 1755 treatise, the Abbé Marc-Antoine Laugier proposed a Paris of wide streets linked by frequent plazas, with building heights to be proportioned in relation to the street widths. In 1767, the architect Pierre Patte advanced Laugier's scheme, but added a detailed proposal for slum clearance, with new streets cut through sclerotic old quarters, to be developed by private parties adhering to a set of unifying codes for new buildings. Patte revised the work in 1769, this time emphasizing the phasing of neighborhood renovations and the sanitary considerations entailed. Sutcliffe writes, "With Patte, architecture, planning, and technology came together for the first time." Consequently, the next set of royal edicts (1783–84) for the first time related maximum building height to street width. The maximum height of the cornice was set at fifty-four feet for new construction in new thirty-foot-wide streets, with as much as fifteen feet additional allowed in attics and roofs, depending on the size of the building lot. More important, a royal office was created for administering the code and issuing permits. This established the convention—especially under Haussmann later on—of architects' being used to working within very rigorous regulations.

The Revolution transformed everything about Parisian life except the essential form of the city. The Bastille was pulled down (completing the demolition of the old military wall). Churches were confiscated and converted into theaters, abbeys and convents shut down, and extensive church lands placed in legal limbo. But the Revolution was so grossly disorganized and politically destructive that it could not manage itself— which is how an astute, capable, decisive army captain from an obscure outland that was barely French seized the levers of power in the vacuum of the late 1790s. The First Consul, and later Emperor Napoleon, was under thirty when he came to power. In the few lulls between his military campaigns, he turned his considerable intelligence to matters such as legal reform (the Napoleonic Code is still the basis of French law), civil administration, and education. He had many hopes and dreams for the renovation of the capital, but his career got in the way. He was able to cut the new Rue de Rivoli through the clutter of slums along the north side of the Louvre, giving a start to the long-needed east-west connector. He provoked the construction of the long-planned Church of the Madeleine, and personally dictated its severe Greco-Roman motif. He simplified the Administration of Paris by creating the city prefecture under the national government. He tried to alleviate the chronic water shortage by building the Ourcq Canal to connect with the Canal St-Martin—it, too, became polluted. Consistent with his ambition to make Paris an imperial capital of Europe, Napoleon entertained the weird idea of bringing the pope there and installing him in a palace on the Chaillot hill (Rome had become a depopulated semirural backwater), but he had to settle instead for the Arc de Triomphe on that site (begun 1806, completed 1836). The rest of his story was military overreach, personal disaster, and an early death. Paris itself remained little changed from its condition in the Ancien Régime.

The regime of Charles X (1824–30) accomplished almost nothing urbanistically, though speculative building as an industry had arrived.[7] Apartment living was already established in Paris, unlike London, where only the single-family house would do. When they could afford it, the Parisian business and professional classes wanted to live in and around the airy and bright Grands Boulevards or in new blocks on the urban frontier of the west end. Meanwhile the vast inner core festered. The growing ranks of the industrial bourgeoisie could not keep pace with the industrial proletariat. During Louis-Philippe's reign (1830–48) the Champs-Élysées ceased to be a monumental country road. The July Monarchy was well-intentioned but weak and financially strapped. As a formal matter that would become highly significant in the next regime, Louis-Philippe's legislative assembly clarified the laws, first advanced under Napoleon I, for the expropriation of land and terms of compensation—in other words, eminent domain. The new law of 1841 gave the prefect of the Seine authority to condemn properties.

Louis-Philippe's prefect, Rambuteau, a relic from the First Empire, was proud of his frugality and could barely bring himself to use the new law on the scale that was required in the old city center. From 1833 to 1843, he cleared forty-nine squalid buildings away from the Place de Grève adjacent to the Hôtel de Ville—the favorite assembly point of angry worker mobs. The neighborhood had also been one of the hardest-hit during the 1832 cholera epidemic, so there was an aura of necessity to the job. In the same campaign, he managed to drive one new thirteen-meter-wide street, now called Rue Rambuteau, a few blocks from Les Halles to the Hôtel de Ville. These were his signal achievements, and to a degree they presaged the methods of Haussmann. Property values along the Rue Rambuteau did rise significantly with the new construction, a circumstance that made an impression on city leaders, and that would later empower Haussmann. Otherwise, the prefect Rambuteau connected a few ancient arteries and realigned others, but the overwhelming infarction of slums remained. Mostly he is remembered for constructing fountains.

In 1848, the second cholera epidemic struck, and the workers staged another major insurrection. The persistent problems of the central slums could no longer be ignored. The government of Louis-Philippe was swept away on a tandem tidal wave of disease and class warfare. Having tried government by restored Bourbons and Orleanists, the French notables who administered national affairs now turned with high hopes to a new and improved Bonaparte.

Coin Tricks

The standard story is that Louis-Napoleon conceived the renovations of Paris solely as a means to quash popular revolt. The new broad, straight boulevards, it is still said, were intended to enable troop movement about the city, prevent barricading of the slum quarters, and permit the effective use of raking artillery fire against mobs, therefore perpetuating the emperor's grasp on power. The trouble with this view, as Olsen points out, is that the rationalist approach to urban design had been dominant throughout the Western world since the sixteenth century, regardless of politics, class relations, or political tensions.

> Long avenues radiating at equal intervals from concentric open spaces can be found in the plans of Wren for London, and L'Enfant for Washington as well as in the Rome of Sixtus V, the Versailles of Louis XIV and the Karlsruhe of Karl Wilhelm. Descartes' preference for straight streets and the geometrically regular was shared in principle by nearly everybody in the seventeenth century and the vast majority in the nineteenth.[8]

In any case, the new boulevards of the Second Empire would prove to be of limited military value later when the Commune seized the city in 1871. The Commune was extinguished no more efficiently than the revolution of 1848 had been. In fact, the Commune managed to wreak far more physical damage upon the city's public monuments than the previous uprising—we will get to it presently. In the time that concerns us, the maintenance of public order was much desired by business and professional classes, but they hoped to achieve it with a competent, decisive, and effective government, if not necessarily a democratic one. For a while, that is what they got in the Second Empire.

Louis-Napoleon had dreamed of renovating Paris since he was a young man in London, which was nearly twice the size of Paris, with sanitary services for the middle if not the lower classes. For years before Haussmann entered the picture, the emperor had actively been working on maps and diagrams of his proposed street realignments and new boulevards. Since the primary records of this period were lost in the torching of the Hôtel de Ville in 1871, it is not always possible to know precisely which ideas originated with the emperor and which with Haussmann and his able deputies, Adolphe Alphand and Eugène Belgrand.

As prince-president, Louis Napoleon was anxious to show that he was in command. In May 1849, his government issued a decree announcing the eastward extension of the Rue de Rivoli—symbolically, a project begun by his uncle, Napoleon I. This would be the long-dreamed-of central east-west crossing, running through the most congested and fractious worker slums of the Right Bank to the Place de la Bastille at the east end of the city. The following year, the government decreed a wholesale clearing of the extensive slums in and around the Louvre-Tuileries and the physical connection of the two palaces. A third project involved additions and renovations to the Hôtel de Ville. These were all continuations of projects conceived by others and started earlier. Louis-Napoleon struggled to overcome the legal and financial obstacles to his more ambitious plans. He prodded the Corps Législatif to further clarify the expropriation laws. They responded with new articles handing the government enlarged powers to acquire slum properties, including lots at the edges of new streets, *and to resell them at a profit*. The revised laws would form the basis of Haussmann's schemes for financing the as-yet-unbuilt new boulevards.

The imperial treasury was but one locus among many modernizing economic institutions, including banks and the capital markets. But some powerful figures in the establishment were among the last to recognize the changes taking place under the industrial juggernaut. To Haussmann's predecessor, Berger, the emperor's notions for building miles of new streets were fantastic, really out of the question. The sums of money required would be astronomical, utterly beyond the logic of normal accounting. Berger's view of city finance was absolutely conventional economic thought of the day. The Rothschilds and other established leaders in finance shared Berger's view, and, in fact, the Rothschilds' bank would not participate in financing the *grands travaux,* the great works to come. Louis-Napoleon enjoyed many prerogatives as emperor, but he could not exact tribute or employ armies of slave laborers. He had to pay for his projects somehow. And he had to operate within the framework of a rational economy composed of ordinary mortals in business to make money.

Haussmann recognized that France had entered new and very different times. The Industrial Revolution, he saw, also entailed a revolution in capital and finance. As the scale of production and commerce grew at never-before-seen rates, the ability to make borrowed money work productively also increased. This was the birth of modern credit. The related idea of deficit spending by government was based on this new calculus: Government could issue bonds, borrow large sums of money, and do important public works that would result in greatly increased productive value in the city, which would in turn increase revenues and allow the government to pay back the bondholders.

Over 80 percent of the revenue collected in Paris at that time came from a tariff on salable goods that entered the city, called the *octroi.* Food, wine, and construction material were taxed, and it all had to pass through the gates of the fortifications built in the 1840s so it could be effectively controlled. The tax was not progressive, either. All classes paid it in costs passed along to consumers. The economy of France accelerated with Louis-Napoleon's coup d'etat, as the prospect of stability and order encouraged investment risk in business based on new and powerful technology. Railroads, new factories, and other large capitalized innovations began paying off in significant gains to the nation's wealth. The Parisian bourgeoisie were the big winners. They provoked a demand for more goods of all kinds, services, and new residential construction, which in turn led to the in-migration of more laborers and artisans. With the rise in population came equivalent gains in *octroi* revenues since everybody, even the poor, had to eat food and drink wine—city water was virtually undrinkable. The rise in population in turn increased the strain on a city lacking viable municipal services, which made self-evident the urgent need for public works to mitigate the terrible problems of housing and sanitation that the newcomers aggravated.

The emperor did whatever he could to help his new prefect of the Seine raise the necessary funds to execute the renovation of the city. Louis-Napoleon was interested chiefly in results, not so much how they were accomplished. Haussmann initially financed his projects with municipal bonds, authorized by the Corps Législatif, and sold to the public at large, using revenues from the *octroi* to demonstrate that interest could be paid on municipal debt. This straightforward procedure was itself a novelty, but Haussmann soon took debt financing to levels of creativity, complexity, and dubious legality not seen in France since the Scotsman John Law organized the Mississippi Bubble scheme there in 1720 (discrediting both banking and paper currency in France for at least a hundred years). One of Haussmann's gambits was to get the emperor to create a separate and mysterious "projects department" (*Caisse des Travaux*) that had no other function except to issue bonds without the approval of the Corps Législatif or the Municipal Council. This was very similar to Robert Moses's later use in New York of a recondite and antiquated legal device called a public "authority" to issue debt instruments and operate beyond oversight. Haussmann added several more obfuscating layers to the process, however. The prefect's office would issue contracts that obliged the demolition and construction companies that worked on the new boulevards to pay indemnities for property that Haussmann had condemned, in effect lending the city money at no interest. The contractors would be stuck assuming full financial responsibility for the project, but with the opportunity to profit hugely in the long term from their development efforts. Typically, this kind of deal would involve millions of francs. In reality, however, the contractors didn't have the money up front to pay off the owners of condemned slums. So, Haussmann got around this by declaring a project "completed" before it was begun and issuing installment payments to the contractors in negotiable proxy bonds, based on the amount owed, which would then be exchanged at a discount to the *Crédit Foncier,* the government's mortgage bank, for cash "advances" to the contractors. To complicate matters—as though that were possible—the proxy bonds (*bons de la délégation*) took on a life of their own and were traded at exceptionally high interest rates, distorting the bond market, and helping to feed a general inflation that constantly raised the cost of Haussmann's expropriations and construction—an unfortunate unintended consequence.

The aim of this scheme was, first, to keep the trail of funding so abstruse and incomprehensible that nobody else in the government could unravel the mysteries of Haussmann's procedures, second, to enable Haussmann to keep an immense revolving credit fund going for years on end under his sole control, and third, to avoid the need for any legislative authorization to do a project or pay for it. It is estimated that by this method of finance Haussmann raised a third of the 1.5 billion francs spent during his time in office on the Paris renovation. Another half billion was raised through increased tax revenues, the balance by regular bonding, the resale of building materials (mostly dressed stone) from the demolitions, and the resale of expropriated building lots—during the period 1853 to 1869, the prefect of Paris was the highest-volume realtor in the city. He had some other devices, too. Sometimes he simply gave building lots to contractors in lieu of payment, an acceptable risk when the value of the properties would be greatly enhanced by their location along brand-new boulevards.

For all the deviousness of Haussmann's methods, they proved very sound in accomplishing his public works goals. Deficit financing of the new boulevards and the sewer and water systems worked, and pretty much in the way that Haussmann had intended. The value of building lots along the new boulevards rose sharply as the new boulevards took shape out of the wreckage of demolition, and the bourgeoisie could sense that something new and exciting was being accomplished. The vacant lots *did* get filled with fine new buildings providing much-improved housing for an expanded upper middle class. Over time, many of the insalubrious old quarters lying between the new boulevards were themselves gentrified, the ancient buildings renovated and lifted greatly in value (the poor shifted more and more to the *banlieue* of the Zone at the city's margin). The end result of Haussmann's financial legerdemain was a great material improvement of the city. The finely detailed boulevards, with their gleaming new limestone-faced apartment blocks, cafés, bistros, theaters, and department stores, became a model for modern urban life all over the civilized world. They generated large volumes of new business that made the quality of life better for all classes.

Haussmann's financial finagling eventually led to his downfall in 1869. But though his methods were savagely mocked in the press, and used as a truncheon to destroy him politically by his enemies, Haussmann loudly declared that he never personally benefited from any of these schemes and, in fact, no evidence was ever found that he did. What's more, he declined a generous consolation payment from the emperor when finally forced to step down, and after Haussmann died, his household furnishings had to be sold to pay off his debts. What interested him was not personal gain but the power to get things done. He had a mystical love and genius for administration.

Haussmann's reorganization of the Paris city government reflected this. As prefect he was the equivalent of mayor. His offices were located in the Hôtel de Ville, the Paris city hall, and he also lived in a sumptuous apartment there. He enjoyed a sizable entertaining budget and both his table and wine cellar were renowned. The prefect presided over, and was at first answerable to, a municipal council composed of three members from each of the city's *arrondissements* or wards (twelve at first and then twenty when the growing suburbs were annexed). The council's chief duty was to approve a yearly budget. As Haussmann's financing became more convoluted and disengaged from normal accounting procedures, the council became an annoying impediment to his projects, and two years after his appointment he got the emperor to alter its charter so that Haussmann personally could appoint all the council members. The prefect did not have a high regard for democratic process generally, but his attitude toward the denizens of Paris was particularly harsh, especially the working poor who made up the majority. They were nomadic renters, he wrote, with no stake in their neighborhoods, prone to excessive drinking, easily excited by transitory emotion, and subject to the manipulations of communist demagogues. Haussmann wished to operate above politics. To him the renovation of Paris was a national project and his role was strictly that of a professional project manager.

The Operations Begin

The first project to originate under Haussmann's administration was the cutting of the new Boulevard Strasbourg. With its eventual extensions, the Boulevards Sebastopol and St-Michel, this would compose the long-wished-for *grande croisée,* a north-south axis across the east-west Rue de Rivoli. Thirty meters wide, the new north-south boulevard would run through the decrepit heart of the city, connecting the Right and Left banks across the Île de la Cité, where Notre Dame stood amid a rickety clutter of slums. The proposed Boulevard Sebastopol would originate at the Gare de l'Est, a new railroad station—one of many being built around the city—that would bring in lines from as far as Prussia, Austria, and Russia.

Haussmann needed to demonstrate that his new boulevards would be powerful generators of business activity and new wealth, and this was not easy to do at first. The projects took a long time. While demolitions for the new Boulevard Sebastapol were underway, the Panic of 1857 occurred, depressing the climate of investment and development very sharply but briefly. This was a time before government had the ability to interfere in business cycles. In the nineteenth century, these cycles tended to be hard and swift, a necessary clearing away of the debris of misinvestment. In these circumstances, Haussmann's scheme for Sebastopol was ingenious, calculated to produce a maximum profit for the city in the sale of buildable lots. Two old existing streets, the Rue St-Martin and the Rue St-Denis, ran north-south, in parallel a block apart, from the edge of town to the Seine. Both were completely inadequate. Either one might logically be a candidate for widening. But to widen either would logically imply that demolitions would occur on only one side of the street. Rather than widen either existing street, then, Haussmann decided to cut a whole new street through the center of the large blocks between them, therefore creating a street with new buildings on *two* sides, doubling the amount of potential building lots for resale. The centers of the blocks between St-Denis and St-Martin were particularly decrepit, since these were the vanished gardens and courtyards where jerry-built additions and shanties had accumulated for centuries, and the land was therefore less expensive to acquire. Meanwhile St-Martin and St-Denis remained intact. The total length of valuable street frontage increased hugely as a result. Subsequently, Haussmann resorted to this strategy of cutting through the interiors of old blocks wherever possible.

The demolitions were massive and traumatic. The scene was one of urban apocalypse. Haussmann's work produced a kind of desolation that hadn't been seen before and wouldn't be seen again for a hundred years. Period photographs show scenes that would resemble Berlin or Rotterdam at the end of World War Two—the ragged shells of tenements standing in vast rubble fields. This was still an age when practically all construction and site preparation had to be done by hand labor, by men with shovels and horse-drawn carts. The amount of earth and rubble moved by these methods was staggering. The new Boulevard Sebastopol opened as far as the Seine in the spring of 1858, beautifully paved, curbed, and furnished with new street lamps, orderly rows of new trees, and broad sidewalks—but as yet eerily unbuilt-upon. The St-Michel extension on the Left Bank opened the following year. The rest of Paris looked on anxiously, uncertain about the outcome.

By 1861 Boulevard Sebastopol was lined with new buildings put up by private contractors. Haussmann had weathered the Panic of '57 and proved that he could renovate on the massive scale, that he could make investors and entrepreneurs rich, employ armies of poor workers, improve transportation tremendously, and produce memorable places that would delight the middle class—all this took attention off a municipal funding scheme that nobody could begin to understand, and that seemed to work magically in any case. As it happened, these first new boulevards, especially Sebastopol, attracted the tremendous pent-up demand for new office space, rather than residential apartments. The difficulty of transportation had long discouraged in Paris the creation of a central business district on the order of London's. The centripetal effect of the railroad and the opening of the city with the *grande croisée* now made the innermost quarters of Paris desirable for business.

Haussmann was ruthless when it came to the Île de la Cité, the island in the Seine that had been the ancient "cradle of Paris." He decided, in effect, that Parisians would no longer live there. The slums around Notre Dame were among the worst in town. Death rates there from cholera epidemics were among the highest in the city. Haussmann was haunted by youthful memories of walking to law school in the Latin Quarter through the foul, decrepit slums of the little island thirty years earlier. It seemed to represent a kind of civic tumor that had to be surgically removed if the rest of the city was ever going to regain complete health. Despite cries of protest, Haussmann demolished virtually every residential structure on the island. He replaced them with civic institutions. The riverside fragment of Philippe the Fair's fourteenth-century palace, the Conciergerie, with its sprightly conical turrets (once the holding tank for those awaiting the guillotine), was grafted onto a massive new complex of law courts, the Palais de Justice. Unfortunately, Haussmann had to lop off the rear building of the triangular Place Dauphine to make it fit. Next to the courts, in what had been an abscess of hovels and tenements, he installed the central police offices, which fronted the now-cleared ("disengaged") plaza before the cathedral of Notre Dame, which was itself going through a very rigorous twenty-three-year exterior renovation led by the gothicist Eugène-Emmanuel Viollet-le-Duc. Adjacent to both Notre Dame and the police headquarters, Haussmann inserted the city hospital, the Hôtel-Dieu. All these are a five-minute walk from the Hôtel de Ville on the Right Bank.

We, in our time and place, are used to thinking of "urban renewal" as a perpetual swindle because the destruction of old fabric in American cities has typically been followed by the insertion of things much worse than the buildings that were knocked down: high-rise welfare housing, freeways, parking lots, blank-walled convention centers, strip malls and other architectural abortions produced by a discredited profession. While many were initially horrified by the scale of Haussmann's demolitions in Paris, they were eventually reassured by the quality and character of the new things that replaced the old. The number of houses demolished within the original twelve arrondissements ran to over 4,300, in the expanded twenty, the estimated figure from 1853 to 1870 was nearly 20,000, with about 44,000 dwelling units (many apartments) taking their places. The Île de la Cité was the only instance where Haussmann's destruction was total. The rest of his work in Paris can be understood as the careful overlaying of new thoroughfares over preserved old fabric, or else in the creation of whole new neighborhoods in what had been the city's semirural edge. It can justifiably be said that Haussmann's operations gave the old quarters a new life. The Paris that is beloved today is exactly that tapestry of narrow medieval streets aerated by the broad new boulevards supporting one another at appropriate hierarchies of scale.

The boulevards today are conspicuously crammed with automobiles. If Haussmann anticipated such an innovation in transport, he did not record it in his extensive memoirs, composed in the 1890s. It is unlikely, too, that he envisaged the volumes of traffic that his boulevards carry today. Certainly the volume was lower in the horse-and-carriage days—though they caused different problems of their own. However, even under the burdens of today's car traffic, the boulevards contain some of the most desirable real estate in the world. People want to live there. This is testimony to the excellence of their design. The central lanes carry express traffic, the outer lanes accommodate slow-moving vehicles, taxicabs, or delivery vehicles searching for a particular address, and the median serves many functions: It is an island of safety to pedestrians crossing a wide street, it accommodates parking at the curb, and the trees planted in the median strip perform their duties of visually narrowing the exceedingly wide streets and filtering the summer sunlight falling on it. The ensemble is completed by the broad sidewalk and the ground floor uses in the buildings, cafés and other magnets of human activity—all despite the tremendous volume of motor vehicles. The boulevards, therefore, function beautifully as a public realm: long, continuous, rich in civic amenity, and beautifully embellished with the meaningful syntaxes of architecture. While it is impossible to see the future, we can imagine the past. The leading painters of the late nineteenth century turned frequently to the boulevards as subject matter. What did they see if not compelling images of something really new, marvelous, and beautiful? Haussmann's Paris was a revelation of how wonderful the city could become.

Who is painting, or even photographing, the strip malls of today?

At Full Speed

There had been a tendency in Paris, as in London, to develop the western end of the city as the more desirable new place for the expanding middle classes to settle. The west ends of both London and Paris are generally upwind, an advantage hard to convey in prose. Haussmann now accelerated the process in Paris. In both cities, the east ends included some of the worst slums. In Paris, Haussmann had the fantastic armature of the Champs-Élysées and the Étoile already in place to work with. Off and around these features he drove a series of new boulevards that would establish a rigorous new standard for modern city housing. At this time, the west end of Paris was still the ragged edge of the countryside requiring minimal demolitions, a nearly blank slate to work on.

Haussmann's premiere project in this district was the Boulevard Malesherbes. Work began early in 1861 and the boulevard opened with great fanfare by midsummer. It ran northwest from the new financial district around the bourse, across the old inner boulevards, to an unbuilt area called the plain de Monceau, a parcel of old Orleanist estate properties that would soon become a very fancy neighborhood surrounding the new Parc de Monceau. The nearby Gare St-Lazare was by far the busiest of the many Parisian rail stations. What was eventually built in this new district ended up in character with the existing fabric of Paris, only very much improved.

Unlike the English, who were disinclined to live in anything but single-family houses, Parisians were accustomed to apartment living. Londoners were used to spreading out. London had industrialized sooner and held about twice the population of Paris by Haussmann's time. In Paris, the old city walls of Charles X had been replaced eventually by the larger ring of

Louis-Philippe's fortifications. London was a horizontal city; Paris was integrated vertically. Until Haussmann, Parisian apartment life had been manifestly inferior in comfort and sanitation to the London row house. But modern technology changed that. With plumbing, new sewers, gas lines, telephones, electricity, and finally elevators, life in a Parisian apartment became fully equal in comfort and healthiness, and perhaps superior in convenience. It tended to produce a denser, more diverse, and more exciting neighborhood fabric. While Londoners may have enjoyed their private gardens in the endless rows of monotonous "terrace" housing, Parisians focused their leisure time on the public furnishings and amenities of the city.

The Parisian apartment building commonly came with ground-floor shopfronts as infrastructure. Napoleon had sneered at the English as "a nation of shopkeepers," but, in fact, Paris had perhaps a richer array of small shops and luxury goods than London. They were deployed more uniformly throughout the neighborhoods and they were purpose-built for commerce, often very elegantly. In London, commercial establishments often had to be retrofitted into the ground floors of former townhouses, a clumsy arrangement still visible today all over the West End. Vertical Parisian urbanism promoted complexity. Directly downstairs from the apartment waited the boulangerie, the pâtisserie, the café, the bistro—life!

Typologically, the apartment houses begun under Haussmann provided luxurious flats for even the wealthiest classes, with large volumes of space, high ceilings, rooms for servants, and increasingly splendid interior appointments. The wealthiest classes of England disdained apartment living altogether. (The "French flat" became a rage in New York City with the result that apartment living eventually became the norm there and the basis for the most familiar New York building typologies.) Londoners had a horror of sharing common hallways and stairs with strangers. The Parisians appreciated the convenience of apartment life and developed a supple social armor to deal with its surprises. The social relations in Parisian apartment blocks built under Haussmann followed the same hierarchical pattern as before his time. The lower floors remained most desirable. The upper floors and attic stories were occupied by the less well-off. The difference now, however, was that the buildings were brand-new, the middle class had grown enormously, and occupants of all ranks could benefit from modern domestic amenities and decent sanitation.

The building lots along the new boulevards were precoded in order to produce a uniform street wall, with a cornice line at 68 feet on streets wider than 65 feet. The transition line at the *piano nobile* was established at 11 meters (roughly 33 feet).[9] A *minimum* ceiling height was set at eight feet. Care was taken to create complex formulas for the roof configuration within a 45-degree pitch to allow sunlight to penetrate the streets (while still affording a lot of livable attic space). As much as possible, Haussmann attempted to regularize the building lots on new streets at roughly 50 or 100 feet of frontage and 65 to 130 feet in depth. Speculative builders were encouraged to fill the entire envelope, and therefore maximize their investment. In many cases the actual façade designs were drawn by city architects and filed at the Hôtel de Ville. Developers were expected to work within the scheme as a condition of receiving the construction permit. In other words, you would buy your building lot(s) and then go down to city hall where staffers would give you the elevation drawing for your new building(s). City architects were also available to advise on design issues. The familiar iron balconies were not required, but they became such a common convention that few buildings from the period are without them. The architects of the time, trained in the rigors of the École des Beaux-Arts, were far less preoccupied with *originality* than architects trained in the elite graduate schools today, and far more willing to work within limitations and unities of urbanistic norms.

As the work continued, there was a tendency for the bigger speculative builders to purchase more lots along the edge of a new boulevard. The resulting buildings were to some extent products of mass production, even if they were built by hand labor and skilled craftsmen. The long rows of apartment blocks, with their uniform cornice lines, decorated transition lines, and unifying buttery limestone façades, produced powerful horizontal compositions, which reinforced the long, straight new boulevards to a degree that could be overwhelming and even monotonous. The long straight street, with its overtones of abstraction, was a residue of baroque civic design. Paris was one of the few places on earth where baroque urbanism was actually employed on the grand scale (Washington, D.C., is another), but, paradoxically, it was accomplished long after the wane of the baroque era. It relied heavily on the drawn diagram. On the ground, it produced some weird results.

Of course, the street was most often experienced at the ground-floor level. The severity of the new boulevards was softened considerably by the lavish use of street trees and elegant street furniture, which took the visual emphasis off the mass of individual buildings and tied the street into a coherent ensemble. The pedestrian often could not see the upper stories under the leaf canopy. All the originality suppressed in the bulk of the façade was let loose on the decoration of the ground-floor businesses, the cafés, and shops, decorated with lavish finishes in order to be as inviting as possible. The boulevards, then, came to be composed of patterned street-walls, like wallpaper, softened with foliage, with a lot of colorful action reserved at the sidewalk level.

Haussmann also attempted to compensate for the tyranny of the straight line by carefully terminating the vistas along his boulevards at compelling public monuments. He used the Arc de Triomphe to terminate twelve streets (creating a future automobile circulation problem). For public buildings he encouraged more exuberant decoration than the apartment blocks, but within the same classical vocabulary.[10] Though the emperor was an Anglophile, he loathed the kind of romantic dark, polychrome gothic architecture that England was producing at the time. The prefect of the Seine was not afraid to use the new technologies of steel and glass frames in assembling grand neoclassical works like the Gare du Nord or the main reading room of the National Library. Classicism therefore was identified with being modern. Conveniently, it also invested the recollection of history, so that Parisians' feelings about the future (their hope) could exist in continuity with their feelings about the past (their memories).

Paris Underground

The new boulevards and all the wonderful new buildings would have meant little unless the city could be adequately watered, drained, and sanitized. At midcentury only 3 percent of the city's dwellings had running water, and it was not clean. Haussmann undertook to correct the situation by tapping new sources of clean water far outside the city. Strangely, he faced a determined opposition of those who felt that the only problem with Seine water was that the city didn't pump enough of it. All that was required, they said, was bigger and better steam engines for the pumps. They maintained that cholera and typhoid fever were spread by miasmas and noxious vapors, not by contaminated water. The hygienist Parmentier had set the tone earlier, in 1787, saying that "the water of the Seine unites all the qualities which could be desired to make it agreeable to the palate, light in the stomach, and favorable to the digestion, and the Parisians are not wrong if they . . . contend with assurance that its waters are the best of all waters." [11] Haussmann undertook to solve the problem by employing the age-old technology that had been used by the Romans: gravity-fed aqueducts. For his part, the emperor was determined to bring Paris up to standards he had already experienced firsthand in English cities, and, as usual, he was far more concerned with results than with the means, but he enjoyed the idea that his Paris would be watered in the same fashion as ancient Rome.

In the early 1860s, Haussmann dispatched one of his chief engineers, the hydrologist Eugène Belgrand, to search for sources outside the Île de France, as the region around Paris is called. After rejecting water from the Loire and Somme rivers, Belgrand located two clean, high-volume springs in the Champagne region at an elevation well above Paris. The first, at Dhuis, was conducted a hundred miles to the city in a masonry aqueduct and collected in a distribution reservoir at Menilmontant at the eastern edge of the city. It was opened in 1865 with a flourish. There, at a little pavilion, the press and public were invited to view a specially prepared pool, at the bottom of which was inscribed in ceramic tile the words "Eau de Dhuis," to be read through fifteen feet of marvelously clear water. The second spring, from Yonne (where Haussmann had served as prefect years earlier, and been impressed with the clean water), did not open until the overthrow of the Second Empire. Between them, however, the two springs eventually sent a half million cubic meters a day to the city under high pressure from a source-drop of over a hundred meters. The combined cost of the two projects ended up at over 70 million francs. The antiquated system of water pumped out of the Seine was kept in operation long afterward for street cleaning.

By 1869, Haussmann had constructed over three hundred miles of new sewers. He laid down the mains, galleries, and trunk lines in coordination with the creation of the new boulevards and widening of the old streets. Haussmann and his engineers were careful to design a system that could be fastidiously maintained over time, so it would not be subject to the kind of permanent blockages that destroyed the old system. The impressive new mains were spacious enough to accommodate specially built barges designed to convey the sewer workers around the system for cleaning operations. A normal person could comfortably stand up even in the smallest branch lines. The results were so stunning that a tour of the sewers became a highlight of the 1867 Paris International Exposition—a world's fair put on to showcase the wonders of the Second Empire. (The sewers remain a tourist attraction to this day.) Paris was now more than fully up-to-date. Its utilities were state-of-the-art. What's more, the city no longer stank.

Louis-Napoleon did not bring an interest in underground utilities to his otherwise ambitious civic improvement schemes. These apparently originated with Haussmann, though the emperor certainly approved of the results. But the idea for a system of urban parks was the emperor's pet project. This, again, grew out of the emperor's experience in England. As all major Western industrial cities reached enormous scale, and were invaded by smoke-belching railroads and surrounded by "dark satanic mills," in William Blake's phrase, and airborne tuberculosis succeeded waterborne cholera and typhus as the dread disease of the period, a universal recognition arose that city air itself was a public health menace. The universal solution was trees, in large quantities. Parks were now considered "the lungs of the city," indispensable to the public good. The actual process of plant respiration may have been no better understood than the germ theory of disease in the 1860s. But there was a large cultural component to the greening of the city, too.

This was a time when large numbers of rural people were flooding the cities and leaving behind traditional ways of life and familiar landscapes.

The nineteenth-century park throughout the Western world was a monument to the landscape that was being lost in the rush to modernization. What's more, typically industrial cities were growing so large that even a brief visit to the countryside was increasingly difficult for ordinary people. City dwellers were now unhappily cut off from the natural world. Hence, the nineteenth-century park movement. Hampstead Heath and Hyde Park in London, Birkenhead in Liverpool, Central Park in New York, and the two great *bois* of Paris represent the attempt to embed an artifact remnant of the rural countryside within the overwhelmingly denatured fabric of the expanding industrial city. In England and America, the emphasis was almost entirely on large, romantically informal constructions, trying to mimic real rural scenery. Louis-Napoleon, Haussmann, and his chief architects Alphand and Davioud employed sweeping romanticism in the Bois de Boulogne and the Bois de Vincennes, and in the smaller but extravagantly picturesque Parc des Buttes-Chaumont, fashioned out of a rugged limestone quarry (and rubbish dump) next to the northeastern worker quarter of Belleville. Both Boulogne and Vincennes had been royal hunting preserves a century before. The emperor himself was deeply engaged in the design details, wishing to create in the Bois de Boulogne a Parisian version of Hyde Park, complete with a watery serpentine lake.

However, the legacy of Lenôtre's baroque formality, still visible in Haussmann's day in the mathematically precise rows of mature trees along the Champs-Élysées, and of the highly formal gardens of the Tuileries and in Marie de Médicis's Luxembourg Palace gardens presented an alternative and very different pattern for emulation. The culture of formality in French garden design prepared Haussmann and his lieutenants to appreciate the special role of greenery in detailing the streets and small squares. Greenery had to be a disciplined part of the greater urban order. Romanticism is, by definition, counter-formal. For reasons of safety, comfort, and orientation small squares must be transparent— that is, you must be able to see through the square to the buildings that compose the street wall on the other side. The small square is not nature in the wild, and should not pretend to be. Nobody should mistake it for rural vignette. The small square must employ as emphatic a formal vo-

cabulary as the architecture surrounding it. Only the materials are different: trees, shrubs, gravel, and cast iron. Ordered nature is itself a powerfully tranquilizing element within the dynamic organism of the city.
London's West End squares, by comparison, often look shaggy, overgrown, and uninviting. (Many of them are also private, locked, accessible
by key only to residents adjoining.) In New York, where Olmsted
reigned during the same period as Haussmann in Paris, street trees are
generally absent, and New York is notorious for its lack of small neighborhood squares.

Haussmann and his architects understood all this. Particularly in the
street setting, they understood the crucial but *limited* role of trees, and they
produced wonderful effects with little more than trees in formal rows (often double rows), a little pea gravel, and some regular deployment of
benches. The greening of Paris, therefore, was more comprehensive at
every urban scale and represents a tremendous accomplishment of urban
evolution. One didn't have to trek across town to see a tree, as in New York.
They were everywhere, and their behavior was consistent with their setting.
When Louis-Napoleon came to power, there were less than fifty acres of
parks in Paris. At the regime's end, the city possessed forty-five hundred
acres in parks.

Let No Good Deed Go Unpunished

Other projects are worth mentioning before the mandatory unhappy
ending. Under the Second Empire, the central markets, les Halles, the
belly of Paris, were transformed from a gigantic rabbit warren of unsanitary, uncleanable decrepit buildings, jury-rigged sheds, vendors' kiosks,
and other temporary structures that had become permanent into a
monumental set of beautiful iron and glass pavilions the size of a dozen
football fields. Work had already started under Rambuteau. But Louis-
Napoleon was displeased by the gloomy masonry structures designed by
the architect Victor Baltard (under commission by the July Monarchy).
He ordered the beginning work demolished and sent Baltard back to the
drawing board, where the architect promptly produced the technologically elegant iron and glass sheds in the spirit of London's Crystal Palace.

When this work was completed, Baltard's false start was forgotten and he received honors.

Under Louis-Napoleon, the population of the Paris rose from 1.27 million in 1851 to just under 2 million in 1870. City revenues tripled. Per capita income nationwide doubled. The railway system was expanded to 23,900 kilometers of track, 26,000 kilometers of carriage roads were macadamized, and a national telegraph went into operation. The emperor quadrupled the art collections of the Louvre. He financed extensive renovations and archeological restorations of provincial towns, deepened ports, drained swamps, and modernized the navy from wood and sail to iron and steam. He was a good emperor, perhaps a model of the benevolent despot, though in actual practice, he behaved more like a modern chief executive than a despot. He was fully engaged in his regime's policies and actions at the detail level. He chose able subordinates and willingly delegated authority. He had a weakness for forgiving his enemies, and perhaps a naively unrealistic view of the human capacity for malice.

Haussmann preceded Louis-Napoleon in downfall. Throughout the 1850s and 1860s, Haussmann had been a magnet for all the ill-will that the empire's opponents could not freely express about Louis-Napoleon. Haussmann made it easy for his enemies. His extremely autocratic personality, his open disdain of democratic procedure, and his supernatural self-confidence made him something of a monster to the republican opposition. His own ceremonial pomposity was more imperial than the emperor's, in everything but costume and sets. His sheer dazzling administrative virtuosity probably also irked the opposition. But since the results of his work in renovating the city were self-evidently excellent, his enemies could only pounce on every opportunity to complain about the costs of accomplishing it.

For seventeen years Haussmann had been able to evade the other branches of government on finance issues. He had so successfully obfuscated the funding trail that his enemies always ran into a disarming fog of numbers. But the sums of money involved grew larger over time, generating ever more anxiety and antagonism. By 1868, major payments finally fell due on notes that had been rolled over for years. Haussmann was forced finally to go to the legislative assembly and request, in effect, a debt consolidation loan for the Department of the Seine.

The result was an explosion of ridicule in the press. His explanations of his financing arrangements were mocked as the *most amazing violations ever committed*—though, as stated earlier, no evidence was ever found that he personally profited. Haussmann had the bad luck of finding an old political enemy, the charismatic orator Émile Ollivier, at the head of the republican opposition in the assembly. (As a provincial prefect in the Department of the Yonne, Haussmann had high-handedly suppressed Ollivier's political activities during the uproars of 1848.) Ollivier and the old political warhorse Adolphe Thiers, later president of the Third Republic, forced the emperor to get rid of Haussmann. The emperor himself was then struggling to "liberalize" his regime by sharing power more with the elected assembly. Haussmann's arrogance proved an embarrassment and an impediment toward that end. The emperor cashiered the prefect just after New Year's, 1870. Haussmann had served at the emperor's pleasure and survived with emperor's support, and without the emperor's favor he was finished—though Louis-Napoleon had made his old colleague a baron as a consolation gift. The title, a mere honorific, came with no land or fortune. Haussmann retired to a small estate in Bordeaux with a pension and lived another twenty years in gathering obscurity, composing his memoirs and enjoying the remnants of his renowned wine cellar.

The emperor Louis-Napoleon, or Napoleon III, met a more unlucky fate than his prefect of the Seine. The crafty prime minister of Prussia, Otto von Bismarck, snookered the French emperor into war. Prussia, only lately patched together into a nation, had been a colorful backwater of comic-opera minor kingdoms and principalities. The first Napoleon had repeatedly thrashed the Prussians in battle. Nobody took them seriously as a major power. The *real* German power in Europe was Austria, so everybody thought. The ostensible reason for the Franco-Prussian War had to do with the proposal to appoint a relative of the king of Prussia to the throne of Spain, by this time a senile, impotent nation. However, within the delicate protocols of the day, this act was construed by Louis-Napoleon's ministers as an attempt to surround the French nation by Teutons, and a great diplomatic insult. Accordingly, Louis-Napoleon declared war on Bismarck's Prussia and rode off at the head of his army to vanquish the impudent upstarts. The French army was promptly trounced. On August 31, 1870, 120,000 French troops collided with 200,000 Prussians at Sedan on the French-Prussian border along the River Meuse. In a decisive battle, Louis-Napoleon himself fell into the enemy's hands. He was deposed as emperor a few days later.

The Prussians then marched relentlessly on Paris and besieged the city from September 19 until late January 1871. Louis-Philippe's fortifications proved very sturdy and the force of 236,000 Prussian troops surrounding Paris did not enter the city. (Wars were still fought on open battlefields at that time.) The city suffered greatly but persevered withal. With provisions cut off from the outside, the desperate Parisians dined notoriously on the inmates of their national zoo. From January 5 to 28, 1871, the frustrated Prussians lobbed thousands of artillery shells over the fortifications. The majority of them, 12,000 strikes, landed on the Left Bank, hitting 1,400 buildings, killing around 100, and wounding 2,700. An armistice was negotiated by Thiers, who went on to organize a new government. The Prussian victors occupied the city for a little more than a month and then marched home, annexing Alsace and half of Lorraine as the winner's reward, and thus laying the groundwork for two world wars to follow in the next century.

A fortnight after the Prussians departed, an urban revolt broke out within the city of Paris. The Commune of 1871, as it was called, was the most destructive uprising since the Revolution. Thiers's government had moved out of the city to Versailles. The new legislative assembly, dominated by provincial members who tended to identify Paris with the dismantled empire and blamed the war on the city, passed measures attempting to disband the national guard. With business and manufacturing crippled by the war, national guard pay was the only income that many working-class Parisians could depend on. And having just spent the winter defending their nation's capital against the Prussians, these guardsmen now went on a rampage, joined by assorted other discontented poor, egged on by a new class of professional socialist agitators who would become stock characters in politics for decades to come.

For the second time in a year, Paris found itself under siege, this time by its own national government. In May, President Thiers sent an army under General MacMahon into Paris to crush resistance. Haussmann's broad boulevards, it turned out, afforded no particular military advantage. MacMahon's forces penetrated Paris by the back streets and retook the city by its rooftops. The Communards responded by setting fires. They torched the Hôtel de Ville, the Tuileries Palace, part of the Palais Royal, the Ministry of Finance, the central police headquarters, and even the Legion of Honor, among other things, 238 buildings in all, before MacMahon ruthlessly restored order. About 4,000 insurgents were killed outright in city fighting. Another 20,000 were executed in the aftermath while 8,700 were deported to the ends of the earth. Two years later, MacMahon took Thiers's place as president of the Third Republic.

Louis-Napoleon Bonaparte, private citizen, was detained by the Prussians only until the armistice of March, and then sailed to exile in the England he had so long admired. Unlike his celebrated uncle, he was not considered a political pathogen. He was sixty-three years old and had suffered quietly from chronic urinary tract disease for at least a decade. In exile, with a fortune tucked away, he lived on an estate with the inadvertently comic name Chislehurst, characteristically maintaining his interest in technological advances and the culture of his time. He died two years later following an operation to remove bladderstones.

Baron Haussmann died in 1891. The last of the debts he incurred for the rebuilding of Paris were not paid off until 1923.

Postscript

Most of central Paris today within the Périphérique freeway that follows the course of the demolished fortifications of Louis-Philippe would be recognizable to the subjects of Louis-Napoleon. The Third Republic, which lasted until World War Two, continued and completed the work of Haussmann exactly as it had been prepared before the prefect's 1870 sacking. President MacMahon dedicated the completed Avenue d l'Opera in 1877. The boulevards Henri IV, Raspail, and Haussmann (finally honored by the city) eventually followed. The Hôtel de Ville was quickly rebuilt in

1874 as a virtual replication of the burned original. The Tuileries, on the other hand, though deemed restorable, was pulled down by peevish radical republicans in 1882, leaving the western end of the Louvre complex unenclosed. The Eiffel Tower went up in 1889 as a kind of technological stunt for the 1889 Exposition and eventually won the affection of Parisians, though it still looks like a UFO landing gantry. The Paris Métropolitain subway system, requiring another heroic truama of excavation and construction, was opened in time for the 1900 exposition. These things completed the familiar Paris of our time, the City of Light, the city of the Lost Generation, the city deemed too beautiful to be burned by the retreating Nazis, the city of Pissarro, Monet, Picasso, Hemingway, Fitzgerald, Colette, Gertrude Stein and Miss Toklas, de Gaulle, Sartre, Piaf, Beckett, Truffaut, Jim Morrison, Chanel, and Mitterrand, of my father and mother, and finally beloved of my own experience and memory. The city of modernism never managed to shake off the formal clothing of the nineteenth century, despite repeated assaults by ambitious mountebanks such as Le Corbusier, and mutilations like the Centre Pompidou and the absurd underground-mall-and-lousy-park-combo that took the place of the beloved Halles.

Aside from some unfortunate boulevard do-overs to accommodate more cars, Haussmann's central Paris remains otherwise intact, perhaps seeming a little embalmed lately, within the greater abscessing megalopolis of greater Paris. In the ring beyond the Périphérique stand office and apartment towers, vertical welfare slums, shopping malls, horrible windswept plazas, parking decks, and all the other soul-annihilating accessories of late-twentieth-century automobile-oriented development. That is not the Paris we go to see. We go to experience the gorgeous texture of Haussmann and Louis-Napoleon's city, the magnificent life of the boulevards, the tremendous, beautiful unity of the architecture (given the exorbitant urban chaos elsewhere, especially America, nobody complains anymore about the excessive discipline of Haussmann's building façades), the grandeur of the monuments, the abiding tranquility of the river quays and the parks.

In the Luxembourg Gardens, there is a little area between the palace and the basin dedicated as an apiary. The posts of the wooden fence enclosing it are surmounted by painted finials in the figure of beehives. I could not help noticing that these finials stood exactly at the height of a perfectly served-up fastball, and it occurred to me that had they been erected in a park anywhere in my country, within a few days some clown with an aluminum baseball bat would have slammed each and every one of the beehives off its post in imitation of Mark McGwire. This is the difference between a city worth caring about and one that is not.

ATLANTA

Does Edge City Have a Future?

They ran the environmental people out of here a long time ago. You've got no trees. You've got no streams. You've got no mountains. It's a developer's paradise.

GWINNETT COUNTY DEVELOPER WAYNE MASON [1]

A *fatal hit-and-run up in Cherokee has got you backed up some on eye-seventy-five,* the radio announcer said, running down the hour's traffic reports as though he were reciting last night's baseball scores. I was at that moment motoring up a freeway myself, in a subcompact rent-a-car, from Hartsfield airport, the megahub of the Sunbelt, toward the postmodern spires of Atlanta. It took a moment to sink in before I understood the import of that little news flash: Some motorist had been killed in a car crash by another driver who then sped away from the scene, up in the northern suburb of Cherokee, or possibly the general vicinity of Cherokee County (whatever)—*and so thousands of other perfectly innocent commuters would now face pain-in-the-ass traffic delays, duration unknown, due to some dad-blamed incompetent driver who had gone and got him- or herself killed at rush hour and therefore upset the supper plans of so many upstanding good drivers, that is, folks who have the goshdarn sense and the decency to pay attention to the road! Well, isn't that enough to piss off the pope?*

It was a very strange moment in America. As a matter of intense current interest, Hurricane Floyd was at that hour churning off the Georgia coast, a few hundred miles away, like a colossal pillar of wrath, and nobody knew which direction it might take next, though Savannah was a good guess. In light of the situation, an unprecedented evacuation was underway along the entire southeast American coast, with horrendous traffic jams along every east-west interstate highway between Jacksonville and Cape Fear. Though the National Defense Interstate Highway System originally had been intended for just such mass evacuations, it had actually never been tested to this degree before. And, let's face it, 1959 standards probably didn't apply anymore. For one thing, the sheer number of motor vehicles was up exponentially. Not in forty-odd years, either, had a hurricane so large and fearsome behaved quite so erratically, and, what with the Federal Emergency Management Agency (FEMA) all cranked up to grandstand for the CNN audience, and virtually every county and municipality along the southeast coast issuing official evacuation orders, the system had clogged up like the porkfat-lined vascular system of a baby boom Bubba behind the wheel of his beloved suburban utility vehicle (SUV), and, Lordy, the entire fretful coastal plain had become a united parking lot.

Of course, this mess was all occurring quite a ways from my then-current coordinates: approaching Ted Turner's new vanity ballpark on the Downtown Connector (the combined I-75/I-85 corridor). The sky was blue, well, bluish-brownish-ochre really, due to the ozone-producing nitrogen oxides and carbon particulate matter issuing from scores of thousands of other cars like mine similarly plying the overloaded freeway system of greater Atlanta that same moment. But this was Atlanta every day nowadays: one big-ass parking lot under a toxic pall from Hartsfield clear up to the brand-new completely absurd Mall of Georgia (which we will get to presently). In fact, the whole city—if that's what you could call this giant hairball of a thirteen-county demolition derby—had come under the most intense pressure to quit doing what it was doing and being what it had become.

In 1998, the Environmental Protection Agency (EPA) had ruled that Atlanta was out of compliance with the 1990 Clean Air Act. The flipping of that little bureaucratic toggle had swift and horrendous consequences. Because of it, the metropolitan area stood to lose over $1 billion in federal highway funds plus, retroactively, an additional $700 million budgeted for road projects that were approved before the EPA ruling. In short, Atlanta would probably not even be able to maintain its existing highway mileage, let alone begin building the outer perimeter northern arc freeway that had been the collective wet dream of all the panting suburban realtors, commercial homebuilders, car dealers, strip-mall developers, parking-lot pavers, and other pathogenic characters who fed off the metastasizing tumors of suburban sprawl.

In the face of this catastrophic funding cutoff, the Georgia state government felt compelled to act. It created a regional superagency called the Georgia Regional Transportation Authority (GRTA). The state vested GRTA with the power to create any kind of public transit system it wanted to in the suburban ring around Atlanta proper—light rail, buses, people movers, you name it—and it could compel each county to pay for it, or else confiscate that county's highway money. GRTA was also given unprecedented powers to kill local developments or road projects of any kind or scope—malls, housing subdivisions, road-widening schemes, anything. The fifteen-member board could just say "no," and that would be the end of it. What's more, the legislation gave Governor Roy Barnes even more extraordinary powers to hire and fire GRTA board members at will. He could dump the whole board with a phone call and appoint a new one, just like that. Of course, the opportunities for mischief in a system like this seemed bottomless (and Georgia had a long and deep record of political chicanery), but so far Barnes was the first governor to enjoy these prerogatives and no one really knew what would happen. Barnes was considered an upright, progressive figure, and he was the first governor in decades to come from the Atlanta metro area itself. Everyone in Georgia politics, friend or foe of the governor's, was so nervous about the GRTA legislation that they referred to it jokingly as Give Roy Total Authority.

There was, however, at the same time, a gathering recognition among the prospering classes that the development explosion of the past thirty-odd years around Atlanta had begun to produce *diminishing returns,* as the geeks in econ might say, tending toward a *decrease in the quality of life*—to use the kind of euphemistic, understated, neutral language that was commonly employed to describe the fucking mess that even hardcore suburban growth cheerleaders, in their narcotic raptures of consumerism and gourmet coffee, had begun to dimly apprehend. Above all, traffic had become intolerable. That was pretty much the sole criterion for the quality of life in Atlanta: motoring convenience (or lack of). You dared not venture out anymore to a restaurant on a Friday evening in Buckhead, the

Beverly Hills of Atlanta, unless you wanted to spend half the night listening to books-on-tape in your SUV. Routine midday trips to the supermarket now required the kind of strategic planning used in military resupply campaigns under wartime conditions. Mothers with children were spending so many hours on chauffeuring duty that they qualified for livery licenses. Motorists were going mad, literally, behind the wheel—one berkserker tired of waiting at an intersection shot out the signal light with a handgun. The people of Atlanta were clearly driving themselves crazy with driving.

Culturally, though, the masses were not disposed to process this information rationally. It went against their current politics, their whole belief system, really, which boiled down to the notion that Atlanta was the ideal expression of democracy, free enterprise, and Christian destiny. There couldn't be anything wrong with the *form* of the city, the way it had crept over the landscape in a dynamic efflorescence of money, power, and *personal freedom,* like a pulsating slime mold. Atlanta was doing what every other place in the country wished it could do, and in spades, producing unprecedented new wealth and prosperity. Atlanta was becoming a collection of fabulous Edge Cities, which, the cognoscenti would tell you, was what the future would be all about—brilliant sparkling satellite pods of corporate high-rise dynamism embedded in a wonderful matrix of leafy, tranquil dormitory suburbs, all tied together by a marvelously efficient personal transportation system that . . . wait a minute. This sounded suspiciously like that old bullshit from Le Corbusier, the Franco-Swiss avant-garde guru-fraud from the 1920s: the *Plan Voison, Le Ville Radieuse,* the Radiant City, the proposal to demolish a big hunk of Paris and replace it with *Towers in a Park* connected by freeways. You mean *towers in a parking lot,* Jane Jacobs had satirized the idea way back in 1961, because that's the way it always worked out in the pathetically innocent, idealistic American experiments of the 1950s and 1960s that inevitably took the form of high-rise subsidized housing, instant vertical slums, the Projects. The idea was so wholly discredited by the end of the century that it is embarrassing even to dredge it up again. Corb himself had tippy-toed back to the Paris authorities year after year from the 1920s to the 1960s with his shopworn, dog-eared *Plan Voison* for the Right

Bank and they laughed at him—even while they were planning La Dé-
fense. The Radiant City was the most conspicuous failure of all branches
of modernism, be it in the arts, the practical professions, or social science.
It had been the butt of ridicule for generations. Nobody with half a
brain took these ideas seriously anymore—except the people of the Sunbelt, U.S.A., a regional group who, culturally speaking, had crawled out
of the mud about twenty-three years ago.

By late 1999, then, Atlantans were having a very hard time understanding any of this beyond the visceral level. Everything in the economy
of the moment was telling them to keep on doing more of the same.
The EPA judgment of air quality noncompliance was an abstraction to
them. It had nothing to do with real life—except perhaps as an illustra-
tion of the evil of Big Gubment. Pretty soon now they (*they,* you know,
them) would come up with cleaner gas, or better catalytic converters, or
some all-new type of fuel, hydrogen cells or what-have-you, and all this
fuss about ozone and carbon particulates would fade away like the head-
lines from the Cold War. Saying there was anything wrong with Atlanta
was like being against America.

Following the Money

I saw all the economic folly of the Sunbelt summarized in three TV
commercials broadcast on *CNN Headline News* in my Holiday Inn room
off the remorseless Peachtree Street strip up in Buckhead. The first ad
was for a financial "product" called the "DiTech 125 percent dream
loan." The DiTech finance company would lend you 125 percent of the
mortgage money necessary to buy a house, up to half a million dollars.
Borrowers could use the 25 percent slopover to pay their closing costs, or
buy furniture (or buy a boat, or go to Vegas for *excitement*). I had heard
many rumors while I was in Atlanta that people knew people who were
buying enormous new houses in the outer limits of the suburbs and living in them without furniture, due to the fantastic and relentless other
costs of living, such as the payments on the his-and-her SUVs that were
indispensable for commuting to work, in order to pay the humongous
mortgage on a forty-five-hundred-square-foot vinyl McMansion. The

next TV commercial, a few minutes later, was for a debt consolidation service, aimed at folks whose finances had gotten a little bit out of hand, who were invited to roll all those depressing bills into *one easy monthly payment*. Of course, this was, psychologically speaking, just another version of the old Polish blanket trick—cutting twelve inches off the top of your blanket and sewing it onto the bottom to make it longer. But, God knows there were enough clucks out there in the Atlanta cable TV viewshed for scams like this to scare up a regular supply of fresh marks. The third commercial was for bankruptcy lawyers. And there you had it: the whole story of a reckless economy, a gigantic Ponzi scheme encouraged by the Federal Reserve's massive inflation of the money supply and hence of the credit supply.

America was at this time near the end of an unprecedented credit orgy, of which the Sunbelt was the prime physical manifestation. The expanding U.S. money supply filtered through the big banks to the regional banks and was expressed as mortgages for ever more suburban houses, loans for gigantic cars, credit card debt for the parallel orgy of consumer spending, or as commercial loans for absurdities like the Mall of Georgia, a triple-decker, $250-million, 1.7-million-square-foot intergalactic mother ship of national chain retail that had landed on five hundred acres of former cotton fields up in the Gwinnett County town of Buford, thirty-five miles from downtown. The month the Mall of Georgia opened, three more regional megamalls were being built and a fourth was in the planning and permitting stage.

The Mall of Georgia, built by the Buckhead developer Ben Carter, was conceived to be a sort of entertainment theme park accessorized by megashopping and featuring a main street "feel," as Carter put it, an "outdoor village." (Whenever the word *feel* is used in real estate development propaganda, it should be understood that the place will be a cartoon of the thing it is purported to feel like.) To make sure that the mall's skin evoked the local vernacular, the developer hired an out-of-town consultant, Communications Arts from Boulder, Colorado, to research architectural motifs that would "relate" to the region's art, history, and natural characteristics. This is how psychotic commercial development has become in America.

Some of the buildings had been plunked down to enfront outdoor walkways. To call them streets would be inaccurate, because they were not public rights-of-way, just mall corridors open to the elements. Anyway, they were surrounded by a wasteland of eighty-six hundred parking spaces. (There is no public transportation of any kind in Gwinnett County.) The mall's central atrium (a fancy name for the franchise fried-food court) was designed to employ decorative elements from Atlanta's old downtown Union Station (long demolished). Unfortunately, a few days before the mall's official opening in the late summer of 1999, several of the major prospective tenants that were to supply the "entertainment" component—Virgin Music, Jillian's nightclub (imagine a nightclub chain!), and FAO Schwarz toys—had nixed their deals and pulled out. What was left was the usual twenty-screen multiplex cinema (yawn), and the state's only 3-D IMAX theater.

Otherwise, the Mall of Georgia's salient attribute was its visible quality of being a fantastic misinvestment. One sensed, gaping at the immense "landscraper"—as Leon Krier has termed these horizontal megastructures—that they would never, ever, sell enough scented bath oil and other unnecessary consumer crap out of the place to justify its existence, even over the relatively short depreciation period of the buildings (after which, for all anyone cared, the place might be sold for use as a for-profit prison or as the world's biggest evangelical roller rink). In fact, the same thing could be said about most of the development on the suburban outskirts of Atlanta: Its tragic destiny was already visible.

You could learn a lot about Atlanta and Sunbelt culture from broadcast advertising. The story of the reckless credit economy continued the next morning on the car radio. I got stuck for half an hour at an intersection cluttered up with yellow front-end loaders and men in hard-hats when a commercial came over the country music station for Joe Ray the bail-bondsman, whose advertising pitch was "bad things happen even to good people." From this notion, caboosed onto the TV commercials of the previous night, you could extrapolate a whole dramatic train of events: Billy-Bob had fallen behind on the payments for his DiTech 125 percent dream loan, debt consolidation had not managed to reduce his indebtedness, and bankruptcy was underway but had left him with no walking-around money, so, in order to feed his family, Billy-Bob had been constrained to rob a convenience store, and the license plate on his getaway car had been recorded by a security video, and, well . . .

This economic recklessness was but one facet of Sunbelt culture that came in over the airwaves. Another facet was the theological one, which plays a large role in daily life there. A memorial service had been held for the victims of the national massacre-du-jour, a lone gunman who had entered a church basement in Fort Worth a few days earlier and slain several children and adults. The media were now on hand for the service, of course. The wife of one of the victims explained from the altar that she would continue to speak of her husband in the present tense because he was "still alive in heaven up with Jesus." What an odd notion, I thought: that when you were dead, you were still alive, perhaps more alive than when you had been supposedly alive on earth. F. Scott Fitzgerald had remarked earlier this century that it was a mark of genius to be able to hold two contradictory ideas in mind at the same time. Of course, he was a midwesterner, but still it was unlikely that everyone in the Sunbelt (formerly the Bible Belt) who subscribed to the fundamentalist Christian idea of heaven as a sort of eternal theme park was necessarily a genius. What it actually prompted one to think was how childishly incoherent Sunbelt theology was, and how strenuously it served to counterpoint another set of Western notions concerning the essentially tragic nature of life. Not only did Sunbelters refuse to accept a tragic view of life, but they liked to decorate their alternative version with satin and lace, like a gift shop welcome sign.

NEWS BREAK

From the pages of the *Atlanta Journal-Record,*

Saturday September 9, 1999

Novice Driver Tragedy
Spurs Flood of Comfort

Comfort and hopeful news are pouring in for the Brown family.

Days after their son Michael, 3, was killed after a 14-year-old neighbor practicing driving with his father hit the toddler and his brother Brandon, the Gwinnett County family has been deluged with offers of sympathy.

"We've been showered with unconditional love and support," said Richard Brown on Friday. "It's overwhelming for us."

Michael died at 8 a.m. Wednesday morning following the accident on Tuesday evening in Buford.

Brandon remains in the intensive care unit at Children's Healthcare of Atlanta at Scottish Rite, but his condition is improving.

Brandon "B.J.," 6, suffered a fractured arm, damaged knees and a collapsed lung that has since recovered.

On Friday, doctors removed his neck brace and hope to take him off an intravenous feeding tube soon.

"He's doing very well," Brown said. "It's steady progress."

The family has received encouragement and offers from family, friends, and businesses around the country, all anxious to help the family, whose van overheated on the way to the hospital and was still in the shop Friday.

One business in Brown's home state of Arkansas offered to purchase playground equipment or books and donate these to a local school in Michael's name.

"It's wonderful to see so much support and love shown," he said.

The funeral for Michael will be 4 p.m. today at the Church of Jesus Christ of the Latter-day Saints in Suwanee, with burial at East Shadowlawn Memorial Gardens in Lawrenceville.

The Brown family has continued to maintain an attitude of forgiveness toward their neighbor, Dimitris Iliadis and his 14-year-old son.

Gwinnett County police say Iliadis was attempting to teach his son to drive when the teen pressed the accelerator and the car took off, striking the Brown children who were playing in their yard.

Police are waiting for blood tests for drugs and alcohol before deciding whether to charge either the father or the son with a crime. That could take months, the police say.

What on earth does one make of a story like this? I conclude that the local culture, in effect, accepts the death of little children like Michael Brown as a necessary cost of doing business. Atlanta's economy is based on suburban development for its own sake. That is, suburban development *is* the economy. This particular pattern of development requires the continual use of personal transport machines, cars, which tend to be dangerous and take some skill to operate. Teaching these skills is the responsibility of the family. It can be hazardous to bystanders. Sometimes members of other families are present in the area of instruction. Sometimes hazards cannot be avoided and injuries or death result. Of course, everybody regrets the loss, but all—including the parents—are eager to forgive and get over the unhappy incident and get on with the next order of business: Real estate must be sold, development deals must be signed, the roads have to be widened to accommodate all the extra cars from the new subdivisions and their accessory strip malls. Children will grow up there, and sooner or later virtually all of them who are mentally and physically able must be taught to drive cars so that they can go out and play their adult roles in the Sunbelt economy.

How It Adds Up

For you statistic hounds out there, here are some facts about life in Atlanta expressed the way America likes to get all of its information, in numbers.[2]

Each week roughly 500 acres of raw land in the Atlanta metro region and its fringes are bulldozed for new suburban development. The metro area lost 190,000 acres of tree cover from 1988 to 1998. There were 2.5 million motor vehicles registered in Atlanta. Each day, motorists rack up over 100 million vehicle miles on Atlanta roads and highways. The average commute reached 35 miles per day, which was half again greater than the figure for commuters in Los Angeles. In 1999, the region produced a record 69 smog alert days. The summer that the Mall of Georgia opened, highway signs urged commuters to eat lunch at their desks. Georgia has the lowest gasoline tax of the fifty U.S. states, and the revenues generated from it can only be used for road and bridge building.

The Atlanta metro area's population density is the lowest of all U.S. metro areas. In late 1999, it was 1,370 per mile, as compared with Los Angeles at 5,400.[3] Growth of the suburbs was one hundred times greater than growth in the city in 1999. The region's population has grown 70 percent since 1980. The population of adjoining Cherokee County doubled from 1990 to 1999. An average of 61,800 people moved into the Atlanta metro area each year during the 1980s and 69,100 during the 1990s. Gwinnett County's population more than tripled since 1980 to its present 523,900. At the end of the century, the ten-county metro area had a population of 3 million.[4] For as long as anyone can remember, Atlanta has been divided racially roughly at its compass points. The northern and eastern areas have traditionally been white; the southern and western areas black. In recent times, that boundary has been delineated by Interstate Highway 20, which runs east-west through the city like the Great Wall of China. By the 1970s, the central city had become predominately black. Along with a wave of white flight, the 1970s also witnessed a movement of middle-class blacks to suburbia. The suburbs, however, also tended toward segregation by race. At the turn of the millennium, one-third of the region's African-Americans still lived in the center city along with 6.3 percent of the region's whites. The poverty rate for the entire metro region was 7.9 percent; in the central city it was 25 percent. From 1980 to 1990 the central city's share of jobs in the region dropped from 40 to 30 percent. The fast-growing northern suburbs' share rose from 40 to 52 percent.

The Pop-Up City

The first white settler arrived in the area that comprises Atlanta's downtown in 1833. A Mr. Hardy Ivy built himself a double log cabin on a 202.5-acre lot and farmed there. He was thrown by a horse and killed in 1842.

You could have barely called Atlanta a city when General William Tecumseh Sherman burned it in 1864. It was a kind of frontier boomtown, composed mainly of pop-up wooden buildings. It developed as a formal consequence of that industrial novelty, the railroad, the means for penetrating the vast, backward interior of the South, which was until then settled only along navigable watercourses. Surveys for the Western and Atlantic line, to run out of Chattanooga, commenced in 1837. The present city of Atlanta would be established in 1838 near the only feasible bridge crossing along the Chattahoochee River, near a Cherokee village that had been called Standing Peachtree.

Atlanta was, at first, named simply "Terminus" because it was to become the far end of the Western and Atlantic out of Chattanooga. Terminus would be an outpost in a major cotton-producing region at the margin of what was still a southern Appalachian highland wilderness. The surveys of the 1830s had determined that the present site of Atlanta was the best place of intersection for several other rail lines started around the same time. The building of the railroad itself *was* the new town's economy—the railroad workers and managers needed places to sleep, eat, and buy things, so boarding hotels, houses, and shops went up in Terminus. In 1843, the trial run of a freight train of the Western and Atlantic line set out from Terminus to nearby Marietta, about twenty miles to the northwest. A year later, Terminus was incorporated as a town and renamed Marthasville, in honor of the daughter of ex-Governor Wilson Lumpkin. Soon, two more railroads converged on Marthasville, the Georgia Line, out of Augusta, and the Macon and Western, connected to Savannah. The town's future as a major inland transport junction seemed assured. In 1845, Marthasville was rechristened Atlanta, said to be the "feminine case" of the word Atlantic by its coiner, J. Edgar Thomson of the Georgia railroad (later president of the Pennsylvania Railroad), in the hopes of stimulating a grander vision of the place's future.

This vision of cosmopolitan glory was as yet belied by the town's actual condition. By 1850, eleven years before the Civil War, the town had only 2,500 permanent inhabitants. Fulton County, which included the municipality of Atlanta, was not incorporated until 1853. By the eve of the Civil War, 1860, the city's population swelled to roughly 8,000, plus another 4,000 rural denizens outside the city line in Fulton County. To give you some sense of scale, this is on a par with today's population of Bennington, Vermont. Seventy-five percent of Atlanta's permanent residents were white. Listed by occupation, the residents included 59 locomotive engineers, 49 prostitutes, 23 saloonkeepers, 9 policemen, 5 bacon dealers, 3 music teachers, and 2 bankers. In 1857 the completed Memphis and Charleston railroad created a connection from the Mississippi to the Atlantic and confirmed Atlanta's status as the transportation hub of what would shortly become the Confederacy.

As the Civil War erupted, Atlanta logically became the Confederate hospital center for wounded soldiers—in battles that ushered in the age of industrial warfare with enormous casualties. The town was geographically remote from the action in the war's early years, but well-connected to all compass points by rail, so the wounded could be transported there expeditiously. Both public and private buildings were appropriated for use as infirmaries. Atlanta also became nearly overnight a workshop for war materials, turning out everything from canteens, to pistols, to cannon, to the steel plates for the South's little fleet of ironclad warships.

In August 1862, the city, as it now thought of itself, was placed under martial law and run as a Confederate garrison. As such, it presented a ripe military target to Union strategists, and in the last full year of the war, 1864, the Federals finally began penetrating the interior of the Deep South by way of Chattanooga, moving south toward Atlanta. The difficult terrain, deeply forested, cut by many unbridged streams and rivers, favored the defenders, under the Confederate general Joseph E. Johnson with fifty thousand troops. Sherman, at a strength of one hundred thousand troops, was instructed with characteristic brevity by the Union's new chief of the army, Grant, to "inflict all the damage you can against their resources."

It was a new kind of warfare. The post-Napoleonic period in Europe had been remarkably peaceful, and the many innovations of the industrial nineteenth century had not yet been tested in combat by the great powers of the Old World. The American Civil War was the first major conflict to employ on a continental scale the new technology of railroads, steamboats, and repeating guns. The carnage was unprecedented. Grant—unlike his predecessors in the top army job, McClellan, Halleck, Meade—did not shrink from the terrifying new scale of casualties and civic destruction. The depressive, fatalistic Sherman, who famously remarked that "war is hell," was the stoical Grant's perfect subordinate. Meanwhile the desperate Confederates replaced the ineffective Johnson with his subordinate, General John Bell Hood. After a long summer of bloody skirmishing around Atlanta, Sherman succeeded in smashing the city's last railroad supply line. On September 1, 1864, the Confederate army abandoned the city, retreating out toward central Tennessee, but not before blowing up seven railroad cars loaded with their own ammunition and powder and trashing the city's steel-rolling mill. Sherman's forces swept in the next day.

The Federals spent the following day ceremonially occupying civic buildings, flying Union flags, playing victor, and taking stock. On the fourth of September Sherman ordered all civilians to get out. It took two weeks to complete the deportations. For two months more—while Federals under General G. H. Thomas pursued Hood toward eventual annihilation in Nashville—Sherman rested his troops and prepared a new campaign designed to cut off at its knees what remained of the Confederacy. On the night of November 14 Sherman's troops went to work methodically destroying Atlanta. They smashed all the remaining railroad infrastructure, roundhouses, depots, and machine shops, and set fire to all the downtown buildings in the vicinity of what had been the old Union Station before the war. From there the flames jumped to the residential streets. No fire companies would be called to save them. No other city during the Civil War endured so complete a trashing, not even Richmond. A few hours later, having destroyed his army's temporary living quarters, and having burned the bridges north and west across the Chattahoochee, Sherman's army set out east on the famously destructive march to the sea.

Atlanta's recovery from the war was brisk, considering what had happened to it and considering too that pretty much all of the defeated Confederacy had entered the equivalent of a one-hundred-year depression. The main thing the city had going for it was its favorable location as a rail center during a period of American history when rail transport drove the national economy. The lines smashed by the Federals in 1864 were rapidly rebuilt. However, by the war's end, the northern states had so far outpaced the battered South in industrial capacity and capital resources that the latter was reduced to a huge agricultural backwater, with overtones of medieval serfdom in the sharecropper system that had replaced slavery. The Atlanta of that long period drew what wealth it could as the depot of a huge, impoverished farming region with little manufacturing and no other cities of any consequence.

It became the state capital in 1868 (replacing Milledgeville). By 1880, with reconstruction (that is, federal occupation) officially over, Atlanta was a city of 37,000, with streetcar lines. It was then forty-nineth on the list of the fifty largest U.S. cities, just below Lynn, Massachusetts. By comparison, St. Louis, Missouri, had reached 350,000 by 1880. Rochester, New York, was then more than twice the size of Atlanta. By 1900, Atlanta was forty-third on the list at roughly 90,000, still way behind Omaha, Nebraska; Toledo, Ohio; and Scranton, Pennsylvania. By 1920, it was thirty-third at 200,000, still way back of Buffalo, New York (over half a million), and Indianapolis (314,00). By 1930, Atlanta's population rose to 270,000. In 1940 it reached 302,000, and in 1950, 331,000.

Atlanta's growth during the first half of the twentieth century was relatively anemic compared to that of places like Cleveland, Detroit, and Baltimore, and other northern industrial cities, and it had a special character that set it apart. Whereas immigration from foreign countries peaked in northern cities between 1900 and 1930, most of the newcomers to Atlanta during the same period were black sharecroppers and poor white farmers fleeing a crisis of regional agriculture. The cotton boll weevil had made its first appearance in the United States in Texas around 1890. By 1914, it arrived in the Georgia–South Carolina cotton belt, with a catastrophic recurrence in 1921 that destroyed crops and pushed many farmers into insolvency and dispossession.[5] The boll weevil crisis was compounded after 1918 in the South by the widespread introduction of mechanized tillage, with tractors replacing draft animals, which led to "sheet" erosion of fragile loam layers atop deep clay soils and ruined more farmers. (A similar process would turn the much drier Texas, Oklahoma, and Kansas into the Dust Bowl.) The social consequence in Georgia was an inflow to Atlanta of people, both black and white, with little experience of urban life, who were poorly prepared for coping with it. The twentieth-century slums of Atlanta, unlike the tenement slums of New York or Chicago, were wooden shantytowns, in effect sharecropper shacks taken out of the rural context. For Atlanta, the Great Depression of the 1930s was a grim overlay on a region that had been economically distressed for generations.

Air-Conditioning, Airplanes, Cars, and an Oil Orgy Create the Sunbelt

In Atlanta, the heat and humidity for a significant part of the year can be debilitating. Before air-conditioning, people got used to it with modifications in their behavior, namely, doing as little as possible. This held for people of all social ranks and was, in fact, a traditional feature of southern culture. People compelled to do hard physical labor would do as little as possible as slowly as possible, but so too would insurance claims adjusters and bank presidents cooped up in offices. Since doing as little as possible tends to produce less of value to human society, it would be fair to say that the climate of the southeastern United States was not naturally hospitable to advanced civilization. Air-conditioning, or "comfort cooling," as the industry likes to describe its product, made modern life possible in that part of the country.

We'll forgo a discussion of the baby steps in its technical development, except to say that practical indoor cooling was first accomplished by mechanically moving air over enormous quantities of ice. By the late nineteenth century, the ice itself could be produced by refrigeration, via steam-driven condensers and compressors (rather than harvested from northern lakes and sent off in sawdust-lined ships and freight trains, which had been the case formerly). In 1880, New York's Madison Square Garden was using six tons of ice per performance to cool its summer patrons. On July 2, 1881, President James A. Garfield was shot by a lunatic at Washington's train station and lingered in critical condition at the White House throughout the punishing Washington summer. Naval engineers rigged an ice-brine cooling drip system that brought down the temperature in the patient's sickroom by a full twenty degrees Fahrenheit (alas, Garfield died anyway in September). In 1889, Carnegie Hall got an ice cooling system, and other theaters followed. All these were extremely cumbersome operations that required physically moving massive quantities of ice.

In 1891, the St. Louis Automatic Refrigeration Company ran circulating pipelines containing ammonia from a central plant to commercial customers in the city. One was a beer hall called the Ice Palace, which featured arctic murals and sleighing scenes on its walls to psychologically enhance the effect. The system was only marginally efficient and prone to breakdown. An ammonia brine system was installed in the U.S. Senate chamber in 1896. Around the same time, the Pullman train company tried a compressed-air system in its passenger cars. Hospital ships in the Spanish-American War, operating in the torrid Philippines, featured air-cooled wards belowdecks.

The premiere modern system using mechanically refrigerated air was installed in the New York Stock Exchange's new headquarters on Wall Street in 1901. It operated only in the boardroom, and was able to lower the temperature from eighty-five degrees to seventy-five degrees. Since cooled air typically gains humidity (heated air dries out), a method had to be devised to reduce the unpleasant dampness of cooled air, and this too was accomplished in the NYSE system, which ran for twenty years.[6]

These room-cooling systems were a wonder to people who had been able to do little besides suffer or jump in the creek in summer heat their whole lives long. By the 1920s, movie theaters that had introduced mechanical cooling enjoyed a tremendous boom. Before that, in some parts of the nation, theaters routinely closed during the summer months. Hotels soon joined theaters, cooling their lobbies and restaurants but not their guest rooms. The first high-rise office building designed with central cooling was the Milam Building in San Antonio, Texas, in 1928. The Tribune Tower and the Wrigley Building in Chicago had it installed in 1934 and 1936.

Up until this point, artificial cooling could only be found in commercial or public buildings. The equipment was awkward, large, and noisy. But parallel developments in home food refrigerators would lead to improved prospects for home cooling. By the 1920s, wealthy people traded in their iceboxes for refrigerators with a mechanical compressor outside the box, typically on top. Electric motors also improved dramatically in power and efficiency. An obstacle to home cooling had been the need to hook up systems to plumbing, to carry away the heat generated by the condenser in the cooling process. Another problem was the relatively meager electrical capacity of a typical American house.

In 1930, the Frigidaire division of General Motors introduced a console-type cooling unit that came in a wooden cabinet like a radio. It, too, had to be hooked up to the plumbing and cost nearly as much as a car. Within a couple of years, other companies introduced home air-conditioners that used metal fins to cool the mechanicals. With this, the room air-conditioner was liberated from the plumbing hookups. But the national economy remained hobbled through the 1930s and few people could afford them. Westinghouse sold its first window-mounted unit in 1941, just in time for World War Two.

Population growth in Atlanta marched in direct relation to the refinements that made air-conditioning common and affordable. The increase from 1950 to 1960 was far greater than the increase from 1920 to 1950. The population of Atlanta proper peaked in 1960 at 487,455. After that, all growth occurred in the suburbs—rocketing to more than half a million outside the city boundaries by 1957, for a greater metro area population of one million. Two out of five newcomers now came from outside the South. From 1960 to 1980, the city's population contracted to 394,000, or more than 8 percent, and stayed at that level into the 1990s. Meanwhile, by 1996, the metro area had ballooned to nearly three million.

There is no question that air-conditioning made this possible. In Atlanta, even the poor in the worst slums have air-conditioning, but of course so does virtually every business establishment and most cars made after 1980 (which, as a practical matter, means almost every car now on the road). In contemporary Atlanta, one need only sweat making the journey from a given parking lot to a given building. Air-conditioning and cars are the primary determinants of life in Atlanta. The city's utter dependence upon them is assumed if no longer completely conscious. Both are, in turn, utterly dependent on reliable supplies of cheap petroleum. Cheap petroleum in reliable supplies has been the condition of the United States for the whole twentieth century, except for a couple of oil market disturbances caused by international politics in 1973 and 1979.[7]

Excluding those anomalies, up through World War Two, American oil imports were fractionally unimportant. During the war, most American petroleum still came out of American wells and the supply was assured—rationing was more a gimmick for boosting war morale than an actual allocation system. The tremendous postwar suburban expansion of the 1950s, including the interstate highway system, began to alter the import picture. Americans were driving exponentially more. Both policy and the popular consensus allowed the car industry to drive the national economy on a permanent basis. After 1960, oil imports increased markedly. Aging American wells would fall off peak production for good in the 1970s.

Apart from the OPEC events of 1973 and 1979, the United State has been perhaps too fortunate in enjoying such extraordinarily stable oil markets. The psychological effect of so much cheap oil has been powerfully narcotic for the American public, especially in the Sunbelt cities. Americans no longer have any idea how tenuous the link is between the life that is considered *normal* in places like Atlanta and the long, fragile chain of our petroleum supplies, more than half of which now come from parts of the world so increasingly chaotic that Western-controlled companies could soon lose the ability to function in them—or sovereign nations themselves, such as Nigeria, could lose control of their own oil production as they dissolve into anarchy. Oil production is complicated and its infrastructure of wells, pipelines, and port terminals is easily subject to sabotage. Atlanta, and cities like it, therefore, are at the mercy of events half a world away. If the international oil markets suffer even moderate disruptions in the years ahead, Atlanta will find itself in deep trouble.

A current popular belief in America these days is that "alternative fuels" could replace gasoline in the vehicles we use and that the system could merrily roll along without petroleum as if nothing had happened. This is a dangerous delusion. The truth is that no known "alternative technology," including hydrogen, fuel cell, electricity, nuclear, or alcohol from biomass, can take the place of gasoline in the way we have organized our lives, especially where cars and trucks are concerned. None of the touted alternative fuels is as versatile as gasoline, or can be produced for anything close to the cheap price of gas we've been accustomed to, or can be stored or transported as easily. The electric car is not going save Atlanta.

The Money Machine

A third determinant of Atlanta's current condition has been the growth of its now-gigantic airport, named after William Hartsfield, who as a city alderman in 1926 lobbied ferociously to get the U.S. Post Office to designate Atlanta as a federal airmail route at the expense of rival Birmingham, Alabama. Hartsfield later became Atlanta's long-time mayor. The federal airmail contract would be hugely consequential after World War Two, when commercial aviation eclipsed the railroads. The airport doubled its number of passengers in 1956 alone, and then went through a never-ending cycle of expansions. The city lavished spending on it like nothing else, even when Atlanta's sewer and water system approached collapse.

The airport, in turn, became a money machine, especially for Delta Airlines, run by a shrewd old ex-cropduster named Collett E. Woolman, a penny-pincher who brought his lunch to work in a paper bag and refused to carpet the corporate headquarters. In the 1960s, an inspired Woolman hired "girl specialists" in sales and promotion to induce conventions of mostly male optometrists, Shriners, and war veterans to hold their annual shindigs in Atlanta by selling cheap Delta round-trip flight packages.[8] Between the late 1960s and the mid-1980s, the airport-convention racket was by far Atlanta's biggest business. Passenger traffic quadrupled from 3.5 million in 1961 to 14 million by 1970. When the airlines went through deregulation in the late 1970s and adopted the hub-and-spoke system, Atlanta easily adjusted by building new terminals and was rewarded with international routes to Europe. In 1999, Atlanta was the world's second-busiest airport (behind Chicago's O'Hare), carrying over 57 million passengers. As I write, another major expansion is underway, estimated to cost $5 billion.

Meanwhile, the conventioneering infrastructure received a Frankensteinlike graft of several ballparks (football, basketball, and baseball), complete with freeway on-and-off-ramp stadium-loading facilities that required the wholesale razing of old neighborhoods and the erasure of existing street-and-block patterns. The result was devastating to a downtown that had been struggling to maintain even the pretense of true urban character. Finally, the Olympics landed in 1996, like a Martian invasion force. The local boosters created a perfect mascot for the games—a purple wormlike creature of no identifiable species that was soon dubbed "Whatizzit," or "Izzy" for short, by wags in the press. "Izzy" had a lot in common with the other things that were being built for the Olympics, like Centennial Park, a concrete pad surrounded by bowling-trophy-like pylons of no identifiable cultural reference, and the World of Coca Cola, a weird shrine/museum/giftshop fronting a wounded little "open space" called Polk Plaza.

The international Olympic site selection committee, it turned out, had been liberally bribed—with everything from cold cash, to free college tuition, to complimentary surgery—so that they might ignore the fact that summertime was awfully hot for running track outdoors in Atlanta. The bribery scandal was still very much alive and generating heated radio chat three years later in the fall of 1999 when I plied the frightening lanes of the downtown connector.

On the Ground

Along Peachtree Street from the city's maimed downtown north to its spatially nebulous Midtown, Atlanta fits all the particulars of that organism described by the *Washington Post* writer Joel Garreau in his famous 1992 book *Edge City*—namely, an agglomeration of inward-turned buildings designed primarily for the convenience of motorists, offering a high concentration of office and retail and, in most instances, no residential. In Atlanta's case, the quality and character of the suburban "edge" had overwhelmed the center so that the whole overblown metropolitan area, including downtown, had become a galaxy of Edge City projects tied together by the freeways and the gruesome multilane "collector" streets, such as Peachtree. The post-modern air-conditioned glass box office towers form a spine of orientation that makes sense viewed from the road at 70 mph, but dissolves into incoherence at ground level, where the towers prove to be miles apart. Between them lies an incoherent streetscape of engineered uniform traffic geometries, curb cuts, cheesy strip malls, parking lots, fry pits, baffling blank-walled museums and a meager residue of prewar fabric—including the three-story Queen Anne style apartment building where Margaret Mitchell wrote *Gone With the Wind*. She literally called it "the dump," though it is now one of the few buildings along Peachtree with any historic character whatsoever.[9]

The utter failure to create any meaningful pedestrian environment (that is, a rewarding public realm) defines the heart of Atlanta today. Every bad idea in the service of contemporary urban design came together here with a public attitude that can be summed up as *the outside doesn't matter.* It was Mayor Andrew Young in the 1980s who famously told embattled preservationists that "Atlanta has no character—we're building it now." Young's view was not altogether accurate, of course, in terms of either the character of the past or the quality of the future. Even if Atlanta's historic buildings had been, on the whole, banal and mediocre, at least there had been a traditional street-and-block-plan armature to hang a city on. The new stuff, both the buildings and the Edge City context created for the buildings, were worse than the old stuff by many orders of magnitude.

The definitive statement was left to an ambitious Atlanta architect-turned-developer named John Portman who, during the "go-go" years of *urban renewal,* designed a particular new kind of heroically grandiose antiurban hotel that became the darling of bigtime commercial developers and *visionary* municipal planning officials all over the nation. Eventually, a whole string of Portman-designed hotel "complexes" would be replicated in Detroit, San Francisco, and Los Angeles. Physically, these hotels looked like elongated silver bullets—and were expected to act like one in economically distressed downtowns, slaying bugbears such as crime, unemployment, and property abandonment, but they never worked as touted.[10]

The prototype Atlanta Hyatt Regency of 1968 is an inside-out building that rejects the surrounding street and attempts to compensate with a seven-hundred-foot-high indoor atrium, along which elevators climb like the projectiles in a theme park thrill ride. The atrium was designed to do one thing—to awe the visitor with insane amounts of interior space. But rather than make people feel grand, the outlandish atrium only made them feel small. In fact it was so overwhelming that it induced vertigo, agoraphobia, and panic attacks. Portman's tower did nothing else well. The circular scheme disoriented casual visitors. Service space was poorly organized. The floor plan for the hotel rooms was clunky and unforgiving. The money had gone into the awesome void in the center of the structure. At the very top of Portman's great silvery glass tube was a revolving restaurant, originally called the Polaris Lounge, as though it were the flight bridge of a gigantic intercontinental ballistic missile, which the building resembled. The hotel was only one part of a complex of office buildings called the Peachtree Center that functioned, in essence, exactly like a suburban office park. The context beyond the exterior curtain wall meant nothing. You were expected to drive there. Besides, what species of *loser* would even want to be out there in the sticky ninety-four-degree heat, melting into the sidewalk on a street that had all the charm of a freeway off-ramp?

Portman's great rival in the late-twentieth-century orgy of terrible Atlanta architecture was Tom Cousins, a former prefab house builder turned megadeveloper who managed to get his hands on the air rights above the old downtown railroad yards, a twelve-acre tract known as the Gulch. Cousins then snatched the glory away from Portman by getting the city contract to build the next-generation convention hall, a leviathan called the World Congress Center, with floor space equal to 108 football fields. The site just west of downtown was a good mile hike from Portman's Peachtree Center and even farther from the old convention center that was the raison d'être for Portman's complex. Adjacent to the World Congress Center Cousins plunked the Omni Coliseum, the basketball arena for his team, the Hawks (since replaced, under Ted Turner's ownership, by the Phillips Arena, which also accommodates NHL ice hockey). These would be joined by the Georgia Dome football stadium for the NFL Falcons. All these were accessorized with a monumental parking structure, known as the Decks. The whole area became a sports-and-convention Edge City that was functionally dead most of the time, except during ballgames, and then it was overwhelmed by vehicles. Physically, it was cut off from the rest of downtown by suburban-style landscape buffers, parking wastelands, and forbidding highway geometrics.

Nobody lived anywhere near the damned things. They did nothing, really, for the life of the city.

At the downtown edge of this giant sports-and-show pod, Cousins undertook a development debacle called the Omni International, which included two office towers, a hotel, six movie theaters, an upscale interior shopping mall (Hermès, Lanvin, Givenchy, and so forth), restaurants, a so-called International Bazaar (imported home decor made by child slaves in Asia), and a ridiculous $14-million indoor high-rise "fantasy park" designed by a couple of guys who produced a TV cartoon show. This awkwardly named venue, the World of Sid & Marty Kroft, closed for lack of business in six months.[11] Even children were confused and embarrassed by it. The Omni International Center eventually failed altogether. The buildings were sold to TV tycoon Ted Turner in 1985 and converted into a headquarters for his CNN empire, which they remain to this day. John Portman lost financial control of the Peachtree Center in 1990.

Adjacent to these things lay one other final oddity of the era: Underground Atlanta, an air-conditioned shopping and eating mall that occupied a layer one story below the street level—or what had been street level at an earlier time, before the capping of the railroad right of ways. Underground Atlanta had the unfortunate effect of draining the little remaining pedestrian life off the surface of downtown and therefore making the historic center look yet more desolate, even at lunch hour on a workday. It also became a notorious attractor of young predator-thugs. Underground Atlanta has been closed, renovated, and reopened over the years, but on the whole it has been unsuccessful, especially as the suburban frontier, with its own malls, crept steadily farther out.

The Omni International, Peachtree Center, the sports stadia, the World Congress Center, Atlanta Underground, all of these things were built for people on wheels, people coming from the airport in rent-a-cars, or suburban commuters coming to work in a downtown that retained almost no character of a real downtown anymore—which, in short, was just another motoring destination among a growing constellation of many others. By the 1970s, the business leadership and the white political establishment were not quite sure what kind of city Atlanta was anymore, or where it was going, or who it belonged to. But fewer and fewer of them actually lived in the city anymore.

The Race Train

Beginning in 1968, a campaign was launched by the last generation of southern progressive politicians to build a public transit system in Atlanta. The greatest beneficiaries of the proposed system would have been the city's poorest citizens, those least in a position to own cars. As it happened, the proposal was killed the first two times it was presented to the voters in the form of bond issues, and, ironically, at exactly the time when white flight had peaked and the city had achieved a majority African-American population. Blacks initially viewed public transit suspiciously as a gigantic pork barrel meant to enrich white contractors and the white owners of department stores that had only just been successfully desegregated a few years earlier. A third referendum took place in 1971. This time, more than $1 billion in federal funds stood behind the proposal. The black leadership had issued a list of twenty-six "concerns" that would determine their support. Sam Massell, the last white mayor Atlanta would elect in the twentieth century, desperately argued that the federal windfall would benefit blacks both in the short term in construction jobs and the long term in civic revitalization. This time the MARTA (Metro Atlanta Rapid Transit Authority) referendum passed by a healthy margin.

MARTA was constructed on an axis following the cardinal points of the compass (largely to take advantage of existing railroad right of ways). The decanting of whites into the suburbs had concentrated them north of the city, while blacks tended to live along the east-west axis and south of the city. There had been a hope and an expectation that MARTA would partially compensate for white flight by bringing white northern suburbanites back into downtown, at least to work during the daytime, and, the hoping went on, to shop, dine, and be entertained at night there. (Some of the northern counties were dry, so you had to go somewhere else to get a legal drink.) At the same time, though, white suburbanites understood that the MARTA line would run in both directions, prompting familiar old xenophobic fears, in this case that blacks would ride the train up to the northern suburbs (with the implication that they would come to commit crimes).

Meanwhile, since MARTA had come into being due to black votes, there was a sense that the needs of the black city-dwelling majority ought not take second place behind the needs of white people who didn't even live in the city anymore. The upshot was that the east-west axis was built first. So through the first years of construction and operation, MARTA was viewed as largely a project for *black* Atlantans. White suburbanites discreetly mocked it, saying that MARTA stood for *Moving Africans Rapidly Through Atlanta*. The center of the system was a station in the heart of the old downtown called Five Points that, by segregationist custom, had been off-limits to African-Americans as late as the 1960s. Now, it became theirs, the crossroads of a demographically black majority city. An increase in crime that was more than just perceptual did occur during the long, lingering recession of the 1970s. Suburban whites gave up on downtown altogether while muggings of out-of-town white visitors increased dramatically around the downtown convention hotels.

A parallel phenomenon was at work during this period: the mass movement of offices and retail out to the suburbs where the office workers had moved with their families. It happened in cities all over America as a kind of fractal efflorescence of the suburban organism. But there had been a considerable time lag, from the 1960s into the 1980s, between the people moving to *new houses* in the 'burbs and the new *business* infrastructure following them. When the corporate boxes arrived in their innumerable pods, they became the basic fabric of Edge City. Why drive into downtown Atlanta when you could have your corporate office right out on the strip in Chamblee or Roswell? It became normal for corporate CEOs to locate their new suburban offices within a five-minute drive of their own homes. So, by the time the north-south line of MARTA opened, a huge exodus of remaining corporate offices from downtown had occurred, and the transit line therefore would not accomplish one of its original goals of bringing white workers back into the heart of town during the day.

MARTA had additional design problems that aggravated the issues of social justice in Atlanta. The rail stations were very far apart—miles in some cases—once you got out of the immediate downtown. The streets of, say, Buckhead, or suburban Doraville were pedestrian nightmares. The sidewalks were discontinuous or nonexistent, the distances between things vast. There was no radial component to the great cross-axis of the MARTA rail line, either. To get anywhere in between the axis lines people relied on a stitched-together system of lurching diesel buses that traveled tortuous routes and stopped, on average, at forty-minute intervals and in some cases only a few times a day. The bus stops, moreover, were dreary, undignified plastic shelters located often in the middle of nowhere out on eight-lane strip highways, usually in poor repair, scrawled upon with graffiti, littered with trash, and poorly lighted at night—the sort of places used only by those with no better choice. MARTA therefore became a second-class transportation system for second-class citizens. Driving was the first-class mode, and compared to the $1.7 billion spent on MARTA, the automobile infrastructure of freeways and free parking amounted to many more multiple billions, a gold-plated public amenity that the public would never deign to think of as government-subsidized.

Edge City: An Experiment That Has Failed

It was ever so ironic, therefore, that in the spring of 1999, one Wayne Hill, chairman of the Atlanta Regional Commission, got stuck in traffic on his way to a meeting of that body where the fate of the proposed "northern arc" freeway that he favored would be voted on. Hill, who was also the highest elected official in Gwinnett County, arrived at the ARC chamber only in time to hear that the freeway had been voted down by the other board members.[12]

In the face of overwhelming evidence that the Atlanta metropolitan region faces a dysfunctional future, most Atlantans cling tenaciously to the illusion that suburban sprawl had been ordained by the founding fathers and God Almighty as the best possible setting for democracy and personal freedom. In early 2000, the metro region was cited by *Physicians Weekly* magazine, as "Fat City," with the worst obesity problem in America, a greater than 100 percent increase in aggregate fatness during the past seven years alone. The study had been done by Atlanta's own Centers for Disease Control, and the shocking result was attributed unambiguously to the region's extreme car dependency.[13]

During the year leading up to the millennium, the expansion into the northern suburbs of Cobb, Gwinnett, and Cherokee counties continued apace, with the obligatory complement of new malls and office parks. Meanwhile, the new GRTA superagency had failed to accomplish anything besides organizing itself bureaucratically. The usual NIMBY psychodramas occurred almost daily in the suburban townships as residents who had already gottem their McMansion on a half acre battled to prevent later arrivals from getting their McMansion on a half acre. In this atmosphere of paranoia and selfishness, the suburban frontier pushed ever farther out to still-rural townships that issued building permits to all comers—until the entire ninety-mile corridor between Atlanta and Chattanooga was in the thrall of bulldozers.

There were a few stirrings of activity at the old center of Atlanta that held some cause for hope for an alternative to suburbia, but the masses were far from convinced about doing things differently. One ray of hope was an announcement by the Bell South corporation that it would consolidate seventy-five far-flung offices with thirteen thousand employees into three mixed-use complexes located on MARTA stops over the next decade. This was based on the recognition by its chief, F. Duane Ackerman, that car dependency and mandatory commuting were reducing all his employees' quality of life to a degree that soon nobody with half a brain would want to live in the region and work for Bell South.

Another bright spot was the ambitious work being done by a big real estate development company called Post Properties, whose CEO, John Williams, had undergone one of those personal transformative experiences that left him convinced that sprawl represented a tragic blunder and that his industry had to find a better pathway into the future. Accordingly, Williams engaged the leading New Urbanist town planning firm, Duany and Plater-Zyberk (DPZ) of Miami, the people who had pretty much founded the New Urbanist movement, starting in 1989 with Seaside, Florida, to design a new urban quarter.[14] Until then, Post Properties had done some apartment complexes with shops around various Sunbelt cities, but never before with a major office component—in other words, a place where you could theoretically live and work and buy groceries. What an idea! DPZ talked them into it, arguing that the retail, the restaurants, the exercise emporium would all do much better with both day and evening trade. The result was a very dense, mixed-use, practically European-scaled neighborhood called Riverside, which would incorporate several hundred apartments with substantial office space and, at the ground floor level where they belonged, shops and restaurants that could easily be used by people on foot.

There were a couple of major problems with it. One was that the property Post had to work with was way the hell out by the intersection of I-75 and the I-285 perimeter freeway, with two major malls—Cumberland and the Galleria—within shouting distance to compete with Riverside's retail. Two, the property was nowhere near a MARTA stop. Also, the parcel's rugged topography, and its location on a bluff beside the Chattahoochee River, made it impossible to connect with the surrounding street system— which was, in any case, an incoherent spaghetti wad of suburban collector streets, superblocks, and residential cul-de-sacs. You had to get there by car, at least for now. DPZ managed to integrate the parking in the interior of the new blocks they created, plus there was a generous amount of curbside parking along the new streets. Well, the land *was* where it *was*. That's what DPZ had to work with.

Variances were necessary from top to bottom to get Riverside built. Under the area's normal codes, everything good about the proposal was illegal and had to be fought over. DPZ more or less fell on their swords in compromise to get the project approved and finished. However well-designed Riverside was internally, DPZ knew that it was essentially a cul-de-sac pod in its own right. The deformities of local culture simply could not be entirely overcome yet. The apartments were even further isolated by a gate, because paranoia about crime (that is, African-American intruders) remained so common. For all its shortcomings, however, Riverside was a raving market success, both for the developer and for the metro region. It was an important step in a better direction—

like the first lurch of a stroke rehab patient without his walker. As a visual model it was swell. DPZ hoped that people would get the message: *This is how well new development can be done. Now go out and find us some decent sites!* It became quite an attraction for curious gawkers from nearby suburban Buckhead and Dunwoody, who, for all the luxurious appointments of their faux Norman castle homes, had absolutely nowhere to go in public but the dreary strip-mall universe of upper Peachtree. Atlanta was so devoid of memorable streets or even fragments of urbanism that Riverside came off like Bruges on the Chattahoochee, and the rubber-neckers flocked to it with their digital cameras.

A much more ambitious proposal on a prime site soon followed. The city had acquired, and sold to a developer, the Atlantic Steel Works property, a 144-acre classic industrial "brownfield" just north of downtown. The topography was much more favorable than had been the case with Riverside. A prewar traditional street-and-block system of steelworker neighborhoods existed adjacent to the parcel, so the old streets could flow into the streets of this proposed new urban quarter. Here, too, however, local culture and local bias (basically the fear of genuine urbanism) undermined the effort to design something truly mixed-use and pedestrian-friendly. All the necessary elements were there—the apartments, the theaters, the offices, the shops—but they were poorly arranged. They didn't connect to each other or to the surrounding city fabric. Each piece was treated as an outparcel. It was an uncooked stew. The design had been based on statistics rather than drawings. In fact, it was a classic Edge City—only it was near the center of the city, and when the *edge* comes to the *center* you have a problem.

DPZ was called in—this time by the Environmental Protection Agency—to "fix" what the local architects had done. DPZ ran a three-day charrette and redesigned the thing entirely. An independent analyst hired by the EPA concluded that the DPZ plan was far superior to the original, but, of course, the extreme perversity of human character was not taken into account in the process, for as soon as his findings were released, the local team gutted DPZ's revisions in an act of vengeance.[15]

During the late nineties, getting around Atlanta had become such a chronic headache that a dribble of gainfully employed people were actually moving back into the city from the far-out 'burbs. A very small number of Atlantans were connecting the dots, realizing that their discontent had to do directly with their living arrangements. So, they opted to live differently. The old streetcar neighborhoods such as Little Five Points, Candler Park, Inman Park, Grant Park, Adair Park, Virginia Highlands, even a tiny cluster of shotgun shacks originally occupied by cotton mill workers, called Cabbagetown, all underwent significant revival. The *risk-oblivious,* usually bohemians or career persons without children, were snapping up loft space in old abandoned industrial buildings all around downtown. Unfortunately, this activity was not happening in high enough concentrations to revive whole undervalued neighborhoods, or to bring back the shopping amenities they required, and the city government was fairly clueless in helping out with code variances, tax incentives, and other concrete measures within their powers.

The Midtown district was getting bombed with substantial apartment buildings. That was the good news. The bad news was that the mid-rise apartment buildings tended to rise in isolation along Peachtree Street, cut off from even the possibility of urban amenities by parking lots, corporate bunkers, landscaping berms, and other dumb-ass contrivances that furnished no places for retail, even if retail wanted to be there. Consequently, even the people who moved into multistory apartment buildings in the heart of town were left car-dependent. Also in many cases, the garage structures behind the new apartments were as bulky as the apartment buildings themselves. Tragically, this was the *better* stuff being built. Run-of-the-mill Atlanta developers had a perverse fondness for a certain type of wooden garden apartment complex on a gated cul-de-sac, and they were popping these things all over Midtown. As a kind of millennium capper to a century of bonehead development decisions, a Wal-Mart "power center" (that is, a giant strip mall) was under construction in late 1999 on the property off Ponce de Leon Boulevard where the old Atlanta *Crackers* minor-league baseball stadium had once stood—yet another megagenerator of unnecessary car trips. The lack of collective vision meant that it might take yet another generation to fill in the holes and blunders created by the current generation of urban infill.

ATLANTA

The Repo Economy

I started this chapter by asking the question: Does Edge City have a future? My answer is a plain *no*. In Atlanta they are constructing a giant misbegotten organism that will almost certainly not be able to function far into the future. Suburbia, more than being a set of *things,* might be described more accurately as a set of behaviors. They were behaviors made possible only under the extremely abnormal conditions of late-twentieth-century life in the U.S.A.: unprecedented political and economic stability, extraordinary immunity to the consequences of bad decisions (really, the ability to mortgage the present against the future), and cheap oil, cheap oil, cheap oil. All these things are apt to change in the years directly ahead.

In the public debates about suburbia, the idea is almost always put forward that suburbia exists because Americans like it and want it. That may have been so. But if so, it may have been a poor choice. What's more, that people like a way of living, or are accustomed to certain behavior, does not mean that circumstance will necessarily allow them to continue that way of living. Junkies like their heroin, too, but after a while their veins collapse, their immune systems switch off, and their organs begin to shut down. I'm convinced that circumstances in the twenty-first century will compel us to live very differently.

The next economy will be the Repo economy when, for example, amazing numbers of "Ditech 125 percent Dream Loans" will be labeled *nonperforming* and seedy-looking men armed with repossession notices show up in the circular driveways of the defaulted-upon chipboard-and-vinyl McMansions in places like Cherokee County, Georgia, to change the locks on the putative collateral. I see this unwinding of credit and presumed wealth evolving into a tremendous political fight over the table scraps of the cheap-oil economy and the dubious material artifacts it produced, pitting neighbor against neighbor, group against group, and region against region.

I believe that the world is entering a long era of chronic instability in oil markets that no amount of wishing or pretending will hold back. By the time this book is published—a year from now—I shall be surprised if we are not experiencing the initial effects. The two oil-producing regions that allowed America to postpone this reckoning for twenty-five years, the Alaskan North Slope fields, and the North Sea fields (belonging to Britain and Norway), are scheduled to pass their production peaks this year, and after that, most of the oil in the world will be controlled by people who don't like us, or contained in regions too chaotic to engage in the complex business of oil extraction.[16] The Middle East regions containing the greatest reserves will be the last to peak, but long before they do, the oil markets will destabilize. In the current American mood of narcotized inattention, the point can't be emphasized enough that it is not necessary for oil reserves to run out before world oil markets are severely destabilized. And when that occurs, industrial economies will be painfully compromised.

We Americans cherish a set of delusions to minimize or deflect the seriousness of this. As already touched on, we believe that we can run a drive-in civilization on some fuel other than petroleum. The actual prospects for this are dim, but we base our belief (a wish, really) on the spectacular cavalcade of technological achievements that occurred in the previous century, one astonishing novelty after another: airplanes, movies, radio, TV, antibiotics, Teflon, computers, automobiles themselves. (The lingering "victory disease" from our great triumph in World War Two still stokes our delusions of invincibility.)[17] Alternative energy sources such as natural gas, biomass, coal, nuclear power, solar power, fuel cells, and so forth, will fall far short of compensating for disrupted oil markets. It will be a hard lesson. The world's fleet of eleven thousand jet airplanes will not run on coal or plutonium. Massive disruptions to transportation and business will occur. The "global economy" as touted in recent years—meaning the long-range transport of enormous quantities of cheap goods virtually everywhere—will join mercantile imperialism in the history books. Food production, which depends heavily on oil-based fertilizers, will be affected by oil market disturbances. The Caesar salad that travels twenty-five hundred miles from California to somebody's table in Atlanta will become an object of nostalgia. Farming will have to become much more labor-intensive, will have to be practiced on a far smaller scale, and done much closer to market. Half a million other products, from medicine, asphalt, paint, and detergent to plastic trash bags, are also derived from oil. As the oil markets destabilize, shortages and fluctuating prices in oil will hinder industry from even addressing the problem of converting societies to other forms of energy.

The fact is that we are an oil-based economy. A peculiar destiny allowed Americans to rely on seemingly limitless cheap oil for the half century following World War Two. We invested hugely in the infrastructure of an everyday life dedicated to cheap oil. Edge City is the climactic efflorescence of that, and Atlanta is the epitome of Edge City. It is also a prime example of what the historian Joseph Tainter called *the overinvestment in complexity with diminishing returns,* an unfortunate human tendency to repeatedly overshoot the limits of growth.[18] The last thing America needed in the late twentieth century was Edge City, and it may be the last big present we can give ourselves.

We are susceptible to another frightening set of interrelated problems: global warming, runaway population growth, and the spread of epidemic diseases such as AIDS and bovine spongiform encephalopathy, with huge implications for economic breakdown and political disorder—but these are topics worthy of whole books and I can only mention them in this one.

In my view, Atlanta has become such a mess that really nothing can be done to redeem it as a human habitat. Like the other great, roaring, car-dependent megalopoli of the American Sunbelt, Atlanta's only plausible destiny at the threshold of the new millennium is to become significantly depopulated.

MEXICO CITY

The End of the World and Other Cataclysms

No it is not a dream. I am not walking in my sleep. I have seen you at last. And now you have come out of the clouds to sit on your throne again.

MOCTEZUMA, UPON MEETING HERNÁN CORTÉS [1]

It was the rainy season, but the rains hadn't come in this super El Niño year. Forest fires raged out of control south of the city in the states of Oaxaca and Guerrero and the air pollution approached supernatural levels. At ground level the ozone concentrations exceeded the national safety standard by 200 percent, and trees were dying in Chapultepec Park. Flying into the airport over the ragged rim of mountaintops that enclosed the enormous basin like an ancient fortification, you saw the city smoldering below like a gigantic ashtray.

It is believed that there may be as many as 30 million people living in the old Valley of Mexico, as this now thoroughly urbanized basin is called, but nobody really knows. The experts at the University of Mexico don't know. They can only guess. In any case, the city's population amounts to roughly one-quarter of all the people in the United Mexican States, as the republic is officially called. The population has become a great mysterious shape-shifting god that expresses itself in conditions as different as the appalling low-rise slums of Chalco in the dried-up lakebed of the same name and the new luxury high-rise condominiums of the Santa Fe suburbs hugging the rugged foothills in the Sierra Madre Occidental. The organism is too big and restless for its constituent cells to be counted. Suffice it to say that Mexico City is at least the second-or-third-most-populous urban place in the world (after Tokyo and Jakarta). Its problems are at once culturally unique and emblematic of conditions in many other poor countries—though whether Mexico is actually a poor or rich country in the first place is hotly debated among Mexican intellectuals.

These unknowable, uncountable, unquantifiable issues of measurement, in a place where not even the ground is solid, do not alter what is visible and palpable in this fearsome metropolis: that it is in a state of crisis verging on breakdown. The government pretends to govern, public safety is a joke, the quality of life is unpleasant for the well-off and atrocious for the vastly more numerous poor, the air is lethal, the water is septic, human waste has nowhere to go, epidemics erupt with medieval virulence, automobile traffic is stupendous and horribly corrosive of public life, trash lies scattered even in the best neighborhoods and the streets smell badly everywhere, a major earthquake could happen at any time (as, indeed, one did in 1985, killing ninety-five hundred citizens), and even the nearby volcano Popocatépetl has stirred in recent years, insidiously venting poison gases into slums that suffer every other conceivable ill to which human settlements are prone. If limits to human growth are comprehensible, then Mexico City presents them in terms that are starkly obvious, beginning with the geophysical setting.

Mexico City and the urbanized Federal District surrounding it occupy a high basin approximately twenty miles wide by forty miles long, 7,350 feet in altitude—about a half mile higher than Denver. The massive high plateau that covers much of central Mexico is poorly drained, and the basin of Mexico City is subject to the worst consequences of this condition. Water running down the surrounding mountain slopes during the rainy season (May to September) has no outlet. The basin formerly contained a set of interconnected shallow lakes, ranging from three to nine feet deep. The largest of these was Lake Texcoco where the Aztecs built their capital of Tenochtitlán on a barren little island near the western shore. The lakes of the Valley of Mexico all had varying degrees of salinity, depending on their depth and the runoff they received. However, rainwater picks up dissolved minerals as it filters down the slopes. Since there was no outlet, the water never flushed out of the basin. It just steadily evaporated, leaving behind dissolved salts, ever-concentrating in their intensity. Lake Texcoco was nearly as briny as the ocean. To the Aztecs, the lake system was a marvelous military resource, a defensive buffer against their numerous enemies, and a tactical benefit for moving large numbers of warriors in canoes quickly around the basin. The lakes were also a source of food, since they attracted migrating waterfowl and produced some fish, as well as the insect larvae the Aztecs incorporated into their diet. The Spanish considered the lakes a noisome, flyblown nuisance and systematically filled them in as their own city took shape over the ruins of Tenochtitlán, but hydrological problems remain today, unseen, beneath the crumbling cathedrals, plazas, and teeming streets.

The encircling ring of mountains also effectively traps air in the valley, especially during the winter dry season. Engine emissions and industrial gases have nowhere to go. Now that the lakes are drained and the beds exposed, wind picks up precipitated salts and metals and adds them to the mix of pollutants. Another ingredient is dried fecal matter turned to dust, which, airborne, transmits diseases ranging from cholera to tuberculosis to exotic fungi, to common intestinal ailments. Things flow into the Valley of Mexico and cannot find a way out. You could hardly select a worse site for a modern, industrial metropolis.

In spite of, or even because of, these geomorphic anomalies, the Valley of Mexico was a congenial site for preindustrial human settlement. The climate of the high plateau is much more temperate than the blistering subtropical or desert lowlands at the same latitude. The annual median temperature is sixty-four degrees. Nights are cool and agreeable. Fossil evidence indicates that humans migrating down the North American continent found in this basin a hunting ground so rich that it resembled a meat market. Unearthed bones of mastodons, camel-like creatures, and wild horses show unmistakable signs of human butchering. These prehistoric people succeeded so well in exterminating the megafauna that their descendants did not possess beasts of burden or any other large domestic animals for work or food. Nor did they ever conceive the technology of the wheel. Yet they developed several high cultures in parallel to, and isolation from, those of Europe and Asia with peculiar features that resonate strongly into the present day.

Aztec Meltdown

Mystery obscures the rise and fall of Mesoamerican civilizations before the Aztecs. Next to nothing is known about the Olmec, other than the gigantic basalt head sculptures they left behind when their culture vanished around 900 B.C. The Maya peaked in the eighth century A.D. at a population estimated at 14 million. They had developed a high culture of mathematics, astronomy, and ideographic writing. Their calendar was more accurate than the Gregorian one used in Europe. They produced monumental architecture and a high order of arts and crafts. The Maya seem to have been overcome by some internal catastrophe, a massive ecological collapse, possibly in connection with rapid population growth or climate change—crop failure, soil depletion, overirrigation, epidemic disease—resulting in administrative breakdown and social strife. We don't really know. Whatever it was, it occurred swiftly. The Mayan capital, Chichen Itza, was wholly abandoned by A.D. 1200 and was eventually swallowed up by the jungle. By the time the Spanish landed, the Yucatán was nearly depopulated. Of the remaining primary Maya records, the Spanish bishop Diego de Landa deliberately destroyed all but three bark paper codices, around 1560.

Another impressive civilization evolved twenty-five miles north of present-day Mexico City, at Teotihuacán, around the same time as Rome. Its chief ruin is the massive Pyramid of the Sun, constructed beginning around 100 B.C., half the height of the Great Pyramid of Cheops, but greater in volume. By A.D. 500, Teotihuacán occupied eight square miles, centered on a monumental boulevard of temples and palaces, surrounded by urban quarters including a mix of villas and multifamily houses. Around A.D. 700, Teotihuacán was mysteriously abandoned. Population pressure, the diminishing returns of irrigation, crop failure, volcanic activity, and climate change are all possible causes. Human skeletal remains indicate that even the Teotihuacán elite suffered malnourishment. There is evidence, too, of a major sacking of the city coincident with the rise of the nearby Toltec culture. Exactly who the inhabitants of Teotihuacán were, or even what language they spoke, is unknown. The names of their gods are lost to history.

Toltec culture is nearly as puzzling. They were aggressively expansion-ist and warlike in a way that hadn't been seen before in Mesoamerica. Ruins of the monumental buildings they left at their colony in Chichen Itza, far away in the Yucatán, are larger than the remains at Tula, their seat of empire and administration in central Mexico, fifty-five miles northeast of Mexico City. Mayan civilization was already in steep decline when the Toltecs established their outposts in the Yucatán, but the Toltecs evidently adopted some of the Maya mythology. By the twelfth century, a great roiling migration of various peoples, the Aztec among them, undermined and subsumed the Toltec empire. Its annals were overwritten by the Aztecs and otherwise lost.

A great deal more is known about the Aztec empire, since its culture collided directly with Europe's and therefore with modern narrative his-tory. What is most striking about the Aztecs was the brevity of their rise and fall, played out in less than two hundred years, from the founding of Tenochtitlán around 1325 to the conquest by Cortés in 1521.

The Aztecs came to the Valley of Mexico around the twelfth century A.D. from Azatlán in the north, guided, they said, by their guardian spirit, Huitzilopochtli, the "hummingbird of the left" (the left being the south-ward edge of the world in Aztec cosmography). They sojourned for sev-eral generations among the Toltecs in their capital of Tollan (now Tula), and probably contributed to the further decline of an already diminished empire. The Aztecs' relationship with the Toltec was parasitical. They acted as mercenary warriors, essentially fighting the Toltecs' battles for them. As a byproduct of this relationship, the Aztecs acquired the Toltec knowledge of agriculture, construction technology, and the calendar, and blended motifs of Toltec history with their own mythology. The Aztec deity Quetzalcoatl derives from the tenth-century figure of a Toltec ruler, Topiltzin Quetzalcoatl, "our young prince, the feathered serpent," who reigned during the period that the Toltecs regarded as their golden age. An important feature of this story involving the forlorn departure of a prince/god figure, and his predicted apocalyptic return in the future was among the mythological baggage the Toltecs had, in turn, adopted earlier from the Maya. It would prove to be a pivotal piece of cultural

DNA in the Aztec meltdown. The Toltecs may also have introduced the Aztecs to a cult of systematic human sacrifice.

By the late thirteenth century, the Aztecs quit Tollan and moved fifty-five miles south into the Valley of Mexico. For a while, they occupied the heights of Chapultepec ("Grasshopper Hill") on the west bank of Lake Texcoco and leased out their services as warriors to the other peoples in the vicinity, the Tepanec, Tlaxcaltecs, Coyoacans, Chalcans, Xochimilco, and others. In 1325, they took possession of an island no one else wanted in the swampy brackish lake and used it as a strategic bastion for fomenting wars between their neighbors. Playing one group off against another, they swiftly came to dominate the complex political life of the valley.

In creating their island capital, Tenochtitlán, the Aztec made effective use of the technology they had absorbed from the Toltec. They constructed masonry and earthen causeways to the mainland and built a complex canal system in and around the fortified island—the Spaniards would compare it favorably with Venice. They organized immense gangs of laborers to build a sophisticated dike nine thousand meters long to raise the level and thus reduce the salinity of Lake Texcoco. They secured fresh water supplies by means of a masonry aqueduct from springs in Chapultepec. Note that they did not employ the wheel in any of these ventures. Nor did they possess any domestic draught animals, no camels, horses, goats, or oxen. They had dogs, fowl, and rabbits, and not much else. Materials not moved by canoe or barge had to be carried by human porters.

The Aztec practiced a highly productive double-crop method of agriculture on small artificial islands called *chinampas,* planting squash, beans, or chili peppers between the rows of maize. In the absence of large domestic animals, they depended on fish, birds, lake shrimp, snakes, and insects for protein, and were known to harvest enormous mats of mosquito larvae and algae from the lake as a supplemental food. Their diet was notably lacking in fats.

By the late 1400s, the population of the valley reached an estimated two million, with Tenochtitlán itself around 250,000—as great as any contemporary city in Europe. Even while warring with one group or another, the Aztecs created a formidable trading network. In fact, they commonly started wars on the pretext that their traders were being molested, and fought ever more far-flung campaigns as their trading territory expanded.

The most dramatic events of the Aztec melodrama were shaped by a single man in the extraordinary persona of one Tlaclaelel, whose very long life spanned the century from 1398 until 1496—shortly before the arrival of Cortés. Never a ruler himself, but the highest official behind several thrones, with more real power, at times, than the monarch, Tlaclaelel was personally responsible for stage-managing his people's most extreme and violent exploits in the era preceding Cortés, including the ceaseless military campaigns against their neighbors, the weird rituals of their diplomatic relations, and the horrific operation of the Huitzilopochtli cult with its extravaganzas of human sacrifice and cannibalism.

Tlaclaelel emerged as a political force during the reign of his father Itzcoatl (1427–40). He was one of innumerable children of many royal wives, received a privileged education in the *calmecac* (a school of leadership for the Aztec nobility), and as a young warrior distinguished himself in campaigns against the Xochimilcos and the Chalcans. Upon the death of Itzcoatl and the elevation of Moctezuma I to the throne, his half-brother Tlaclaelel was appointed to the singular position of *cihuacoatl,* chief advisor to the ruler. The Aztec king, by the way, bore the title *tlatoani,* meaning "first speaker," a curious detail.

The psychologist Julian Jaynes, trying to account for the conquest of the New World empires by comparatively tiny bands of Spaniards, has argued that New World human consciousness might not have developed analogously with European consciousness, leaving groups such as the Inca and the Aztec vulnerable to behavior that they could not comprehend.[2] It is a controversial theory, developed by Jaynes in the 1970s. Jaynes's hypothesis rests on the idea that consciousness is a "learned cultural ability," not a genetic program, and that what we understand to be *modern* consciousness is superimposed over a "vestigial substrate" that he calls the "bicameral mind." Jaynes argues that many intellectual constructs taken for granted by Europeans of the 1500s—notions of self, of time and causality, for instance—did not spring fullblown into human culture but rather evolved with the development of language and our ability to create increasingly complex metaphors for describing objective reality. He argues that such building blocks of modern consciousness had not yet evolved into regular features of New World culture, indeed that New World consciousness was limited in ways that are almost impossible to imagine today.

To put it as simply as possible, Jaynes proposed that New World peoples as late as the fifteenth century A.D. experienced their own thoughts not as we do, but in the rudimentary form of "hallucinated" voices—the remembered voices of leaders and kinsman, living and dead. That is, they didn't recognize thought *as* thought per se, as something emanating from their own minds. They didn't know that they were thinking, were neither conscious nor self-conscious of *being* conscious in the way we understand all these things. Jaynes went further to propose that, lacking these abilities, the New World peoples were unable to differentiate between the authority of others and the authority of an autonomous self. Central to Jaynes's argument is that the notion of an autonomous self is a relatively recent achievement of human cultural evolution. Large, complex civilizations, or "literate bicameral theocracies," in Jaynes's terminology, were able to flourish, he said, in the absence of mental mechanisms we take for granted as being somehow essential to hold such a human society together.

Jaynes finds abundant evidence for all this in the record of relations between archaic people and their "gods," literally the statues, idols, and figurines housed, fed, and tenderly cared for as though the statues themselves possessed animate spirits, literally *were* the gods. Indeed, Jaynes implies that among the crucial concepts missing in the bicameral mind was any firm distinction between what was living and what was not living—a residue of which exists in the animism of surviving older cultures around the world today, in which rocks, trees, animals, people, corpses, statues, figurines, all things contain spirits. In bicameral culture, *the houses of the dead,* especially dead chieftains, were built in order to amplify the remembered "voices" of the formerly living, aided by chanting, music, and other typically right-brained mnemonic devices that we regard as mystical or "religious." Over time, *the houses of the dead* evolved into temples, the houses of the gods, of departed heroic ancestors conflated through the rich embroidery of storytelling (that is, the practice of language) to mythic status, who "spoke" to their subject-descendants from a hidden realm and directed their activities with supernatural powers and the sheer authority of their status.

Jaynes's hypothesis finally poses the sequential breakdown of the bicameral mind in different parts of the Old World—Egypt, Israel, Mesopotamia, Greece—at various times in the centuries before Christ, and locates with some precision the rather swift propulsion of these bicameral cultures into a truly modern sensibility. It is a short step, that is, from the bicameral world of *The Iliad* (transmitted orally in chanted mnemonic bicameral verse), in which such emotions as wrath, fear, and desire are literally confused with the names of organs such as the heart, the stomach, the lungs—and the functions of these organs, the spurting of blood, hunger, nausea, breathing—to the world of Plato and Aristotle, around 360 B.C., with the fantastic coadvancements of language, abstract thinking, and real knowledge of the objective world that blossomed around them.

The Aztec fit the description of just such a "literate bicameral theocracy," and the level of ritual violence in their society suggests in Jaynesian terms a culture undergoing the painful first stages of the breakdown of the bicameral mind. It also seems possible to infer on the basis of the evidence that in the time that concerns us, the period around A.D. 1500, while most Aztecs did not possess a modern conscious sensibility, a few might well have achieved something like it, including perhaps the crucial consciousness of an autonomous self, or at least the fearful recognition of leaving a familiar state, in which one's activities are always directed by thoughts experienced as "voices," for a new and uncertain state of self-sovereignty. Imagine the anxiety such conditions might have provoked, and the extraordinary behavior in response to such overwhelming anxiety. The huge scale of human sacrifice in late Aztec culture suggests that the voices of the "gods," especially Huitzilopochtli, might have been literally fading away, and with them such fundamental assurances about life and survival as the very rising of the sun, and that the massive ceremonial slaughter was a desperate attempt to get back the attention of their chief god, guide, and protector.[3] Another way of stating this is that the Aztecs were so frightened by the acquisition of consciousness that they mistook it for existence itself.

As one of an elite possessing the ability to know *that* he was thinking, and *what* he was thinking, a privileged figure like Tlaclaelel therefore might have functioned administratively as a sort of exalted ventriloquist, using a succession of "first speakers" as his dummies, in order to direct the affairs of his people in a time of terrible uncertainty, anxiety, and upheaval when the gods seemed to be abandoning them. This hypothesis of the nature of Aztec consciousness may also account for the apparent mental confusion and fatal indecisiveness shown by Moctezuma II (reigned 1502–20)—who assumed his throne six years after the death of Tlaclaelel—when Cortés and his eerie band of strangers did confront the cannibal empire.

The actual procedure of Aztec sacrifice, well-documented in their own annals and in those of the Spanish conquerors who witnessed them, was a wholesale feeding of human hearts to the statue who "dwelt" in a house at the top of their largest pyramid. The explicit purpose was to fuel his journey across the sky, in the persona of the sun, and thus keep the Aztec universe in motion. At first, the victims were war captives, an estimated ten to twenty thousand per year. They were ritually butchered with obsidian knives and their extracted hearts were stuffed into the mouthlike aperture of the stone statue or burned with copal resin in stone censers. In the event, the "first speaker" himself customarily performed the first several killings and then turned over the proceedings to more muscular priests. Sometimes, captives were roasted alive in gigantic braziers. Other times they were flayed, and the Aztec priests danced in their skins.

It is not known exactly when the Aztecs began the practice of eating these sacrificial victims in more than symbolic portions—but their empire was so short-lived that it could not have been a long leap. Cannibalism of one kind or another is a common feature of archaic cultures around the world. Cannibalism turns up in annals from across North and South America. The early Jesuit missionaries of Canada record regular instances of it among the Huron, and certain Amazonian tribes were notorious up into the twentieth century. The question is not so much whether the Aztec were cannibals—this is beyond dispute—but why they practiced cannibalism on such a colossal scale.

In the 1450s, during the reign of Moctezuma I, a series of natural disasters, crop failures, a plague of grasshoppers, and floods occurred, placing the rapidly growing population at hazard of famine, and it may have been during these vicissitudes that large-scale cannibalism was institutionalized as a survival mechanism. As the practical troubles of the kingdom multiplied, the volume of sacrificial victims needed to mollify the angry gods increased dramatically. The sheer numbers of bodies certainly would have presented disposal problems. (The later eyewitness diaries of Cortés and his circle say that the Aztec were fastidious about the treatment of the lake surrounding their city, and had strict rules against dumping offal or human waste in it.)

In the face of famine and political breakdown in the mid-1400s, it fell to Tlaclaelel to contrive a system that would produce a steady supply of fresh sacrificial victims without the cost or bother of actual battle. He therefore instituted a diplomatic policy of ceremonial "flower wars" (*xochiyaotl*) with the Aztecs' neighboring vassals. It amounted to a sort of protection racket. At the conclusion of a staged combat, a prescribed number of prisoners were turned over to the Aztecs for sacrifice. Meanwhile, the royalty of the victim group would be escorted inside Tenochtitlán, taken up to the stagelike platform at the top of the main temple, close to the place where the sacrifices were carried out, like playgoers at the theater, and screened from the general view by a trellis of roses—hence "flower wars." During the grisly proceedings, which could occupy several days and nights, the visiting dignitaries were fed hallucinogenic mushrooms and treated to dishes of human flesh stewed with chilis, squash, and maize.[4]

The anthropologist Marvin Harris, drawing on scholarship by Michael J. Harner,[5] proposes that Aztec cannibalism was a "state-sponsored system geared to the production and redistribution of substantial amounts of animal protein in the form of human flesh," in compensation for recurrent crop failure and a lack of large domestic animals.[6] Harris points out, however, that institutionalized cannibalism did not result in improved vigor for the average citizen of Tenochtitlán, but only the staving off of social collapse by selectively rewarding the ruling elite. For those tempted by more sentimental explanations for such horrific behavior, Harris explains, "People can learn to like or dislike the taste of human flesh, just as they can learn to be amused or horrified by torture. . . . The unique contribution of [the Aztec] religion was not the introduction of human sacrifice but its elaboration along certain destructive pathways."[7]

By 1487, on the occasion when the final reconstruction of the main temple to Huitzilopochtli was consecrated in what is today the center of Mexico City, Tlaclaelel staged the greatest spectacle of his long career. An estimated fourteen thousand sacrificial victims were assembled in a line that extended four abreast down the steps of the temple, across the city, and along the causeway that led off the island clear to the mainland, and systematically slaughtered over several days. Around this time, too, the merchant and artisan classes were admitted to the status of human flesh-eating, while Aztec commoners, including children, joined the ranks of the victims. Within twenty years, the Aztec empire collapsed.

"Nowhere else in the world," writes Harris, "had there developed a state-sponsored religion whose art, architecture, and ritual were so thoroughly dominated by violence, decay, death, and disease. Nowhere else were walls and plazas of great temples and palaces reserved for such a concentrated display of jaws, fangs, claws, talons, bones, and gaping death heads."[8] When Cortés and his men arrived for the first time in Tenochtitlán, they found a monumental rack of human skulls (*tzompantli*) on display, calculated by the Spaniards to contain more than one hundred thousand heads. Cortés and his party were led proudly to see Huitzilopochtli's slaughtering room at the top of the great pyramid, crusted with human blood and reeking so horribly that the Spaniards could barely wait to leave. A while later they discovered the two basements (*netlatiloyan*) where the Aztecs collected whole flayed human skins.

It was a death-driven culture and its constant undertone was the imminence of cosmic doom. Their universe was unstable and subject to predestined cyclical destruction. The entire purpose of Aztec existence was to provide Huitzilopochtli with his daily ration of human hearts, and Aztec society was wholly organized for and devoted to this task. The sacrificial victims—generally warriors—were assembled and lined up in masses equal to whole armies, and there are no recorded incidents of revolt. They shuffled up to the blood-drenched alter like so many sheep. The accompanying pageantry—music, drumming, chanting, the crowds, amplified with hallucinogenic drugs—may have served as a potent mechanism of social control, but a lack of some critical subjective mental ability seems inescapable.

The evolution of a modern consciousness must have been accompanied by the terrible recognition of individual mortality as central to the human condition. And the questions that mortality raised for both the individual and the group must have produced enormous anxiety. It would appear that the Aztecs projected these anxieties over an already frightful collective world-view—obsessed with the foretold collapse of their universe and confused about their role in it—while acting out scripts of violence and terror in daily life that could only have reinforced their state of anxiety. Note also that saints, angels, and agents of goodness or mercy do not exist in the Aztec cosmography.

When the Saints Come Marching In

Moctezuma II came to the throne in 1502, at age thirty-five, seventeen years before the Spanish landed. Tlaclaelel was gone, but the complex death machine he had set in motion carried on its massive operations without him. Young Moctezuma II had already gained renown as a philosophical prince of exceptional humility, who often retreated to meditate alone in the desert. But upon ascending the throne he soon became erratic, unreliable, indecisive, and prone to depressions and rages. Early in his reign, Moctezuma conducted extravagant purges of the enormous palace bureaucracy, declared himself a God incarnate, and demanded that no one, including the most exalted nobles, look at him directly. The top-heavy apparatus of Aztec government began to groan under his rule. It is a matter of the most astonishing historical synchronicity that Moctezuma's most dire fears jibed so seamlessly with the apocalyptic mythology of his people and the fantastic succession of real events that followed.

No one believed the Quetzalcoatl myth more fervently than Moctezuma himself. The myth stated that this historical figure cum deity had
fallen out with the other gods over the practice of human sacrifice, was
consequently overthrown and banished, and had vowed to return from
exile at a specified time from somewhere across the "divine water" beyond the sunrise to overthrow the bloodthirsty Huitzilopochtli and bring
on a new cycle of life on earth—presumably a better one than the san-
guinary nightmare that life in Tenochtitlán had become. The date of
Quetzalcoatl's return was specified, under the Aztec calendar system, as a
"One Reed" year. One Reed years recurred in cycles. The years 1363
and 1467 had been One Reed years, but Quetzalcoatl had failed to materialize. The next One Reed year was 1519. This was the year Cortés
landed, on the very day, "Nine Wind," that represented Quetzalcoatl's
name day in Aztec theology.

Moctezuma's chief duty as theocratic head of state was to protect the
Aztec world against occult threats. He was surrounded by a corps of ma-
gicians, astrologers, sorcerers, priests, mediums, and wizards, whose job
was to determine the moods of their ill-tempered gods, and to direct the
elaborate ceremonial rites of appeasement. Their "science" was extraordinarily complex. Maurice Collis writes:

> It is no exaggeration to say that the government of Mexico was
> organized from top to bottom so as to be able to sustain, and
> therefore mollify, the unseen powers with as many human hearts
> as it was possible to give them. . . . The religion had become
> such a tangle of rites and counter-rites that the Mexicans them-
> selves had great difficulty in understanding it and knowing the
> right course to take in moments of crisis. . . . In result, the Mex-
> ican government and its priesthood lived under very great strain.[9]

The years of Moctezuma's reign had been filled with portents. A
comet flared in the sky over Mexico. Earthquakes disturbed the lakebed
and caused floods in the city's streets. Volcanic vents issued foul-smelling
gases. Nezahualpilli, "fasting prince," ruler of the neighboring vassal
state, Texcoco, a renowned astrologer and poet in his own right, predicted

in so many words to Moctezuma in a personal audience that the Aztec empire was about to meet its destruction. From this point on, according to the annals of Spaniards later well-acquainted with the Aztec king, a deep fatalistic depression gripped Moctezuma.

A year before Cortés's venture, a Spanish party led by Juan de Grijalva had landed near Tabasco and provoked some bloody skirmishes there, so the people of Mexico were alerted that strange bearded white-skinned men had indeed come from the water beyond the sunrise in impressive vessels powered by clouds (sails). The image of Quetzalcoatl in Mexican statuary was customarily represented with a beard and a conical hat. The Spanish, in their beards and iron helmets, fit this description closely. Cortés landed first at Tabasco, April 22, 1519. It was Good Friday and the captain happened to be wearing a black suit of clothes—another characteristic of Quetzalcoatl, who was always depicted in dark raiment in the Aztec codices. Moctezuma's agents were watching and waiting ashore, and duly noted it.

Cortés came in eleven ships, bringing six hundred soldiers and sailors, and sixteen horses. A delegation of Aztec messengers, priests, soothsayers, and wizards came out to greet him. They showered him with gold and silver gifts and presented the feathered, jeweled, and gilt regalia of Quetzalcoatl—but they brought additional costumes suitable for other gods in case there was a mistake regarding his identity. Cortés also got a vivid preview of the Aztecs' main cultural preoccupation.

> Moctezuma . . . sent along some captives to be sacrificed because the strangers might want to drink their blood. The envoys sacrificed these captives in the presence of the strangers, but when the white men saw this done, they were filled with disgust and loathing. They spat on the ground, or wiped their tears, and shook their heads in abhorrence. They refused to eat the food that was sprinkled with blood.[10]

The Spaniards' distaste for human sacrifice was also duly reported to Moctezuma, and only reinforced his conviction that Cortés was indeed an incarnation of the "Feathered Serpent," Quetzalcoatl. Cortés at first had no idea that he had been assigned this role in a religious melodrama of messianic prophecy, or that his very presence had provoked a kind of nervous breakdown in the kingdom. But he was a person of exceptional mental agility and as the script was revealed to him, he took every advantage it presented. He considered the whole Quetzalcoatl fantasia a "miracle" without which his tiny force could never have conceivably dared to even penetrate the empire.

Following this initial contact, Cortés sailed farther up the coast, established an official "settlement" he called Veracruz, and had himself "elected" its governor. This was a legalistic ploy that allowed him to act as a direct agent of King Charles in this new land, by-passing his immediate superior, the meddlesome governor Velázquez in Cuba. Then, in a gesture of extreme bravado, he torched his ships to obviate any question of retreat.

Half a year of delicate maneuvering ensued during which Cortés steadily advanced inland toward Tenochtitlán, gathering intelligence, receiving lavish gifts from Moctezuma—which only magnified the scent of golden fortune—and recruiting as allies a large force of Tlaxcaltecs, a nation who had been used by the Aztecs as a sort of human meat market for decades. The population of Tenochtitlán at this time is estimated to have been 250,000, and the valley as a whole two million. As the Spanish pressed on, Moctezuma issued a string of threats and blandishments to keep them away. He always maintained a glimmer of hope that Cortés might be induced to go back where he came from, if given enough presents. But at the same time, he nervously expected the more likely destruction of his world. The ideas that held Moctezuma in thrall seem to us starkly contradictory, and may, in fact, have been sufficiently confounding to Moctezuma himself so as to prevent him from taking any action. His theology demanded that he accept the divinity of Quetzalcoatl, but to do so would mean an end to the practice of feeding hearts to the other gods, which kept the universe from collapsing. Quetzalcoatl had supposedly returned to bring a new golden age of peace. But Aztec well-being depended on a constant state of war, their mechanism for harvesting hearts. To accept Quetzalcoatl meant renouncing Huitzilopochtli, meaning the sun itself. If they insulted it, and failed to feed it its favorite food, it might not return from one of its nightly journeys beneath the horizon. How would the world survive without a sun?

> Moctezuma was distraught and bewildered. . . . He could not run away, could not go into hiding. He had lost his strength and spirit and could do nothing. . . . Therefore he did nothing but wait. . . . He mastered his heart and waited for whatever was to happen.[11]

Cortés entered Tenochtitlán in November 1519. The scale and material wealth of the city stupefied the Spaniards. The Aztec multitudes were equally shocked to see the strange steel-clad white men mounted on armored horses, towing their cannon, brandishing powerful crossbows, rifles, pistols, and steel weaponry. Moctezuma lodged these sinister, powerful strangers in his father's former palace and kept them liberally supplied with food and women. Apparently convinced of their authenticity, and resigned to a foretold fate, Moctezuma kept up an elaborate theater of ceremonial palaver with the Spaniards, stalling, negotiating, and bargaining desperately like someone under a death sentence. The Aztec monarch became, at first, a psychological hostage, and very soon a hostage in body as the weeks went by, while Cortés systematically melted down as much Aztec gold as his men could lay their hands on. The whole Aztec people became psychological hostages.

From the time of their first meeting, Cortés had routinely denounced the pantheon of Aztec gods as a pack of "devils" and endeavored to Christianize Moctezuma. He never succeeded. Moctezuma never even pretended to understand. He seemed as bewildered by Christian theology as the Spanish were disdainful of his. They might as well have come from separate planets, and to some degree the New World *was* another planet, so different were the Aztec and Spanish interpretations of reality. In any case, human sacrifice at Tenochtitlán continued at a rapid pace even with the disapproving "Quetzalcoatl" in residence through the spring of 1520. Moctezuma increased his personal participation in it as his anxiety intensified. He kept a private stock of fresh captives in a palace jail as well as a private sacrificial stone in his quarters. Despite all this, the Spanish soldiers gained considerable respect for him as a generous, warm, and straightforward personality, and he came to be regarded, according to the chronicle of Bernal Díaz, with more genuine affection than even their cunning, resolute leader, Cortés.

However, the official Spanish answer to all this bloodletting and deviltry was to set up a shrine to the Virgin Mary at the top of the chief temple. They went about this with a deliberate bashing and mockery of the Aztec figurines already housed there. According to Díaz, this indignity finally prompted Moctezuma to tell Cortés that Huitzilopochtli "had commanded us to make war on you and kill you and drive you back across the sea." [12] Coincidentally, Cortés had decided this might be a good time to gather up as much treasure as he could carry, leave for the coast, build some ships, and return to Spain.

Meanwhile, though, another Spanish force, this one of twelve hundred men under Pánfilo Narváez, landed on the Gulf Coast. Moctezuma learned of this through his network of spies and runners, who could cover the two-hundred-mile journey by relays in twenty-four hours, and Cortés got the news, too. Moctezuma had persuaded himself that Narváez was sent to defeat Cortés (which was true) and to free him (which was only wishful thinking on Moctezuma's part). Anyway, Cortés hurriedly departed Tenochtitlán to deal with Narvaez, leaving behind his hoard of gold with a garrison of eighty Spanish soldiers under a hot-blooded subaltern named Pedro de Alvarado. Cortés had good reason to be suspicious about Narváez. Indeed, Governor Velázquez had dispatched him from headquarters in Cuba to arrest Cortés and commandeer his loot. But the wily Cortés, with native auxiliaries beefing up his forces, succeeded in a rainy night ambush of Narvaez's troops. Narváez himself was wounded—he lost an eye—and taken prisoner. Cortés assumed command, rallied the new arrivals with tales of the treasure that awaited them inland, and marched a reinforced army (including over eighty fresh horses) straight back to Tenochtitlán. One of Narváez's men, a Spanish Moor, was carrying smallpox.

As this was happening, however, Alvarado lost control of the situation back in Tenochtitlán. According to Bernal Díaz, Moctezuma, wishing to be permanently rid of Cortés/Quetzalcoatl, gave permission for a big celebration in honor of Huitzilopochtli, with the usual sacrificial goings-on. Alvarado's men rushed into the plaza and broke it up just as the music and dancing had gotten underway, lopping off the arms and heads of the musicians in the process. Alvarado later claimed that he'd acted in self-defense, saying he'd been informed of a plot to massacre his men. The incident finally provoked an Aztec uprising, led by a faction opposed to Moctezuma. Alvarado's men holed up in their quarters to avoid being slaughtered. In the event, and after a month's absence from the Aztec capital, Cortés rode into an ominously quiet city on June 24, 1520. Moctezuma must have been devastated to see his nemesis return in even greater strength than before. Within a few days, a council of nobles formally deposed Moctezuma, elected a new *tlatoani,* Moctezuma's brother, Cuitlahuac, and declared their intention to decisively run the Spaniards out of town. None of them doubted that Cortés still was an incarnation of Quetzalcoatl; rather they had firmly decided to take sides against Cortés/Quetzalcoatl with their god of war and the sun, Huitzilopochtli. Cortés and his army barricaded themselves in the royal quarter of the city as the Aztecs prepared to destroy them. On the second day of the siege, Cortés asked Moctezuma to negotiate a truce. The deposed and dispirited ruler stepped out on the palace roof garbed in all the splendid regalia of former office. When he spoke to his people, a shower of rocks answered. One struck him on the head, and three days later, he died. His persistent vision of doom, though inaccurate in so many details, proved to be eerily correct in the deepest sense: The end of the Aztec civilization was at hand.

What followed was an epic rich in drama but somehow anticlimactic to the collision of worlds that led up to it. Cortés and his soldiers escaped the city after a terrible night battle with a tremendous loss of life. More than half his soldiers and all but twenty-three of the eighty horses perished. Many of these men—and some of the horses—were captured, sacrificed, and eaten, their heads fastened to skull racks for display. Cortés and his remaining troops retreated east and fought another pitched battle with a massive Aztec force at Otumba on July 7, 1520. They were vastly outnumbered, exhausted, wounded, hungry, and lacking gunpowder, but managed to prevail for two reasons. First, the Aztecs' peculiar military tactics were based on capturing the enemy alive for later sacrifice, so they took pains to avoid killing, while the Spanish tactic was to kill the enemy as expeditiously as possible. Second, they managed to kill the Aztec chief-in-command, a figure called (weirdly, because he was a man) "the Serpent Woman," an action that apparently so confounded the Aztecs' magical auguries that they simply gave up and left the field of battle.

Cortés attributed his miraculous victory to Christ's power and mercy over a host of cannibal heathen. He retreated to the nearby city of his allies, the Tlaxcalans, and recovered there for six months under their care. While he did, a plague of smallpox broke out back in Tenochtitlán. The new king, Cuitlahuac, was among the many thousands of victims. During the autumn of 1520, several ships sent to relieve Narváez landed at Veracruz. Cortés exchanged a quantity of captured Aztec gold for gunpowder and munitions and recruited more soldiers with the promise of immense fortune waiting inland. Rested and reinforced, with a hundred thousand Tlaxcaltec auxiliaries, Cortés and six hundred Spaniards set out once again for Tenochtitlán just after Christmas 1520.

From January through May 1521, he busied himself destroying every Aztec outpost along the way and subduing all the towns around the lakes of the Valley of Mexico. In May he put the beleaguered Aztec capital under siege, cut off food supplies, broke up the aqueduct from Chapultepec that was Tenochtitlán's sole source of drinking water, and tried to persuade the city to surrender. The Aztecs refused under their newest and last *tlatoani,* twenty-six-year-old Cuauhtemoc, a nephew of Moctezuma. Their decision is said to have been reached because of an astronomical event involving the periodic disappearance, precisely at sunset, of the planet Venus, the evening star, which in Aztec theology was yet another incarnation of Quetzalcoatl, and signified a period of weakness when he might be overcome in battle. The Aztecs, therefore, mounted a final furious resistance.

Cortés then commenced the methodical destruction of the whole city. It took many weeks of harrowing street-by-street combat with an awful loss of life. There were times during the battle when Spanish soldiers were dragged by their hair shrieking up the temple steps and sacrificed in view of their comrades fighting below. Díaz tells it thus:

> When they had hauled them up to a small platform in front of the shrine where they kept their accursed idols we saw them put plumes on the heads of many of them; and then they made them dance with a sort of fan in front of Huichilobos [Huitzilipoctli]. Then, after they had danced the [priests] laid them down on their backs on some narrow stones of sacrifice and, cutting open their chests, drew out their palpitating hearts which they offered to the idols before them. Then they kicked the bodies down the steps, and the Indian butchers who were waiting below cut off their arms and legs and flayed their faces, which they afterward prepared like glove leather, with their beards on, and kept for their drunken festivals, Then they ate their flesh with a sauce of peppers and tomatoes.[13]

The Spaniards persistently advanced in the face of these appalling spectacles. Eventually, they fought their way into the heart of the city, torched the sanctuaries at the top of central temple, and systematically pulled down every building they captured. Many a vacated chamber, they discovered, was filled with heads and corpses and the stench was fantastic. Cortés could not entirely control his Tlaxcaltec and Texcocoan allies, who were now disposed to feasting on the flesh of their hated oppressors. Aztec women and children in despair flung themselves into the lake and drowned. Out of an estimated 300,000 Aztec warriors gathered from all the outlying towns around the lake to defend their capital, 240,000 were killed. Almost all the Aztec nobility was exterminated. At least 30,000 Tlaxcaltec and Texcocoan auxiliaries of the Spanish died in the fighting. Cuauhtemoc—whose name could be translated as either "Falling Eagle" or "Setting Sun"—was captured trying to escape across the lake with an entourage of fifty canoes. The date was August 13, 1521, roughly two and a half years after Cortés first stepped ashore at Tabasco.

When it was over, the civilian inhabitants who were not killed outright were nearly dead of thirst and starvation. It took three days to get them all out of the city. Díaz wrote that the place "looked as if it had been ploughed up." Every living plant had been eaten, including the bark of trees. Cortés's men at once set about pulling down the abominable temples, stone by stone. The canals were filled with rubble, debris, and thousands of rotting bodies. The floating gardens lay trashed. A city that had been the equal of Venice lay in smoldering ruins.

For the sake of perspective, consider that when all this happened Michelangelo was in the prime of his life. That same year, 1521, Martin Luther defended himself before the Diet of Worms. William Shakespeare would not be born for another forty-three years. The Jesuit order had not formed yet. The Pilgrims would not set foot on Plymouth Rock for another century.

"Do Little and Do It Slowly"

The Spaniards themselves were hardly Boy Scouts. They were adept at terror and torture, too. The behavior of the Aztecs might have validated the most extreme European fantasies about New World cannibal heathens, but the conquest of Mexico took place at the onset of the Spanish Inquisition, a disabling cultural convulsion that has left an enduring imprint in Latin America. The first inquisitor general, Tomás de Torquemada, was appointed in 1483.

Both as a symptom and a contributing cause, the Inquisition had a self-reinforcing corrosive effect on the decline of Spanish power. It induced a culture of treachery and paranoia in which denouncing one's neighbors, scheming against one's confederates, and spying on one's family became normal. In destroying the Jewish community of Spain, the Inquisition eliminated the most economically dynamic portion of its middle class, and indeed sabotaged the continuing evolution of a modern middle class in general, so that Spain actually reverted to near-medievalism at the very moment when the rest of Europe was waking to the high Renaissance. The crown even barred Spanish students from attending Catholic universities in other kingdoms, further isolating Spain intellectually from the flowering of knowledge. What became a culture of permanent Inquisition would infect operations in the viceroyalty of New Spain for a long

long time, indeed through virtually the whole colonial period (until Napoleon Bonaparte put a formal end to the Inquisition in 1803), and it is the thesis of this chapter that the spirit of both the Inquisition and the Aztec Death Machine still haunt contemporary life in Mexico City.

Cortés operated from the start as a renegade. He thoroughly distrusted his superiors and constantly went over their heads, sending a stream of letters directly back to King Charles justifying his actions after the fact. In the yawning intervals between communications, Cortés behaved as though he had tacit permission to do whatever he liked. He knew that he was exceeding his authority in Mexico and he availed himself of every device to continue doing so, even attacking his own countrymen when they were sent to rein him in. What's more, he established a pattern of rogue behavior that others emulated throughout the century of conquest in the Americas—for instance, Pizarro's brief, lucrative career in Peru, rife with conspiracy, ending with Pizarro's own assassination in 1541—and that continues to affect official conduct in Latin America even today.

The government established in colonial Mexico was a direct extension of a mother country that was failing to develop the crucial institutions of modernity—due process of law, banking and finance, scientific inquiry for its own sake, a reformed clergy, a bourgeoisie with a work ethic, and an economy based on the capital creation of value. Spanish Mexico was essentially medieval and it remained that way long after the Revolution of 1821 and through the many regimes that ruled afterward. The Mexican economy was organized around "bullionization," the extraction of treasure, the exploitation of minerals, and Indian peonage. The tone of colonial administration was set by the first viceroy, Don Antonio de Mendoza, whose most memorable utterance was, "Do little and do it slowly."

It is estimated that somewhere between 12 and 25 million Indians lived in all of Mexico when Cortés arrived. One hundred years later, after the introduction of smallpox, typhoid, measles, mumps, and bubonic plague, 1.5 million Indians remained. With the steep decline in population and the introduction of cattle, sheep, and goats, the frightful Aztec theology that supported mass human sacrifice and organized cannibalism withered away to a residual folk-fetish for skeletons and a jokey attitude toward death, under a broad but thin lamination of Christianity. The colonial administration was not devoid of humanism. The viceroy abolished Indian chattel slavery in 1550, and various unsuccessful attempts were made over the centuries to reform peonage. But for their part, the Indians inherited a vanquished, fragmentized culture characterized by poverty, despair, and violence. Among those who came to reinhabit the old central quarter of Tenochtitlán, the drinking of *pulque,* the fermented juice of the maguey, a species of century plant, reached levels as lethal as the epidemic diseases, and persisted longer as a permanent feature of culture. Not until the twentieth century did the population of Mexico City exceed the quarter million who dwelt there in the last days of Moctezuma.

In his 1852 *Historia de México,* Lucas Alaman called his native land "a nation that has leapt from infancy to a state of decrepitude without ever knowing the vigor of youth."

Anarchy Inc.

It is against this extraordinary historical background that we consider the continuing catastrophe of Mexico City today, a hypertrophied metastasized organism that seems destined to devour itself, like a snake that would swallow its own tail, or die trying. A nation founded on culture-streams of theocratic despotism, institutionalized death worship, paranoia, and treachery is hard put to support a meaningful social contract, and indeed as it exists in modern Mexico City the social contract is a flimsy and provisional thing. Rule of law is an illusion

As long as anyone can remember, there has been in Mexico City no clear line distinguishing the activities of civilian criminals from the police. In practical terms, the police *are* the chief criminal organization in town. When they are not actually committing crimes themselves, the police are supporting the gangs that do in an institutionalized "protection" racket that distributes the gross profits between the police and the criminals. When I was there in June 1998, three major robbery programs had become regular features of daily life in the city.

One was the standard kidnap-for-ransom operation, in which well-heeled citizens (or visitors) were systematically plucked from the streets, often in broad daylight (and commonly from their cars while stopped at red traffic lights). The latest victim while I was there was a prosperous car dealer from the upper-class inner suburb of Coyoacan—once an Aztec satellite village, where Cortés lived just after the conquest. The car dealer was held for weeks and released only after his family paid a substantial but unspecified ransom.

One particular kidnapping outfit, the Arizmendi gang, was renowned for cutting off its victims' ears. It started out as a way of getting the full attention of their victims' families, but eventually evolved into a kind of artistic trademark, to distinguish their work from that of rival operators. That the Arizmendis were officially "wanted dead or alive" by the government indicated that they had crossed some invisible line by maiming the relative or business associate of a police official—not a difficult mistake to make within such an inbred network of mafias.

I was strenuously advised not to go to the police if I had any problem on the city streets, and urged, in the event that I accidentally fell in with them, to observe the highest possible degree of politeness. Likewise, citizens whose homes are burglarized tend not to report the crime, since the police, in the process of "investigating," have been known to come in and take anything of value that has not already been stolen. One police officer actually caught on videotape in the act of robbery, I was told by someone in a position to know, was far more concerned about his mother finding out than about any theoretical trouble he might find himself in with the magistrates.[14] In Mexico City, family values trumps the rule of law.

Another type of state-of-the-art banditry that had reached epidemic proportions was the ATM joyride, often performed with the city's huge fleet of green Volkswagen taxicabs.[15] In this rip-off, an unsuspecting tourist would hail a cab from a hotel, or the airport queue, and climb inside the cab to find an armed accomplice on board. Mr. or Ms. Feckless J. Tourist would then be driven around to every ATM machine in the city until the victim's bank and credit card accounts were drained. Since ATM machines are programmed to dispense only a set amount of cash per customer per day, the perps would keep a victim with a high credit ceiling or a fat bank account in custody past the midnight hour, and then revisit all the ATM machines as soon as the date changed, sometimes over a period of several days. It was like driving around with a golden goose in the backseat. Just after I departed the city, in fact, a Swiss diplomat was shanghaied into an official police car waiting in the porte cochere of the downtown Crowne Plaza Hotel, taken on just such a joyride, made to drink a large quantity of tequila, and eventually dumped half-dead along the highway to Chalco, the enormous new slum in the old mud flats beyond the airport.

A third form of criminal styling has been the restaurant takeover robbery, which is carried out in the manner of a military operation, the restaurant patrons robbed en masse. Since there is no particular distinction between the ruling class who patronize the restaurants and the criminal mafias that carry out the robberies, one can surmise that these are cases of a social group robbing itself, in other words, treachery, another residue of conquistador culture. It has not been uncommon for one bistro to be hit three or four times in a year, and the fact that these establishments are able to remain open for business after such a stigmatizing trauma suggests how normative robbery has become. Consequently, a major new service industry in contemporary Mexico City is private security. Every restaurant, shop, or even office of any pretension employs a squad of guards armed with automatic weapons to stand around the doorway—a daunting sight as one plies the streets, for instance, of the Zona Rosa, a central district near the old Aztec temple quarter that was once Mexico City's equivalent of New York's Upper East Side. All these characters lurking in the shade brandishing rifles, dressed in ill-fitting uniforms that appear to be castoffs from the Manhattan doormen's union, give the impression of a city under military occupation by scores of different armies. To make matters worse, many private security guards are, of course, in league with the police and the various mafias who carry out the robberies, and either actively assist in the robberies, or do nothing to interfere. Then why bother with private security at all? It gives the illusion of safety in a city where the illusion of anything is an acceptable substitute in the absence of the real thing.

There was another consequence of this behavior: Under the law of diminishing returns, as crime increased, a *tipping point* was reached where the patronage of restaurants in the Zona Rosa fell off, so that what once had been the city's premier neighborhood was slipping into a self-reinforcing downward spiral of decay and despair.

While robbery of all kinds is hardly new in Mexico, the volume of activity has gone up 80 percent since the collapse of the peso in 1994 and an ensuing deep business recession in the late 1990s.[16] This extraordinary increase of incivility is provoking a nearly complete withdrawal from public life by those lucky few—the 10 percent of the population—who are not desperately poor. In a sense, though, these conditions only aggravate a long-standing pattern. While the open central plaza is a wonderful convention of Latin American urbanism, the ordinary streets of even the fancy neighborhoods are almost always closed and grim. Spanish culture, under Moorish influence, produced an urban house that typically faced inward, away from the street, to an interior courtyard. The pattern originated in the desert heat of North Africa and had analogs in Aztec architecture. Today, the pattern has been taken a step further. Private homes in the wealthy barrios of Coyoacan or San Angel are virtual fortifications. Well-off families live behind walled compounds topped by broken glass, razor wire, motion detectors, and video cameras. Driveways and the few doors and windows facing the street are protected by forbidding steel grates. The streets in these residential neighborhoods take on the dreary look of a maze: endless corridors of blank walls. Behind any drab stucco wall may be a luxurious villa, but you'd never know it. Sensible people don't advertise their prosperity.

Domestic labor is very cheap and even a middle-class household can have several servants, so there is always someone at home. The relationship is overtly paternalistic, but then servants are the most *fortunate* of the poor, and it is considered a privilege in Mexico City to be so well-employed. It may be among the few reliable social conventions in a culture otherwise subject to treachery. Practically all government officials of any standing have personal drivers both to protect their cars against theft and to provide at least the illusion of security while in transit. As mentioned earlier, traffic intersections are prime carjacking zones. One drives around with the doors locked and the windows closed. Every intersection in even the best neighborhood is clogged with street vendors hawking anything from single sticks of chewing gum to narcotics. Though Mexico City is a nightmare to get around on its surface streets and horrible freeways, many middle-class people will not take the subway, which was completed in time for the 1968 Olympics, and which miraculously survived the intense earthquake of 1985.[17] Today the subway is used almost exclusively by the least poor of the poor, the upper poor, shall we say, while the poorer poor take lumbering jitney buses, which are horribly crowded, agonizingly slow, and routinely subject to wholesale stick-ups.

When not actually committing crimes, or standing around brandishing their machine guns outside the skyscrapers along the grand Paseo de la Reforma, or shaking down the thousands of poor street vendors in front of the National Cathedral off the Zocolo, the police serve as parking valets (tipping mandatory) along the downtown side streets.

The latest sociopolitical feature of this life in a continual state of siege was explained by my hostess, an American woman married to a Mexican treasury official: "We were at a cocktail party recently," she said, "and all of us were talking about the incredible amount of crime, the kidnappings, and the taxi robberies. Everyone in the room was either in the government or connected to the power structure. Yet, oddly, nobody knew who in the hierarchy was in charge of the crime. This is a new thing. In the old days, you always knew who was running the mafias, even if there was nothing to be done about it. These days, even the mafia doesn't know who's running things. That's how out-of-control it's gotten."[18]

A Broken Ecology

Homero Aridjis lives in the heights of Chapultepec, a posh neighborhood in the foothills a few miles west of the city center. The mostly suburban-style, single-family houses nestled in subtropical shrubbery along steep, antiseptic-looking streets date from the 1960s. Dropped there blindfolded, you might think you were in Sherman Oaks, California—but looking closer you notice that the split-levels and raised ranches have been heavily fortified over the decades. Virtually all the picture windows are protected by steel grates and many driveways are gated and locked, too.

Aridjis, sixty-two, is a successful novelist and journalist, but also one of the nation's leading environmental figures, president of an organization called *Grupo de los Cien,* which is roughly equivalent to the Sierra Club. He speaks English very well in a deep bass voice, and what he has to say carries the weight of a biblical lamentation.

"Mexico City, founded on water, may die of thirst," he told me in his spacious living room, lined with thousands of books and decorated with colorful folk art. Even in Aztec times, water had to be transported by aqueduct from outside the city. Today it travels vast distances from lower-lying terrain and is pumped at tremendous cost across mountain ranges. This causes several layers of political problems. One is that the neighboring states are not rich in water, either, and they would like to keep it for themselves. Central Mexico is mainly desert. The neighboring states also resent the rate that city dwellers consume water: an average sixty cubic meters per second compared to thirty-six cubic meters per second in areas outside the Federal District. Another problem is subsidence. The water in question comes not from rivers or reservoirs, but from aquifers. Pumping out these underground lakes causes the land above to slump and shift. The center of Mexico City is thirty-four feet lower today than it was in Moctezuma's time, and the entire valley continues to sink at the rate of eleven centimeters a year as the aquifers below are steadily drained.

"There is no official threshold," Aridjas said, "but we predict at the most it can last ten more years. The issue is too frightening for politicians to think about."

Once used, the "black waters" (sewage) have to be pumped back out of the closed hydrologic basin. The amount of electricity needed just to move this sewage is equivalent to all the electricity that would be consumed daily by a city of three million. A great many households in the sprawling slums lack elementary plumbing, anyway. The sewage just goes a few feet into the ground and percolates back up to the surface in the rainy season where it eventually turns to dust, contributing disease-causing bacteria to the atmospheric soup of the city's spectacular air pollution.

On the government's own scale, Mexico City's air is unsatisfactory more than three hundred days a year. When I was there, just breathing anyplace downtown was like perpetually standing behind the exhaust pipe of a seventeen-year-old delivery truck in need of a ring-job. Mexico is a major oil-producing country. The industry, a vast corrupt bureaucracy run by the government, is the establishment's second-most-important source of income after drug smuggling.[19] By world standards gas has remained relatively cheap in Mexico. America represents the world's largest supply of used cars, so affordable vehicles are plentiful in Mexico City and therefore it is clogged with motor vehicles.

The government tried to regulate car use by restricting odd and even license plate numbers from the streets on alternate days. But they left a loophole of designating the digit 0 for use any day, and the digit 1 for any day except those during officially declared air pollution emergencies (a category above merely "unsatisfactory" rarely invoked). License plates with these special digits were sold at a premium in huge quantities. And because used cars are so cheap and plentiful, many families also simply got another car with an odd or even plate as their case required.

"The city is an urban disaster." Aridjas said, dolefully. "The physical pollution is a product of the moral pollution of the Mexican political system."

Chalco

The old dried-up bed of Lake Chalco, fifteen miles east of the city center, is the site of Mexico City's newest giant slum. Chalco is the successor to Nezahualcoyotl, popularly called Neza, northeast of the city, the previous generation of giant slum built beside the city's old garbage dump, where Neza's impoverished eked out a living picking bits of salvage out of the city's vast stream of waste. Neza has graduated over the decades from a hell-hole to a more complexly organized peasant barrio, as its sprawling shacks have been continually added to and upgraded by a hardworking population moving out of absolute poverty into regular menial jobs with cash pay, so that many of them now have running water, sewers, electricity, and telephones. Chalco may not be so fortunate in its future cycles of existence.

In the late 1990s, Chalco was said to contain a population of 2.5 million, but it was another one of those phantom statistics that no one could verify. If anything, the slum was growing steadily larger every day, like a great exurban tumor. The economy of rural Mexico had become so hopeless that even Chalco was a step up for the newcomers who flocked in every hour from the desert or jungle hinterlands. As a physical artifact, Chalco had the character of an immense junkyard laid out incongruously over a highly regular orthogonal urban grid. The terrain of the old lakebed had a bleak surrealist flatness that evoked the nightmare landscapes of Tanguy and Dalí. The yellow-gray sky above seemed abnormally heavy, as though it could compress any living organism impudent enough to lift its gaze back into the hardpan desert floor. The squat individual buildings and dwellings were assembled out of bits and pieces of wood, tin, and concrete block, the industrial effluvia of the city. You could look up the very straight streets for a mile and see not a single object that wasn't broken, twisted, rusted, cracked, bent, corroded, leaning, tattered, or shot up. The majority of houses had dirt floors. In the rainy season they became fetid, muddy cesspools. Being one of the lowest points in the Valley of Mexico, Chalco had a particularly bad problem with sewage percolating to the surface from the fractured lines leading out of the city as well as the jury-rigged septic infrastructure and shallow latrines of Chalco itself. The periodic, but unpredictable, venting of volcanic gases made things worse. The public health consequences were overwhelming. Practically everyone there suffered from chronic infections, airborne parasites, and fungal skin disorders. Cholera broke out at regular intervals. The leading cause of death, however, was violence, followed by the effects of chronic alcoholism and drug abuse. Feral-looking children teemed in the dusty, unpaved streets, hurling rocks at an inexhaustible supply of panting skeletal dogs while impassive adults in shredded clothes sat here and there on overturned plastic buckets stuporously surveying the scene.

Slums like Chalco and Neza were outgrowths of Mexico's land reforms of the 1930s, following three decades of continual and inconclusive revolution. Under the reforms land was given not to individuals or heads of households, but to whole groups, and held in common. These *ejidos* were worked cooperatively by the class of peons who had been previously tied to the great haciendas as virtual serfs. Consequently, a body of property law evolved in which the terms of ownership were ambiguous and provisional, and under which it was never quite clear who owned what. *Ejido* land could not be mortgaged or used as collateral. It was not until 1992, when the constitution was amended, that *ejido* land could be sold under any circumstances. An exploding population, massive internal migration out of the impoverished countryside, and the accustomed ambiguity of Mexican property law, in turn, spawned the *terranos invadidos,* the invaded lands movement of the postwar era, gigantic squatter colonies at the city's edge, usually organized with the protection of politicians. One day there would be nothing, the next day, thousands of shacks. The squatter shock troops were nicknamed "parachutists," though they did not literally arrive by that method. After five years, such an area could legally declare itself an *ejido.* In time, the political protectors would see to it that electricity and water lines were extended to the invaded lands. This was the origin of Nezahualcoyotl and, twenty years later, Chalco.

The peculiarities of Mexican property law reverberated through the whole city. Under the perverse effects of the reform laws, renters' rights ended up trumping the rights of property owners. In the scores of large, prewar apartment building in the heart of the city, rents had been frozen as low as thirty cents a month, and apartments could legally be passed down in wills. There was no legal remedy or recourse for the building owner. Consequently, the building owner performed virtually no regular maintenance on the building, nor could he sell it, for no other prospective buyer might operate the building in a rationally profitable manner under the terms of the law. For all practical purposes, it was an abandoned building occupied by legalized squatters. In general, Mexican property owners were no longer willing to engage in formalized rental relationships because they might never get rid of their tenants. Rental housing for all classes was therefore terribly scarce. So the institutional defects of the law made it necessary for the poorest Mexicans to form enormous slum settlements at the distant edge of the city, where, if nothing else, the inhabitants "owned" their own miserable housing.

Chalco, with its population of more than 2.5 million people, had formed this way in a mere decade. It was the kind of place that even well-intentioned, unselfish, educated, idealistic Mexican progressives regarded with dread, as though they were looking through an occult window into their nation's grim future, as palpable to them as the end of the universe was to their Aztec ancestors. A constant tremor seemed to run through the body politic at all levels. It accompanied the frightful recognition that a tipping point had been reached in Mexico City's ability to continue as a viable collective organism. The crime, the pollution, the poverty, the drug abuse, the misery, the decay, the distrust and treachery, the prospective scarcity of civilizational goods and graces, gave every evidence of climbing further up a cataclysmic curve in the years ahead. And, of course, one lived in this part of the world with the knowledge that it had happened many times before, that cities every bit as important in their own terms and epochs had vanished into in the silence of history, leaving behind only their mute stone skeletons.

BERLIN

The Paradoxes of History

The history of this century is a violent catalog of aberrant and erroneous behavior by national and ideological interests; no-where is this more evident than in the history of Berlin.

ALAN BALFOUR

There is a map on the wall of a bookshop on the Friedrichstrasse in what was formerly East Berlin, very near the site of that Cold War oddity, Checkpoint Charlie. The map shows all the World War Two bomb damage in blue ink. Areas of total destruction are indicated in dark blue, partial destruction in light blue. The whole center of city on this map is blue.

The Allies bombed Berlin around the clock steadily from October 1944 until April 1945. The Americans bombed it by day, the British by night. In the spring of 1945, the Soviet Red Army closed in on the city from both the north and the south in a pincer movement designed to capture what was left of the German high command, most particularly, Mr. Adolph Hitler in his bunker off the Wilhelmstrasse at the very center of town.

The Soviets met stiff resistance in these final weeks of a long and terrible struggle that had already consumed millions of lives. In the campaign for Berlin, the Red Army lost over one hundred thousand dead, five thousand alone taking a single building, the Reichstag—defended desperately despite the fact that there had been no German parliament through the years of the Third Reich. Many of Berlin's remaining defenders were old men and boys. They were holed up in a rat-maze of urban fabric— the most difficult type of battle terrain—and their gunfire was no less lethal for their age or youth. The Red Army's approach to urban combat, like all things Soviet, was crude, remorseless, designed to operate at outlandish scale, and without regard for human dignity, history, or culture.

Thus, wherever some German hold-out popped up in a window, standing policy was to level the whole city block around him with artillery. To complicate matters, a remaining skeleton crew of true-believer Gestapo officers monitored the devastated streets for signs of surrender, and wherever they saw a white flag hanging from an upper story, they slipped inside and shot the occupants as traitors. Under the circumstances, the overall damage to the city was rather apocalyptic. Berlin was such a smoldering wreck at war's end that serious proposals were made to abandon it altogether as a monument to the futility of war.

From May until July 1945, when the Americans and British arrived on the scene, the Russians had Berlin to themselves. They had a lot to be sore about—the perfidious backstabbing following the 1939 nonaggression pact, the awful siege of Stalingrad, the 20 million Russian war dead—and they expressed their feelings in an orgy of hands-on destruction. With the arrival of the other Allies, basic order was finally restored. The city was divided into American, British, French, and Russian administrative sectors. Over the next several years, as the "Iron Curtain" descended across Eastern Europe and Soviet-sponsored communist governments took over in one country after another, Berlin found itself an urban island marooned within a sovereign communist German Democratic Republic (GDR). The destiny of Berlin remained highly uncertain in these early postwar years. Ideological lines hardened as the Soviets developed atomic bombs and confidence in the righteousness of their worldwide socialist crusade. By 1948, they flexed their muscles by cutting off rail and highway lifelines to Berlin from the west. The West responded with the Berlin Airlift. As we now know, a forty-year stalemate ensued. This stalemate eventually took the form of a competition, with Berlin as a sort of demonstration project showcasing the vaunted merits of Christian democracy on one side and socialist collectivism on the other.

In Living Color

I visited Berlin for the first time in the summer of 1997, eight years after the fall of communism and all its dreary agencies. It was a trip fraught with bizarre personal discoveries. For instance, I was strangely startled to find that Berlin did not exist in black-and-white. After a lifetime of watching World War Two documentaries on television, I was conditioned to think of Berlin in grainy black-and-white images. What a surprise, then, when stepping off the airplane at the Berlin-Tegel Flughafen to see that Germany existed in high-resolution color, just like the rest of the world. A second striking impression was the complete absence of anything relating to the former existence of Herr Hitler and his minions. I had semiconsciously expected his baleful visage to hang over the city like a permanently moored zeppelin, blotting out the sun—with Goering, Himmler, and Goebbels floating subserviently around him like Macy's Thanksgiving Day balloons. But there was not the slightest residue of Nazism besides the obvious war damage. Not the shadow of a swastika. All vestiges of Hitler-the-personality had been utterly swallowed by time. The chancellery was a vacant lot with mature trees growing over it. A block away, the Gestapo and SS headquarters on the Prinz Albrecht Strasse were long gone and the street name changed to Nieder-kirchnerstrasse.

Yet another jarring perception was that, whatever awful vicissitudes it had suffered this century, Berlin at the turn of the millennium was palpably in far better shape than many comparably sized American cities I'd been to in recent years, including Detroit, St. Louis, Cleveland, and Baltimore.

Since 1989, scores of billions of Deutschmarks had been spent on reunification and the rehabilitation of the city's shabby eastern side, with hundreds of billions yet to come. The scars of division were still conspicuous. The chief scar was the broad swath of still mostly vacant land that had contained the wall and its devilishly complex death strip—composed of raked sand concealing trip-wired flares, explosive mines, coils of razor wire, tank barriers, five-inch steel-spike tire traps, plus 260 watchtowers and 267 guard dog impounds, plus masonry fortifications. The East Germans officially referred to the whole ensemble not as *the wall,* but as an "antifascist protective rampart."[1]

By the late 1990s, almost all of the tilt-up concrete slab wall itself was gone. Parts of it had been auctioned off for souvenirs around the world. A large remnant of it was stockpiled in a northern industrial district called Pankow, where it was being crushed by machines for reuse as gravel. The old border strip had become a gigantic linear construction zone, with hundreds of acres in various stages of site preparation for new buildings, restored streets, and new subway lines. The city's famous bright sandy soil lay exposed in an open gash that ran from Kreuzberg to Moabit.

There was a particularly vexing hydrological problem here. Berlin's water table lies within a few feet of the surface. Many of the new buildings were designed with underground parking garages up to five levels deep. The scale of the excavations was awesome. It was like gazing down into one of those open-pit copper mines in the American West. In some cases foundations had to be poured under water by scuba divers. In the meantime massive quantities of water had to be pumped out of the excavations continually. Drainage pipes painted in primary colors ran out of these pits and formed a dense network of plumbing ten feet above the sidewalks, like the gaudy ductwork outside the Pompidou center in Paris. Squadrons of front-end loaders and bulldozers moved about this eerie zone like latter-day panzers engaged in a massive military operation. In the mother of sandpits, the old burned and bombed-out Reichstag rose cocooned in a web of blue nylon tarps and steel scaffolding, under renovation to house the federal legislature, the Bundestag, in the twenty-first century. One was struck by the sheer optimism this represented in the face of so much cumulative historical catastrophe. An average of three unexploded bombs per day were still turning up at excavation sites in central Berlin in the 1990s. (In 1994, one exploded, killing three and injuring seventeen.)

I stayed in a brand-spanking-new hotel off the Unter den Linden, formerly East Berlin, complete with CNN on cable TV, a lap pool, an immense Teutonic breakfast buffet, and chocolates on your pillow, for less than one hundred dollars a night. The adjacent streets were all obviously struggling back to long-banished normality. Stores and restaurants were beginning to open here and there but all seemed short of customers. Waiters congregated on the sidewalks smoking cigarettes outside their empty new cafés, peering anxiously up and down the street as if, any time now, battalions of tourists might materialize to save the day. Across the street from my quarters stood one of the few large hotels left over from the communist period, a farcical modernistic assemblage of dingy, faded, multicolored aluminum panels that looked like an institute for training circus clowns.

The surrounding blocks of this neighborhood, called Friedrichstätte, had been the city's banking and newspaper publishing center before the war. Hitler's headquarters had stood nearby, so you can imagine the attention it received from Allied bombers. The place felt like an organism slowly returning to health after an extraordinarily long and dire illness, and it was still far from the norm of urban vitality found in, say, Paris or Barcelona. What interested me was how the cultural memory was still in force, and how that memory was guiding the organism of the city back to structural integrity, as DNA will regulate the knitting of bones and healing of flesh in a body.

The Unter den Linden had been the principal monumental avenue of the city through the nineteenth century and the first half of the twentieth. It was a broad, baroque boulevard more than one hundred meters wide with a generous green median. Off and around the east end of it stood the great historic buildings of the city: the architect Karl Friedrich Schinkel's opera house, his National Gallery, the Crown Prince's palace, the royal library, the Cathedral of the Dome, the Zeughaus (arsenal), and much more. The king's palace, abode of all the Friedrichs and Wilhelms, had stood there, too, vacated after World War One, discreetly ignored by Hitler, bombed by the Allies in 1945, and finally demolished by the communists. The west end of the great boulevard was anchored by the Brandenburg Gate, leading into the Tiergarten, Berlin's central park. The Reichstag lay slightly off-axis two hundred yards north of the Brandenburg Gate.

Every major monument except the Reichstag had stood on the former eastern side. Most of these structures still bore the acne of bullet holes from the war. Some of them had undergone painstaking restoration. For instance, Schinkel's little neoclassical gem the Neue Wache (new royal guardhouse) had scores of big and little marble grafts embroidered into its façade. No matter how skillful the masonry, however, the colors were always a little off, like mends in a precious old family teapot, painstakingly glued back together time after time. The prewar apartment buildings still standing on this side of the city were also uniformly pockmarked with bullet holes, but there had been hardly any effort over the years to repair them cosmetically. It was all the impoverished East Berliners could do to keep the battered old structures habitable.

Also on the eastern side of the wall had been the city's most vibrant prewar commercial node, a pair of conjoined civic spaces called the Potsdamer Platz and the Leipziger Platz. They anchored the southeastern corner of the Tiergarten. The Potsdamer Platz was just the oddly shaped intersection of five major streets, not a work of civic design so much as an accident of urban circulation. The adjacent Leipziger Platz was a formal baroque octagon (*Achteck*) that had begun as a marketplace on the city's western edge in the 1700s—the gated country road leading out of it had led eventually to the royal villa at Potsdam. The Leipziger Platz had been part of an ambitious urban extension by Friedrich Wilhelm I in the 1730s, which also included a circular plaza at the Halle Gate (now Mehring Platz), and a square plaza at the western end of Unter den Linden, which would eventually become the Pariser Platz just east of the Brandenburg Gate.

Several proposals, never realized, had been drawn up in the early 1800s for a huge monument to Frederick the Great at the Leipziger Platz. All that got built, however, were two cute little Greco-Roman gatehouses by Schinkel to mark a formal entrance to the city. By the twentieth century, with Berlin's extremely rapid industrialization, the city spread west, and the conjoined Potsdamer and Leipziger Platz became the commercial crossroads of Germanic Europe. Dozens of new trolley and then subway lines intersected there. The city's premier hotels, restaurants, saloons, and department stores operated in the vicinity. Hitler's huge Reich Chancellery was built around the corner in 1937. Naturally, this area was bombed to smithereens, too.

After the wall went up in 1961 the whole district was incorporated into the death strip. All that was left of the Leipziger Platz during the communist interregnum was the pentimento of granite curbing that faintly outlined the old *Achteck*. Wildflowers grew there and for thirty years the only inhabitants were border guards and rabbits.

THE CITY IN MIND

The Curse of the Modern

The urban rehab policy in place since reunification had been dubbed *critical reconstruction* by city planning officials. In essence, it was a repudiation of the aggregate twentieth-century architectural fashions, theories, fantasies, and dogmas that had insidiously degraded the public realm since the days of Gropius and Le Corbusier—the modernists' disdain for the street. There was, by the 1990s, a very specific sense of fatigue with the Brave New World *weltanshauung* of the modern. It had failed every conceivable belief system, including especially the dominant postwar politics of statist socialism and democratic liberalism. It had failed as art theory and as pseudo social science. In Berlin, both the East and the West had had their love affairs with architectural modernism and it had turned out pretty badly on each side of the wall. But the cultural war over modernism had taken many curious turns.

An emblematic case was Erich Mendelssohn's Columbus Haus on the Potsdamer Platz. Mendelssohn was born in 1887, two years before Hitler, to an affluent Jewish family in what was then East Prussia, now Poland. He fought for the kaiser in World War One and afterward enjoyed ready success as an avant-garde architect in Weimar Berlin, despite the economic chaos of those years. Intellectually, what grabbed him was the astrophysics of Einstein, not the socialist therapeutics of Gropius's Bauhaus. He had perhaps more in common with the cult of the solitary artistic genius (a position favored by Hitler) than with the spirit of the modernist collective, and yet he produced for one of the most important sites in the city a building that expressed every cliché that we now associate with the modernist movement.

The ten-story-high Columbus Haus of 1933 was the prototypical steel-and-glass box with alternating horizontal bands of windows and masonry, and a flat roof. (Mendelssohn claimed later that his client insisted on the masonry courses in order to hang neon advertising signs on the building. Otherwise it would have been all steel and glass.) You could plunk Columbus Haus down today in any Edge City office park from Walnut Creek to Waltham and it would be perfectly camouflaged among the credit unions, the software companies, and the commercial leasing agencies. It was touted at the time as representing up-to-date *Amerikanische* verve, the sleek, industrial, streamlined look of an enormous object in motion, an ocean liner, a locomotive. Speed was an inescapable metaphor permeating early-twentieth-century high culture, uncritically embraced, as chaos and contradiction have been by the avant-garde in our time. That speed might lead directly to blitzkrieg and the intercontinental ballistic missile was not anticipated by the giddy cutting-edgers of the interwar era. Columbus Haus's first major ground-floor tenant, in fact, was the American merchandiser F. W. Woolworth.

The building opened for business in January 1933. Adolph Hitler became chancellor on January 30. A month later, the Reichstag was burned. Hitler proclaimed extraordinary police powers under an emergency decree (supplied by the aged, ailing, and confused President Hindenburg) under Article 48, the Enabling Act, of the Weimar constitution. The decree suspended due process of law, the free expression of opinion, the right of public assembly, and other civil liberties, and allowed Hitler to hold political opponents in detention for three months on the mere suspicion of anything. In March, officers of the Nazi SS—headquartered around the corner on Prinz Albrecht Strasse—leased the top six floors of Columbus Haus and began to use it as a detention and interrogation station for prisoners bound for the newly opened concentration camps outside the city. Columbus Haus was a perfect setup for the SS. It was a block away from the chancellor's headquarters on the Voss Strasse. The open floor plan allowed for easy conversion into holding cells and torture chambers. A rear alley allowed the unobtrusive delivery of suspects. In full swing there were accommodations for three to four hundred prisoners at a time. Meantime, Woolworth's continued dispensing hairbrushes, spools of thread, and goldfish from its ground-floor shop and Berlin life seemed to go on with a veneer of normality.

At this early stage of the Reich, the Nazis were equal-opportunity thugs. They were at least as interested in rounding up suspected communists, assorted dissidents, deadbeats, layabouts, petty criminals, Gypsies, and homosexuals as in persecuting Jews. But unlike some other groups, the Jews of Berlin possessed considerable assets in both real property and fungible paper, and the Nazis set about to seize invidiously whatever they could before any of this wealth might be sent safely abroad. Mendelssohn was among the fortunate Jews who sized up the situation early. He left Germany just weeks after Hitler came to power, hopped from Brussels to London during the thirties, and eventually got to the United States in 1941. He spent his last years designing synagogues and community centers in places like Grand Rapids, Cleveland, and St. Paul, dying of lung cancer in 1953 in San Francisco.

The fate of Columbus Haus was more doleful. The building survived the bombardments of World War Two as a steel-and-concrete shell at the edge of the new Soviet sector. Since the surrounding devastation was so complete, anything even partially standing had relative value, so Columbus Haus was soon reused. In 1946, a vestigial version of the once-immense Wertheim's department store—its great gothic headquarters on the *Achteck* reduced to gravel—opened in the ground-floor space that had formerly contained Woolworth's. The upper six floors, where the SS had plied its grisly trade, remained vacant and open to the weather. By 1951, as the city's political division into east and west assumed permanency, the new East German regime kicked out Wertheim's and installed a state-owned store. Two years later, riots rocked East Berlin as construction workers revolted against the communist regime. Again Columbus Haus sustained shell damage from Russian tanks brought in to quell the rioting. By the following year, as the Potsdamer Platz took on its bleak character as just another patch of contested border strip, the building was abandoned. In 1957, Columbus Haus was carefully dismantled. Its steel skeleton was carted off for salvage. By the 1960s, native shrubs of the Brandenburg Plain were growing on its former site. The wall was up. The crossroads of Germanic Europe had become no-man's-land.

Germania

To understand Hitler's Berlin, a few historical notes are in order.

Berlin is a younger city than London or Paris. In 1800, the population of London approached a million inhabitants, Paris stood at half a million. Berlin in 1800 was a provincial backwater of 150,000. Berlin's growth during the next hundred years was therefore comparatively explosive and traumatic. In 1800, Germany was not a nation, but a crazy quilt of more than a dozen kingdoms, duchies, baronies, principalities, landgraviates, and margraviates, including Prussia, Bavaria, Hanover, and Saxony, and scores of now-forgotten entities such as the Barony of Fulda, the principality of Ottingen, and the Duchy of Gotha. It took the genius of Otto von Bismarck to pull them together into a modern state.

Bismarck (1815–98) was the son of a Brandenburgian squire. His mediocre college career was distinguished only by a heroic capacity for drinking. He took his law degree into a brief and hapless stint with the Prussian civil service, from which he fled in anomie back to the family estate. For ten years he helped his father run the family lands and became increasingly drawn into local politics, for which he began to show a pronounced gift. Election to the Prussian Chamber of Deputies took him to Berlin where, with industrialism rising, he witnessed the urban disorders that swept Europe in 1848. In these struggles, Bismarck first formulated his notions of "realpolitik," the art of playing one group against another by manipulating political rewards and penalties. His talents soon propelled him into ambassadorial posts at Moscow and then Paris, where he was able to observe the canny Napoleon III at work, and also the operations of Georges Eugène Haussmann, prefect of Paris, who was directing an immense physical renovation of that city. Bismarck was called back to Prussia in 1862 to become simultaneously prime minister and foreign minister under the young king Wilhelm I.

Until Bismarck, Austria had been the dominant Germanic power in Europe. The functions of the old Holy Roman Empire—the pope's instrument for controlling northern Europe—had devolved upon the House of Habsburg, which still exercised hegemony over the other German-speaking states, including those with a Lutheran majority. At times, Austria also ruled outright in all or parts of Hungary, Bohemia (the Czech and Moravian lands), Slovakia, Romania, and scraps of the Balkans. Bismarck, using the growing industrial and military might of Prussia as a lever, set out to compose a north German empire that would overtake Austria in continental importance. He accomplished this by diverting Prussia's political energy from domestic squabbling into the conduct of several swift strategic wars, first against the Danes in 1864, to wrest away the duchies of Schleswig and Holstein, then Austria in 1866, and France in 1870. Austria came out of its six-week-long clash with Prussia a much-diminished power, France was surprised and humiliated in its brief war, and when it was over, the south German kingdoms, duchies, and principalities happily merged with Prussia and its dependents into a muscular new German Empire.

Germany's swift rise as an international power was necessarily accompanied by rapid industrial development. Bismarck managed this momentous transformation with two central tactics. The first was an innovative social welfare system of old-age pensions and subsidized medical care, which purchased the loyalty of the expanding working class. The second, and more sinister, tactic, when he had concluded his expansionary wars, was Bismarck's cultivation of a national siege mentality, portraying the Germans as a people encircled by scheming, jealous enemies from an alien culture, a world-view that would have terrible repercussions a few decades hence. It fostered a radical sense of apartness from the rest of European culture, one outgrowth of which was a virulent strain of anti-Semitism that became institutionalized in science, literature, and higher education. The historian Paul Johnson writes:

> [The] ruling caste hated the West with passionate loathing, both for its liberal ideas and for the gross materialism and lack of spirituality which (in their view) those ideas embodied. They wanted to keep Germany "pure" of the West, and this was one motive for their plans to resume the medieval conquest and settlement of the East, carving out a continental empire for Germany which would make her independent of the Anglo-Saxon world system. These Easterners drew a fundamental distinction between "civilization," which they defined as rootless, cosmopolitan, immoral, un-German, Western, materialistic and racially defiled; and "culture," which was pure, national, German, spiritual, and authentic. Civilization pulled Germany to the West, culture to the East. The real Germany was not a part of international civilization but a

national race-culture of its own. When Germany responded to the pull of the West, it met disaster; when it pursued its destiny in the East, it fulfilled itself.[2]

A substantial portion of the German intellectual establishment was therefore at odds with the idea of the modern city, which is what Berlin had become by the early twentieth century, with a population above four million. As a locus of industrial activity in Europe, it was exceeded only by London. The Berlin of the years before World War One was vibrant, protean, fast-paced, cosmopolitan, and full of new things, in the way that otherwise only American cities were at the time. Even among cultural conservatives, the German sense of being in the vanguard of history was vivid and had been bolstered by a half-century of stunning success in technology and power politics. But Bismarck was dead by 1900, and none of his immediate successors matched him in stature.

World War One was initially an attempt by Germany to consolidate these gains and become the dominant power of all Europe; Germany came close to prevailing in that unexpectedly protracted struggle. Bismarck's three wars had been remarkably quick and decisive. The longest, the Franco-Prussian war, lasted less than a year. The German general staff and Kaiser Wilhelm II expected the new conflict with Britain, France, Russia, and others to go accordingly. But the technology of combat had improved dramatically by 1914. Rapid-fire artillery stymied the capacity of either side to advance their positions on the ground. All the combatants were capable of immense industrial-scale slaughter, and the struggle stalemated in the inconclusive nightmare of the trenches. The Germans' tactical blunder of drawing the United States into the conflict in 1917, through unrestricted submarine warfare, finally broke the stalemate and lost the war for them. The shock of surrender brought on a national nervous breakdown.

The kaiser fled to exile in Holland, the Prussian military establishment slunk back to headquarters in paranoia and ignominy, and the German world turned upside down. The Weimar Republic of the 1920s was everything that Bismarck had hated: It was urban, cosmopolitan, leftist, pacifist, atheist, libertine, and irreverent. Revolutionaries, Jews, and homosexuals were heavily represented in the lively arts. A strident new cultural "modernism" declared its opposition to history, middle-class convention, and artistic tradition. "Outsiders" took over bastions of the cultural establishment. The young Bauhauslers became the official government architects. This brash new culture was on conspicuous display in Berlin, a city that had not been the least physically damaged by the First World War and that remained a bustling urban colossus despite the economic vicissitudes of the 1920s. It was also the site of much of the political street violence and disorder that helped to usher in the regime of Hitler.

Adolph Hitler never felt at home in Berlin. He was not from there. He was neither a northerner, a Prussian, or even a German, by strict definition. He was born and raised in Austria. The convulsion of World War One found him serving the German kaiser in the trenches of France and Belgium as a message runner. He attained the rank of corporal and won two Iron Crosses for valor. Had the war ended differently—and it easily might have—one result probably would have been the complete absorption of Habsburg Austria under an enlarged, unified, and Prussian-led German Empire run out of Prussia's capital, Berlin. But the war ended, rather, in the disgrace of Prussian authority, and it was in this vacuum of authority that Hitler, the talented demagogue outsider, found himself magically rising.

His National Socialist party had never gained a majority of Berlin votes in any election up to the time of his appointment as chancellor. The city's sympathies were decidedly leftward; Berlin was the epicenter of German bolshevism. Hitler in Berlin was therefore always something of an alien, and indeed when the Second World War got going in earnest, he spent as much time as possible away from the city, at first in the Bavarian Alps and then, as the war went increasingly against him, in remote and austere military camps.

Hitler's consolidation of power in 1933 had been so swift and total that he neutralized all opposition in the first weeks, and reembarked on the imperial project, begun by Bismarck, that had been derailed in the fiasco of World War One. Hitler's postwar career as a frustrated young artist has become a cliché of history. To describe him as "a failure," however, misses the point. His political career was performance art, with many explicitly theatrical touches, and it was such a smashing success until the last few disastrous years that he was rewarded with a kind of absolute temporal power not seen since the Roman emperors. Among other things, it enabled him to practice architecture on the grandest conceivable scale, through his surrogate, Albert Speer.

Back in 1924, while serving a year in Landsberg prison for his Munich insurrection against the leftist Bavarian government, Hitler had made sketches of a soldier's monument—a triumphal arch akin to one depicted in a painting by Schinkel, but never built—and a domed government hall of gargantuan proportions. Both these fantasies reemerged ten years later virtually intact when Hitler engaged Speer to collaborate with him on an ambitious scheme to transform Berlin into a world capital. By then, Hitler had erased the boundaries between the party, the state, the economy, and his own personality, and anything seemed possible.

Hitler neither lived in nor disturbed the palace at the end of the Unter den Linden where the kings of Prussia had lived. He just ignored it, so as to avoid stirring up any memories of its former inhabitants. The adjoining Lustgarten, the royal square, came in for some modification, however. The Führer had it paved over (in granite, not plebian asphalt) to facilitate military parades. He did not further molest the virtually decommissioned Reichstag after the 1933 fire. Upon becoming chancellor, Hitler moved into the prime ministers' traditional quarters off the Wilhelmstrasse, which he referred to as "fit for a soap factory," and unsuitable for someone who aspired to be "master of the world."[3]

Speer soon replaced it with an enormous, somberly classical edifice, more than half of which was occupied by a sequence of vast ceremonial courts and corridors designed to cow visiting diplomats as they marched hundreds of feet on slippery marble floors from the front entrance to Hitler's office. Even so, this chancellery building was intended only as an interim establishment, with a more suitable palace to come later. As a matter of style, Speer's version of classicism was not so far from the spirit of Art Deco, which could be described as classicism mechanized and streamlined for speed; Nazi architecture was classicism further simplified to express power minus distracting eroticism. It differed from Art Deco chiefly in eschewing any hint of feminine curves. Up the street from Hitler's chancellery, Reichs Marschall and air force chief Hermann Goering, more lustful for material gratification than the abstemious Führer, had commissioned Speer to design a palace that made the chancellery look like a filling station in comparison. Even Hitler was dismayed by the saturnalian excess of it, but he needed Goering (a celebrated pilot in the First World War) and did not interfere. To protect Goering's top-floor apartment, Speer designed a bombproof roof garden with thirteen feet of topsoil, deep enough for mature trees to grow. To facilitate the Reichs Marschall's lavish scale of entertaining, the two-and-a-half-acre roof garden was to include "swimming pools, tennis courts, fountains, ponds, colonnades, pergolas . . . and finally a theater for two hundred and forty spectators."[4] In any case, construction had to be postponed due to the war.

Speer, still in his twenties, was eager to please when Hitler took him on as an artistic protégé-collaborator. Together they conceived a scheme for turning crass, dynamic, workaday Berlin into an imperial city of somber monuments. Hitler intended to rename it Germania when he had secured the boundaries of his empire. The main ingredient was to be a mammoth mall-like boulevard running three miles at a north-south axis to the east-west Unter den Linden.

The south end would be anchored by the immense soldier's arch, the north by the Grosse Halle, a domed colossus nearly a thousand feet high, sixteen times the volume of St. Peter's Church in Rome. The oculus at the top of the dome would exceed the diameter of the ancient Roman Pantheon! In it, at some future point in midcentury, with his expansionary struggles of empire completed, Hitler imagined himself a gray eminence triumphantly performing his oratorical hoodoo before crowds of several hundred thousand gratefully enthralled subjects. Though the Führer himself disdained religiosity in his subordinates, the Grosse Halle's only conceivable purpose would have been Hitler-worship. The Reichstag, occupying an adjoining site, would be dwarfed by it, a vestigial organ of government. Himmler was preparing to organize an army of slave laborers for these projects when the war intervened. Demolitions were carried out for the north-south boulevard even while the war raged in Russia and

North Africa, but only one building in the general scheme was ever constructed, the "House of Tourism" (1940), and Allied bombers would eventually complete the Nordsud demolitions in an entirely different spirit.

In those heady days before America entered the war, when France had been conquered, and Paris occupied, and England was reeling from the Blitz, and the Russians were mollified with a nonaggression pact, and America dallied in denial and isolationism, and the prospect of a quick Nazi victory did not seem so far-fetched, Hitler had loved nothing better than to adjourn a dinner party at the chancellery and lead his guests to Speer's headquarters next door where they could ogle a huge, elaborately detailed scale model of the Berlin project, with Hitler wielding a flashlight to illuminate dramatically the various buildings and urban features while he discoursed for hours on his plans to build a city that would exceed ancient Rome in its magnificence and timelessness. In Hitler's scheme of things, the war was just an unavoidably messy phase of a large construction project.

The wish to overcome time itself was never far from Hitler's thoughts in this enterprise. He and Speer had even formulated an explicit "theory of ruin value" (*theorie von ruinenwert*) in anticipation of the inevitable distant point when, by definition, history would leave behind the Thousand-Year Reich. Under this theory, steel framing and reinforced concrete were not acceptable building materials because they would not result in aesthetically pleasing ruins. Therefore, all National Socialist buildings would be composed of granite and marble. As it happened, these standards were too rigorous even for the Nazis, who more often resorted to conventional techniques of the steel framework with brick and concrete walls clad in limestone veneer—including the chancellery, which was erected in less than a year by thousands of workers laboring in round-the-clock shifts. In any case, the theory of ruin value was tested during Speer's own lifetime. It turned out that bombs and artillery do not fashion ruins quite the same way that time and weather do. By 1945, the chancellery was reduced to a jagged dusty shell and its remains were eventually bulldozed by the Russians in 1949. The chocolate-brown marble from its interior was taken to decorate the subway station nearby under the Mohrenstrasse. To this day, the site of Hitler's former headquarters remains vacant save for its eerie little forest of shrubs and trees. Ambitious reconstruction goes on all around it, but the site remains untouched. There are no historical markers, nor even graffiti identifying the empty lot on the corner of the Wilhelmstrasse and the Voss Strasse. An aura of historical toxicity lingers there, contaminating with poisonous shame not so much the soil but the persistent collective memory.

Clashing World-Views and Competitive Modernism

By the early 1950s, the first tentative efforts at reconstruction were undertaken in East Berlin. One of the first and most prestigious buildings, the Soviet embassy on Unter den Linden, was exuberantly neoclassical. It fit in pretty well with the Schinkels and the royal monuments that remained, however fragmentary, in the old center of town, which the Russians controlled. The new embassy building was the product of Soviet state architects. Why did they employ the stylistic idiom of the nineteenth-century bourgeois "owner" class instead of the futuristic egalitarian language of industrial modernism? One might get very giddy and *deconstruct* the "dialectics" of post-Leninist Soviet social realism and its relation to a servile, capitalist functional modernism. But the truth, I believe, is simply this: Stalin and henchmen were quasi-educated provincial rubes for whom neoclassical architecture invoked the visual symbolism of authority—specifically *their* authority.

The plans drawn up in 1952–53 by East German officials for major reconstruction of the old center of Berlin, Colln Island, the Mitte District, and Friedrichstadt look like Daniel Burnham's turn-of-the-century plans for Washington, D.C., or Chicago. The communists never had the money to carry out much of the plan, but it was utterly old-fashioned. For them, the Bauhaus modernism of the Weimar Republic era was anarchic nonsense, just as it had been for Hitler. Paradoxically, the opprobrium that Stalin and his fellow tyrants expressed against modernism only boosted its legitimacy in the West, where it became by default *the architecture disliked by fascists and communists,* and therefore *the official architecture of democracy and human decency.*

One of the showcase projects, however, was the last truly monumental baroque boulevard to be built in Europe along principles established by Haussmann out of Lenôtre: the Stalinallee, a broad tree-lined street, in the spirit of Unter den Linden. The apartment buildings that lined it were intensely neoclassical. Thus, the proletarians of the *workers' paradise* were provided with exactly the sort of housing that the reviled bourgeoisie had striven to acquire in the previous century. The high neoclassical period of East Berlin reconstruction would only last until the mid-1950s.

Perversely, postwar West Berlin, the island of liberty in a sea of socialist oppression, became a showcase of monumental Bauhaus-inspired modernism composed of intrinsically despotic buildings that made people feel placeless, powerless, insignificant, and less than human. The Christian Democrats actually paid workers to remove ornament from old buildings. Since all the major old museums, libraries, and public monuments lay in the communist sector, West Berliners felt compelled to construct a new alternative cultural center of their own. This Kultur Forum, as it was called, made possible a grand reunion of two old modernist buddies, Hans Scharoun and Ludwig Mies van der Rohe.

Scharoun was the only major modernist architect to remain in Germany during the war. He did so, according to Balfour, out of "an intense belief that his work was rooted in German culture" and that "he could act only in relation to German culture."[5] Though classified by the Nazis as a "cultural Bolshevist," Scharoun was appointed to serve during the height of the war as Berlin's chief inspector of bombing damage. It was his job to go around and determine whether a given building was still safe to occupy. Under the circumstances, he was an exceedingly busy man. After the war, like many former minions of the Nazi regime, Scharoun was "rehabilitated" and reintegrated into West German civic affairs. Before long he became the director of city planning for West Berlin. When the Kultur Forum was proposed, he grabbed two of the major building commissions for himself: the Philharmonic Hall and the new City Library. Was this not a dream come true for the now-aging idealist who had managed to survive the nightmare of the Third Reich?

The buildings Scharoun designed now stand in a desolate pod that is the equal of any Motor Vehicle Regional Title Processing Center out of the California suburbs. In their quixotic attempt to overcome the catastrophes of history, they end up negating all history, including whatever good things ever developed from the long history of architecture. Both the library and the symphony hall are UFO-type inward-turned structures with no recognizable façade or street orientation and the full complement of parking lots, which seems as much a part of this aesthetic as the engaged pilaster and pediment were of Nazi architecture. They are covered with golden anodized aluminum panels of the type found on American suburban roller-skating rinks of the same vintage (1964). The streets they are on were tweaked into a suburban curvature that is completely at odds with the orthogonal layout of the adjoining city neighborhoods. Today, the Kultur Forum is a dispiriting mess. After nearly forty years, the gold anodized panels have collected a dingy patina of auto emissions, and the buildings look unspeakably filthy and tired. The meaningless berms and medians that float in the Kultur Forum's asphalt lagoons are littered with trash because no one walks here; no one feels any civic ownership of the site.

The other major component of the Kultur Forum is Mies van der Rohe's New National Gallery (in distinction to Schinkel's Alte Museum, the *Old* National Gallery). Mies, a successor to Gropius in directing the Bauhaus, had actually worked on commissions for the Nazis, but his aesthetic predilections were not to their taste, and in 1937 he bailed out in disgust and frustration for the United States, where he eventually became a superstar. His Seagram Building (1958) on Park Avenue in New York City became the ultimate model for the modernist corporate status box. It was natural, then, that Scharoun would extend to Mies the honor of designing West Berlin's new temple to modern art. And, by the way, Mies just happened to have a perfectly good, previously owned, slightly-used design for a large glass box. . . .

The New National Gallery building was originally intended to be the Bacardi Rum corporate headquarters in Santiago, Cuba. The design was completed just in time for Castro's revolution of 1958, as a result of which American-backed corporations, including Bacardi, had their property seized and were chased out of Cuba. The only substantial change in the design when it came to Berlin was a steel, rather than concrete, roof. The New National Gallery was completed in 1968.

Apart from its formal merits or shortcomings, the most peculiar thing about Mies's gallery is how poorly it functions as a place to hang paintings. Summer days in the northern European latitudes are very long. The sun comes up before four in the morning and stays out until nearly eleven at night. Because of the earth's rotation, the sun describes a rather low arc along the horizon this far north. When I was there a few weeks after the summer solstice, the sun would hang just above the horizon for hours before sunset. As one walked around the outside of the National Gallery, you could see the sun well under the overhanging steel roof, its rays streaming through the glass walls and bombarding the paintings inside with ultraviolet radiation.

West Berlin had also been subjected to other depressing modernist planning schemes that, more fortunately, didn't pan out. The most notable was Le Corbusier's plan of 1957 done for the great international competition of that year organized by the Federal Republic (West Germany). For Corb, the wartime destruction of Berlin was a fortuitously necessary convulsion of urban renewal that had removed all the accreted claptrap of the city's history at one stroke. It presented exactly what he had been longing for in Paris back in the twenties, when he had proposed, in his *Plan Voison,* the complete replacement of a substantial part of the Right Bank with a series of colossal high-rise slabs set among a matrix of urban freeways and grassy voids. This was back in the days when Corb was solidifying his position as the guru-in-chief (Dogma Division) of the modernist juggernaut. The *Plan Voison,* of course, was the product of a man who loathed everything about cities, but especially the street, cluttered, as it was apt to be, with other human beings.

Berlin presented Corb with the longed-for clean slate. His *Haupstadt Berlin* plan looks like an overblown version the 1964 Flushing Meadows World's Fair, a composition of eccentric pavilions set in suburbanoid landscape pods. The Friedrichstrasse would have been turned into a freeway. The centerpiece of the scheme would have been a sixty-five-story government tower that Corb named, apparently without irony, the House of Bureaucracy. His entry did not even place among the finalists—although the winning entry by the Berlin architects Spengelin and Pemplefort looked little more inspiring than the postwar addition to the campus of a midwestern land-grant diploma mill. Scharoun's entry, done with Wils Ebert, which was along the similar lines, placed second. A casual observer could conclude this much: They weren't any worse than the atrocities of "urban renewal" being perpetrated on New Haven, Connecticut; Worcester, Massachusetts; or scores of other American cities. The Berlin plans from the 1957 competition at least had the virtue of never being carried out.

Back over in East Berlin, an interesting architectural revolution had occurred. Joseph Stalin died in 1953. After a few years of jockeying for power, Nikita Khrushchev took charge as general secretary of the Communist party. In 1956, he denounced Stalin's character and malfeasances in the councils of government, and set out to reenergize the turgid, boring, insolvent, reactionary Russian state. Among other particulars, he denounced boring, backward-looking Stalinist architecture. The 1957 launch of Sputnik, the first artificial earth-orbiting satellite, made Russia seem stunningly, shockingly, more advanced—perhaps, the West feared, even technologically superior. At a stroke, the Russians had equaled all the Buck Rogers–style bravado of the West in an amazing bravura deed of the collectivist spirit—becoming the first pioneers of outer space! In this flush of confidence, trying both to bury the memory of Stalin and to make socialism appear more futuristic, Khrushchev threw the sponsorship of his government wholeheartedly behind architectural modernism. Henceforward, all communist buildings would be slicker and sexier than the bourgeois corporate clubhouses of the West. Soviet classicism was dead.

East Berlin accordingly entered its golden era of communist modernism. The tourist hotels that looked like clown colleges went up. Modernist apartment tower slabs went up for the paradise of workers. (It turned out they were built out of a subpar concrete containing too high a proportion of sand, and they began exfoliating in a few years.) Alexanderplatz, the most prominent civic space on the east side of the city, was given a surrounding skirt of apartment boxes that looked like a joke version of the Cabrini Green projects in Chicago grafted onto one of Victor Gruen's prototype 1960s American shopping malls—minus real shopping (since the communists didn't believe in commerce). A twelve-hundred-foot-high TV tower that looks like a Christmas tree ornament impaled on a medieval lance has loomed ever since the 1960s a block from the Alexanderplatz, hogging the view down Unter den Linden looking toward Moscow.

Perhaps the most contentious and pathetic product of GDR architecture was the so-called Palace of the Republic or People's Palace, a modernist bronzed-glass box monstrosity that had all the charm of a Soviet Ministry of Prosthetic Limbs. Built on the site of the former Royal Palace, it was the seat of East Germany's pretend parliament, combined with a bizarre array of entertainment venues for the masses, including two theaters, thirteen bars and restaurants, and a bowling alley. The old Royal Palace proper, home of the last kaiser and his predecessor Hohenzollerns, had been heavily damaged by Allied bombers. The remnants were dynamited in the fall of 1950 by the GDR, which could neither abide its symbolism nor afford to restore it. Adjoining the site was the former royal square, the *Lustgarten,* which Hitler had paved for Nazi rallies, and which the communists now greatly enlarged, along the lines of Moscow's Red Square, to accommodate political demonstrations on a greater scale than the Nazis'.

After the Wall fell in 1989, the Palace of the Republic became an instant anachronism. The emotion unleashed by the surprising and rapid events of that year led to proposals for razing the building out of sheer disgust for the toppled regime and all the wickedness it had embodied. Few regarded the building itself as having any inherent architectural value. Nevertheless, the building's fate generated tremendous political controversy. Many who had hated both the East German government and the dreary building itself were distressed by the notion that yet another chapter of German history would be lost, torn down, demolished, swept away, in an orgy of shame and recrimination. They argued that the Palace of the Republic had to be preserved if only to sustain the memory of what had happened. Another faction wanted to rebuild the old Royal Palace, though it was nearly impossible to justify on any grounds—other than a nostalgia for lost baroque urbanism at the epicenter of the city. There hadn't been a kaiser for eighty years and there was no prospect of a new one. Anyway, the debate over the building's fate was halted in 1990 by the discovery that it was hopelessly contaminated with asbestos. Three years later, after more handwringing, the federal government finally decided to demolish it. Except that the announcement only reenergized the debate over the destruction of history, and in the end, nothing was done about it. The building remains, an empty wreck deemed unsafe for visitors, and the old *Lustgarten* (Marx-Engels-Platz for fifty years) is alternately a parking lot and a rock concert site.

The Pain of a Dream Realized

As the war faded into history, and apart from extraordinary interventions like the Kultur Forum, West Berlin carried on and redeveloped more or less like the other wounded cities of Western Europe. Deeds and titles were reestablished, property was bought, sold, built upon, rehabilitated, neighborhoods were stitched back together, shops opened, the Kurfurstendamm (with its signature department store, KaDeWe) became the commercial spine of the half city. This was all made possible by generous infusions of Free World financial life-support in order to make West Berlin a demonstration project of political liberty, but it produced an abnormal economy. With major industry and business fearful of locating there, and its future darkly clouded, the half city became a haven for bohemians and other marginal personnel. In fact, it became very much like the old Weimar Berlin that Adolf Hitler had worked so furiously to extirpate—a magnet for artists, sexual explorers, and political adventurers.

Because West Berlin was an "island" locked within the communist GDR, it never developed postwar suburbs and urban extensions of the kind built in London, Paris, and elsewhere after World War Two. There were no daily commutes into and out of the city. Nearly a decade after unification, the streets of the city center were eerily tranquil after six o'clock in the evening. Plenty of people strolled the Ku'dam and Unter den Linden after work, but there were few cars in motion *because practically everybody who worked in the city lived there, too.* Suburban development was coming, though. Now that the enormous blank slate of former East Germany had become market real estate, there was tremendous pressure to emulate the worst of American suburban development practices, which were primarily designed to generate short-term profits. Projects were just then going through the extremely rigorous and time-consuming German permitting process. The hope of some that Berlin would become a new kind of "green eco-city," a twenty-first-century showcase of *sustainable* urbanism, was fading, but there was still tremendous activity in the city proper—especially compared to similarly sized American cities. Also, unlike Americans, Berliners still maintained a fundamental belief that city life was a valid aspiration for normal people.

As a technical matter, the Berlin block was a peculiarity of local urbanism that also had a major effect on redevelopment. Oversized by the standards of other Western cities, it was an oddity of Berlin's extremely rapid urban development in the nineteenth century, and the building typology it promoted took on the name of *Mietskaserne* or rental barracks. Ladd explains that this was a direct outgrowth of Berlin's earlier history as a garrison town, where the military was the city's chief industry and its workers (soldiers) were customarily quartered in people's houses.[6] The nineteenth-century *Mietskaserne* blocks, which composed much of pre-1945 Berlin, put the prosperous middle class in spacious apartments along the outer block edge, where there was plenty of air and light. Poorer people occupied quarters built very densely around multiple courtyards in the interior of the block, which also commonly contained small factories and workshops. The further inside the block you went, the worse the conditions became—less light, less air, smaller quarters, less amenity, more industrial nuisance.

During the bombardments of 1945, the majority of Berlin blocks were at least partially destroyed. Afterward, it became a conventional idea that this form of urban organization was no longer desirable. In the West, when repair was addressed, only the block-edge buildings were replaced or rehabbed. The bombed-out centers of the blocks were left open as courtyards. In the east, every scrap of habitable building was needed for housing and whatever the blocks contained was patched back together. In some of the more intact districts, such as Prenzlauerberg in the East and Kreuzberg in the west, these old buildings were taken over by risk-oblivious bohemians or Turkish immigrants, who discovered that in a city lacking masses of industrial workers, *Mietskaserne* could be reconfigured as spacious living quarters or studios—even if the view from the window was lousy. Rent control in both east and west also helped on the demand side, though it had the usual long-term pernicious effects on the supply side (in the west, disincentives for landlords to maintain their buildings, the abandonment of some property, the loss of value and revenue, and in the east, a suspension of market forces and ownership responsibilities altogether).

After the fall of communism in the east came the enormous problem of establishing legal title to urban properties. Many of the prewar deeds and records had been destroyed or lost. The GDR had tried to abolish the idea of private property anway, so in the decades from 1945 to 1989 they had done absolutely nothing to reconstruct the title record. In theory, all occupants of East Berlin buildings had been paying rent to the government. At unification, the task of reestablishing private ownership titles was given to a federal office called *Treuhand,* the truth company. The backlog of cases ran years behind. Thus, the redevelopment of East Berlin's general fabric was bogged down by legal disputes that were in some case unresolvable.

Additional huge problems appeared when the mist of euphoria over reunification lifted. Fully 10 percent of the Brandenburg state surrounding (and including) Berlin had been composed of military bases. East Germany had been the tank and heavy truck repair depot of the entire communist world for forty years. Many of these sites were toxic to a ninety-foot depth below ground from washing off vehicles contaminated by the residues of tactical nuclear weapons. (Strange to relate, when the GDR fell, the West discovered that the Soviet soldiers posted on these bases were living in such desperate conditions that they had turned basements into pig-raising operations and mushroom farms just to feed themselves.)

Yet another set of problems for the city concerned infrastructure. The subway lines between two sides of the city had been disconnected for years and had to be reestablished. The telephone wires in the east were in wretched condition. By the time the Federal Republic asked for bids for reconstructing it, several companies, including AT&T, proposed to do away with wires altogether and just give away free cell phones to the *Ossies.* These many problems led to the call to move the main offices of the Federal Republic from the provisional capitol at Bonn back to Berlin, the historical capital. The physical unification of East and West Berlin was going to be so costly that only such a bold stroke could politically justify the government expenditure. The response from both Germans and the rest of the world was surprisingly tame, as though it were self-evident that sooner or later Berlin would be reestablished as the national capital, and under the circumstances, with democracy well established and benign institutions running in the Federal Republic, it had just as well happen sooner rather than later.

By the 1990s the signal failures of modernist city planning had helped induce a search for a less hysterical approach. This was *Critical Reconstruction* under Hans Stimmann, the city's planning director, a reformed 1960s modernist, who remarked that the contemporary mess of Berlin could no longer be blamed on the World War Two bombing, but was a result "of politics and bad planning by people who were against history."[7] Critical Reconstruction aimed to restore the primacy of the street and the block as the fundamental units of design. Henceforth architectural "creativity" and "genius" would take second place to the ordering principles of traditional urbanism. "Let's stop with the experiments," Stimmann had said. Unities of design would be regulated: heights of the buildings, the relation of the façade to the sidewalk, cladding material, color, fenestration formats, roof configuration, pavements, and so on. This seemed despotic to some people highly sensitized to Germany's recent experience with despotic government. It certainly aroused the antagonism of most of the superstars of contemporary architecture, who were all clamoring for work in the bonanza of RFPs that flew out of the city in the nineties. They bid for the work, but sniped about it constantly. For instance, the American superstar Richard Meier (The Getty Center in Los Angeles) said of Stimmann that "he single-handedly ruined Berlin." The British starchitect Richard Rogers called *Critical Reconstruction* "ridiculous," but that didn't stop him from joining his old partner from the Pompidou Center in Paris, Renzo Piano, on a huge nineteen-building complex for the new Daimler-Benz headquarters on the Potzdamer Platz. The truth was that Critical Reconstruction was no more rigorous than the design system that produced present-day Paris. Perhaps even a little less so. After all, both Daimler-Benz and Sony's European offices (seven buildings) were allowed variances to exceed the height restrictions.

The planning ideas spawned by the modernists had been perhaps an understandable reaction to the shortcomings of the nineteenth-century industrial city, the bad sanitation, the terrible crowding, the perpetual twilight of the slums. The worker housing slabs of the Bauhaus had been conceived to bring air, light, and exterior open space to apartment dwellers who had previously known only the dreary *Mietskaserne*. The Bauhaus program had tried to be humanist, but its many negative consequences wounded and even destroyed cities everywhere. Now these planning ideas were in discredit with virtually everybody *except* the international celebrity architects and their cheerleaders in the universities. Critical Reconstruction was a way of saying that the twentieth century had been a disaster where city life was concerned, and the only way to truly correct things was to reach back to the last period in German history when the essential dignity of the civic culture had not been compromised by war, politics, or harebrained aesthetic theory. It was hard not to sympathize with this point of view.

In any case, the rebuilding of the nineties brought to Berlin an elephant stampede of architectural superstars, who whined all the way to the bank about the restrictions on their tormented genius. Norman Foster won the contract to refurbish the Reichstag (after the "artist" Christo completed his stunt of wrapping the old ruin in pink fabric—wow!). Piano and Rogers (mostly Piano with a pinch of Arata Isozaki) got Daimler-Benz on the Potzdamer. Helmut Jahn got Sony. José Rafael Moneo of Spain got the Hyatt Hotel. Frank Gehry bagged the Deutsche Genossenschaftbank's vanity headquarters on the Pariser Platz, adjacent to the Brandenburg Gate. (The exterior of Gehry's building had to conform to the height, cladding, and fenestration regs, so he knocked himself out turning the interior into a warped steel uteruslike atrium. Peter

Eisenman had actually gotten in under the unification wire, with a commission to design a piece of "social housing" for the GDR a year before the Wall fell. Eisenman's Checkpoint Charlie House on the Friedrichstrasse (1988), as it is called, is today renowned as the only apartment building in Berlin that has a waiting list *to get out of.* Since then, Eisenman, with the American sculptor Richard Serra, was awarded the job of designing Berlin's primary new Holocaust memorial. On a site about the size of two football fields, in the historically toxic zone off the Wilhelmstrasse, near the site of Hitler's bunker, a concrete field of twenty-seven hundred cement cenotaphs (originally four thousand) will memorialize the six million Jewish victims of Nazism. Culture Federal Minister Michael Naumann scorned the concept as a "wreath-dumping ground" whose grandiose scale recalls the projects of Albert Speer.[8]

Making plans for its own accommodation in a town that is trying to— but certainly never will—overcome the whole idea of politics, the Federal Republic made arrangements to convert Goering's old Air Ministry building nearby into the Finance Ministry. The building that housed Hitler's central bank will become the new Foreign Ministry headquarters. The Defense department will move into the Third Reich's War Ministry, where in 1944, the Nazis executed Count Claus Schenk von Stauffenberg, who had failed in his attempt to assassinate Hitler.

The great postunification project for Berlin has been the enormous task of simply becoming a normal major city again, as indeed the great cultural task for the German people and nation was to become normal again after all the vicissitudes, horrors, and lunacies of the twentieth century. Normality had to be accomplished without any artificial reinforcement of the national sense of self-esteem. If anything, group self-esteem has been viewed by Germans for the past half-century as a deadly vice, something to be avoided at all costs, the doorway to the abyss. The goal of normalization in Germany, and in the once and future capital city, Berlin, has pretty much been attained now, at the threshold of the twenty-first century.

Here in America, meanwhile, the attendees of all our conferences and symposia on urban problems tell us that injections of self-esteem will lead to the reconstruction of American cities. And every day Cleveland, St. Louis, Baltimore, Detroit, Buffalo, Hartford, Indianapolis, Nashville, Houston, Birmingham, Richmond, Raleigh, Topeka, Des Moines, Scranton, Worcester, Louisville, and other cities of the victorious United States, leader of the Free World, look as if the enemy bombers flew over them yesterday.

LAS VEGAS

Utopia of Clowns

They say that Antarctica is the worst place on earth, but I believe that distinction belongs to Las Vegas, hands down. For one thing, Antarctica is more pleasing to look at. The natural scenery is about equal to Nevada's in desolate grandeur, but Antarctica's man-made artifacts are less distressing to an average human being's neural network. The population of Antarctica, though tiny in comparison, is better-educated, less transient, and employed in more honorable work. Las Vegas certainly leads in cheap buffets, but the result is a shocking rate of obesity with attendant medical disorders. Some might even argue that overall Antarctica has better weather. In Las Vegas, a baby left unattended in the backseat of a car for nine minutes will fricassee before its mother returns with the dry cleaning.

As I write, Las Vegas is the fastest-growing city in the United States. For a culture that understands things only in terms of numbers, this supposedly proves that it must be a splendid place. I've heard it touted often as the American *city of the future,* the prototype habitat for a society in which the old boundaries between work, leisure, entertainment, information, production, service, and acquisition dissolve, and a new, exciting, colorful, pleasure-laden human metaexistence finds material expression in any wishful form the imagination might conjure out of an ever-mutating blend of history, fantasy, electrosilicon alchemy and unfettered desire. If Las Vegas truly is our city of the future, then we might as well all cut our own throats tomorrow. I certainly felt like cutting mine after only a few days there, so overwhelming was the sheer anomie provoked by every particular of its design and operation. As a city it's a futureless catastrophe. As a tourist trap, it's a metajoke. As a theosophical matter, it presents proof that we are a wicked people who deserve to be punished. In the historical context, it is the place where America's spirit crawled off to die.

The trouble with Las Vegas is not just that it is ridiculous and dysfunctional, but that anybody might take it seriously as a model for human ecology on anything but the most extreme provisional terms. That they do might in itself be proof that American civic culture has reached a terminal stage. Even the casual observer can see that Las Vegas is approaching its *tipping point* as a viable urban system, particularly in the matter of scale. In evolutionary biology, at the threshold of extinction organisms often attain gigantic size and a narrow specialty of operation that leaves them very little room to adapt when their environment changes even slightly. This is the predicament of Las Vegas. Its components have attained a physical enormity that will leave them vulnerable to political, economic, and social changes that are bearing down upon us with all the inexorable force of history.

Las Vegas evolved as a crude extrapolation of several elements of American culture: the defiance of nature, abnormally cheap land, vast empty space for expansion, and the belief that it is possible to get something for nothing—these elements all presenting themselves there in the most extreme form. The trouble with extrapolation as a growth model is that it assumes the continuation of all present conditions in the future, *only more so.* Since this is not consistent with how the world works, systems organized on this basis fail. Anyway, to extrapolate urban growth based only on extreme conditions invites certain catastrophe, since the law of unintended consequences will produce ever more compounded skewed outcomes. The destiny of Las Vegas, therefore, would seem bright in the same sense that a thermonuclear explosion is bright. I view it as a model for the extinction of the system I call the National Automobile Slum.

The Brief History of a Place That
Laughs at the Idea of History

Las Vegas means "the meadows" in Spanish. In a valley where the Mojave and Sonoran deserts meet, between thrust faults, which the geographers call basin and range and geologists call *horst* and *graben,* three potable springs flowed out of the cementitious sand into what is considered the harshest climatic region in North America. The ancient Anasazi people established a farming civilization centered east of these springs in what are today Arizona and New Mexico during a favorably moist weather cycle between A.D. 700 and 1200. Las Vegas lay at the edge of their territory and they used the swampy oasis as a camp in a trade route that connected New Mexico to turquoise mines near present-day Baker, California. After A.D. 1200, altered rainfall patterns in the Southwest severely reduced agriculture and, with it, the Anasazi. By 1519, Hernán Cortés was in Mexico, destroying the Aztecs and permanently disrupting the web of native cultures that emanated from them, and soon the Spanish penetrated what is now the interior western United States. For decades, the Spanish maintained a trail from their outposts in Colorado to their mission at San Diego, with Las Vegas as a midway watering hole. After 1600, Spain declined steadily as a world power. Its colonial enterprises languished in this forbidding region, but the native cultures never recovered either.

By the mid-1800s, Mormons ventured from Utah into Las Vegas long enough to build an adobe scouting station, but soon decided the extremely hot and isolated basin was beyond even their ability to make deserts bloom. When a U.S. government expedition finally got there, the area around Las Vegas was inhabited by fewer than a hundred very primitive Utes, who survived by the most marginal scavenging. Captain John C. Fremont disparagingly called them "the Diggers."

Toward the end of the nineteeth century, as railroads criss-crossed the Great American Desert, Las Vegas became a place where steam locomotives stopped to fill their water tanks, the classic jerkwater. It was incorporated as a town in 1905. The Hoover Dam project on the Colorado River—thirty-odd miles from Las Vegas—brought thousands of well-paid federal employees to the area between 1929 and 1935. The state of Nevada legalized gambling in 1931 and for a while Las Vegas benefited by hijacking federal paychecks. When the dam construction was complete, in 1935, the place languished again. During World War Two, the army set up an artillery training range just north of Las Vegas, cycling thousands of trainees through every couple of months. For all this federal life-support, Las Vegas remained a desert tank town with a few honky-tonk casinos until after the war. It was hard to get to, hellishly hot half the year, and offered the kind of sordid attractions geared only to nine-teen-year-old soldiers.

That changed with the federal highway program, air-conditioning, and a national syndicate of criminals whose specialized skills in the art of the grift were perfectly suited to a state where grifting—formalized as casino gambling—was perfectly legal. We all know by now the story of Ben-jamin "Bugsy (don't call me that!)" Siegel, the Los Angeles gangster and business partner of the New York gangster Meyer Lansky, and how the Flamingo Hotel was built with mob money, establishing the original template for both the physical planning and financial infrastructure of postwar Las Vegas. Siegel was murdered for grifting his grifter associates as soon as the Flamingo was up and running, but the experiment of Las Vegas as a mob money machine proved highly successful. More low-slung, cheaply built, tilt-up modernistic motel-casinos were quickly es-tablished on the highway outside the Las Vegas city limits proper and the place entered its classic era—mid-Elvis, early Rat Pack, quickie divorce and marriage capital of the United States, desert laundromat of mafia money. Elsewhere, in "normal" America, gambling was still considered a crime and a sin.

By the early sixties, the original casinos with their attached sleeping quarters were growing outdated and shopworn. To enlarge, refurbish, and reproduce casinos, the mob concocted a scheme for funneling addi-tional enormous sums of money through the Teamster's Union regional pension funds—which became, in effect, the chief investment bank of Las Vegas. A quirk in Nevada law had made it impossible for publicly held corporations to own casinos (under the law, every single stockholder would have to be individually licensed to operate a casino), so "normal" capital was unavailable to the gambling "industry." The quaint system of using sanitized front men to pose as owners for shadowy partners left Las Vegas a socially medieval society of mob lords and vassals glossed with the trappings of hypermodernity.

The night before Thanksgiving, 1966, billionaire Howard Hughes, erstwhile Hollywood movie mogul, aviation pioneer, founder of Trans World Airlines, and increasingly delusional recluse, moved into a penthouse suite in the Desert Inn on the Strip and began buying up approximately half the action in Las Vegas for reasons that are still largely mysterious, but may have had to do with a conjunction of his morbid terror of microbes, the clean desert air, the fact that he had a mania for controlling his surroundings, and that he had the financial means to do it. As the sole stockholder in the Hughes Tool Company, and head of its Las Vegas spinoff, the Summa Corporation, Hughes alone of all his employees and factotums needed a casino license to carry out operations. By this time, the founding generation of Las Vegas gangsters was growing old, and they were happy to sell out to Hughes for tens of millions of dollars to retire in splendor from the toils and hazards of gangsterdom. Hughes ruled his empire from the unreal isolation of his penthouse sickroom, his instructions carried out by a few handpicked morally hygienic Mormon executive aides whose rectitude in business matters was a stark contrast to the anarchic gangster folkways of the old guard, with their gauche bundles of cash, notorious skimming operations, and liberal application of "muscle" in employee relations. Hughes himself remained so generally invisible and unavailable to the public, including federal officials who vainly called him to testify before this or that subcommittee, that the newspapers retailed wild stories about his ever-weirder life in seclusion, the length of his hair and fingernails, his dietary peculiarities, and his neverending war against germs.

Perhaps fearing the prospect of a Hughes-dominated city, the state legislature in 1967 rescinded the law that had prevented publicly held companies from owning casinos. This made available for the first time gigantic streams of "normal" American investment capital, just when the scale of construction and operation in Las Vegas began to require larger sums of money than the criminal underworld or individual eccentric tycoons could provide. Meanwhile, Howard Hughes became increasingly crazy and physically ill. He departed Las Vegas in 1974 in a desperate journey between disinfected hotel suites in Europe and around the Caribbean, and he finally expired under mysterious circumstances during an airplane flight from Mexico to Houston in 1976, though his Summa Corporation remains to this day a major landowner in Clark County. The Hilton, Ramada, and Holiday Inn hotel chains soon stepped into the vacuum left by Hughes to buy several old established casinos, including Bugsy Siegel's Flamingo. Banks in New York and California began for the first time to regard Las Vegas as a wholesome place for investment. By 1980 half the action was owned by publicly held corporations.

In the 1980s, beginning with Atlantic City, New Jersey, gambling rapidly became legalized in many other parts of the United States, creating an enormous problem for Las Vegas. Folks in Rochester or Tacoma could piss away their paychecks in a local casino now without the bother of an airplane trip halfway across the country. Casino riverboats opened on the Mississippi where any soybean farmer could drop his life savings at a blackjack table and drive home in time for the Eleven O'Clock News. Every state cooked up a lottery. Video poker machines appeared in convenience stores all over South Carolina.

Through a loophole of federal law, Indian tribes were licensed to operate casinos on reservations, and they built some gigantic ones in, of all places, Connecticut. Few Americans knew that there *were* Indian reservations in this part of the country. Even the locals had not known their neighbors were Indians. But it was part of the oddball epidemic of political correctness ideology of the same period that gambling licenses became the de facto national reparations program to compensate Indians for the wholesale theft of their homelands—and one did not have to be fractionally much of a Native American to qualify. Some putative Narragansetts and Pequots in Connecticut might have had a Native American great-great-grandfather, but meanwhile they were fifteen-sixteenths Italian, Portugese, Irish, Polish, Ukrainian, Hungarian, French-Canadian, Serbo-Croatian, Anglo, and Dutch—which is to say of mixed heritage like most other Americans. They owned gas stations, plumbing supply stores, insurance offices, optometry practices, drove Mercury Montegos, and dressed in mail-order casuals like anybody else. But now, through some freaky caprice in federal statute, they were all candidates to become multimillionaire casino operators. By the mid-1990s, all but a few states had Indian casinos. Legal gambling had become nearly as ubiquitous on the American landscape as "factory outlet" shopping.

The response to this in Las Vegas was interesting. First, the official gambling trade association (and political lobby), in a swift semantic move, changed its name to the National Gaming Entertainment Association. This was intended to flush the last vestige of stigma out of it, to make gambling seem a normative, socially acceptable behavior, just another form of entertainment, in a culture that was finding it increasingly difficult to maintain boundaries between what was entertainment and what was not, what was decent behavior and what was was socially or personally pernicious. Henceforth, gambling would be just another *game,* like basketball, Nintendo, pin the tail on the donkey, or the stock market. Gambling was now *play!* And what was more innocent, in the popular jargon of psychotherapy, than *play?* Little children play. Kittens and puppies play. Gamblers were no longer skeezy, profane, overweight, alcoholic, cigar-chomping, wife-beating, acne-scarred losers in stained polyester suits with matching white leather belt and shoes. Now they were *players,* like members of the world championship Chicago Bulls, or partners in a Wall Street brokerage. Players could be sleek and fit! Buff men in hiking shorts, gals in spandex aerobic outfits. Moms and dads could be players! Playing was good, clean American fun.

Next came the campaign to turn Las Vegas into a *family vacation desti-nation,* like Disney World or Colonial Williamsburg—along with all the physical infrastructure needed to support it. The idea was to make gambling seem incidental to the family vacation, just something that happened in the background, like sunshine in California or Muzak in a Disney "theme" restaurant. To this end, the casinos went through another incarnation of massive renewal and reinvention. Hotels were built that had some of the rudimentary features of theme parks. Steve Wynn's Mirage was the prototype. It featured a fire-spewing volcano on the hotel's front apron along the famous Strip that erupted at hourly intervals, like Old Faithful up in Yellowstone, with better lighting effects. Even with the kids in tow, sooner or later the lure of gambling (that is, the possibility of getting something for nothing) would overtake the flash of the "family entertainment" come-on. You could eat all the tater tots in the world at the $7.95 buffet, buy the souvenir rubber rattlesnake, and finally catch Siegfried and Roy's magic show, but the scent of *winning big* always lurked in the background like an especially potent pheromone, igniting irresistible fantasies of unearned riches. A nation in denial of all its bad habits and lapsed standards of decency wanted to believe that Las Vegas was a perfectly wholesome place to take children. The themed spectacles just provided an excuse. The fact that Las Vegas pulled it off with hardly a peep from society's moral guardians attests to the flimsy pretense of *family values* politics.

If you visit Las Vegas these days, you will most certainly find yourself in the company of many people with children in tow, families who have done time in the Disney Worlds, Sea Worlds, Six Flags, Universal Studio parks, et al., and are seeking evermore thrills in themed togetherness. The volcano at the Mirage has been joined next door by a pirate ship extravaganza, in front of the Buccaneer Bay Resort, complete with cannon fire and live swashbuckling actors, enacted every two hours. The Circus Circus offers big-top thrills and chills along with blackjack. An enlarged Caesar's Palace contains a Last Days of the Roman Empire shopping mall. The Luxor has a Gunite sphinx with laser-beam eyes guarding the door, an indoor boat ride down a simulated ancient Nile, and a reproduction of King Tut's tomb, not to mention a video game arcade and several swimming pools. New York, New York, has, on the outside, an enormous roller coaster weaving up and around the cartoon skyscrapers of its fanciful façade. Inside it offers a food court done up in a pastiche of Greenwich Village and Times Square (yeah, both in the same place, why not?). Across Tropicana Avenue stands the Excalibur, featuring more magic shows, jugglers, acrobats, medieval banquets, and jousting tournaments. Across the street—that is, across the ten-lane Strip—from Excalibur looms the baleful glass box of the MGM Grand, the casino of which is larger than Grand Central Terminal. The MGM Grand has an adjoining mini "theme park," which is transparently a glorified babysitting service. Visible from every compass point in the Las Vegas valley is the Stratosphere Hotel, Tower, and Casino, at eleven hundred feet nearly as tall as the Empire State Building. It anchors the north end of the Strip and boasts a revolving restaurant with a roller-coaster grafted atop it, like a freakishly tall person wearing a crown of orbiting horseflies. The broadcasting needle at the tippy-top does double duty as the armature of a kind of zero-gravity-drop ride called the Big Shot that gives thrill freaks a taste of what a pleasure defenestration might be.

Recently opened are Steve Wynn's $1.8 billion Bellagio, a Lombardy-themed colossus with a twelve-acre simulated Lake Como atop the front parking lot, plus (drum roll) a collection of real European paintings, including such superstars of *plein air* as Van Gogh and Renoir (twelve-dollar entry surcharge); the Venezia (same thing as Bellagio only Venice-themed with a canal inside); the Parisian (ditto, Paris, the River Seine, half-sized Eiffel Tower, and so forth); and the Mandalay Bay, a sort of Indiana Jones–style generic South Seas fantasy featuring an artificial surfing beach with wave machines. All the foregoing are essentially the same building type dressed up in different costumes, just as the old Strip casinos were just hypertrophied versions of a basic roadside motel dressed up in different neon flavors. The Bellagio's Stripside main sign is housed in a structure nearly the size of New York's Flatiron Building, and at least as ornate. Locals joke that the way things are going, somebody will eventually have to build a Las Vegas, Las Vegas—a miniature version of the Strip inside a hotel on the Strip, so you can avoid the Strip and still experience it.

Which is something the casual visitor might dearly wish to do, because the experience of actually being on this gigantic motorway lined by buildings of such monstrous scale—or, at some stretches, vacant lots that appear to be the size of Rhode Island—is not apt to gratify many human beings with normal neurological equipment. In fact, if ever a setting was designed to ravage the central nervous system and induce acute agoraphobia, the Strip is it.

The Physical Layout

Originally there was downtown Las Vegas, platted in 1905 by the San Pedro, Los Angeles, and Salt Lake Railroad into forty three-hundred- by four-hundred-foot blocks, subdivided by alleys. This was a normal American urban grid pattern of the time, producing optimal frontages and building lots organized for rapid sale and easy development. The drawback, common in the American West, was a monotonous geometry unrelieved by focal points, terminal vistas, diagonal thoroughfares, or other grace notes of civic design—though one block at center was reserved for "public purpose"—say, a courthouse or a plaza. The streets, at eighty feet, were uniformly too wide to produce a pleasing ratio of spatial enclosure—another common western practice. They were designed to permit horse-drawn wagons to turn around without circling an entire block. (This was a cultural carryover from earlier times that would shortly be obsolete; 1905 was only two years before Ford's introduction of the Model T.)

The town had a Main Street, but it lay along the railroad right-of-way, really the edge of town. The building lots on Fremont Street were oriented narrow-end-to-shopfront in order to locate the business district there, and indeed Fremont became the commercial heart of town. Las Vegas quickly acquired a school, a bank, shops, hotels, and the other common furnishings of American life. The surrounding desert remained, of course, a forbidding wasteland in every direction, lending the town a permanent air of desperation. It wasn't the end of the world, but you could see something like it shimmering in the heat out in the buzzard flats beneath the Spring Mountains.

The modern, post–World War Two Las Vegas of the famous Strip, Highway 604, now Las Vegas Boulevard, lies wholly outside the incorporated town and its original grid. It is under the jurisdiction of Clark County. The Strip developed where it did for several reasons: Taxes on gambling and hotel rooms were lower outside the city proper, desert land outside town was very cheap, and the bulk of visiting thrill-seekers arrived by car from Los Angeles, a seven-hour drive then, four hours nowadays, and they expected the usual autocentric amenities associated with L.A. life—that is, parking, parking, parking. The El Rancho Vegas, Siegel's Flamingo, the mob's Desert Inn, the Frontier, the Sands, the Sahara, Riviera, Dunes, Stardust, Aladdin, Tropicana, and so on were thus deployed at half-mile intervals along the highway to provide a certain cushioning separation between establishments. Under this system, there was plenty of room for each hotel to expand as necessary—indeed no sense of limits. Around and behind the casinos, well into the 1960s, there was virtually nothing but sand, creosote bush, and tarantulas.

By the late 1960s, the desert to both the east and west of the Strip began to fill in with houses and apartments for the ever-growing population of hotel and casino workers and with el cheapo shopping plazas to service the houses. The Strip runs basically north-south, with a slight northeast dogleg halfway up. The major east-west arteries were named after the casinos that occupied each regular interval of the Strip: Sahara Avenue, Desert Inn Drive, Flamingo Road, Tropicana Avenue. The problem from an urbanist's point of view was that this pattern for future development was based on blocks one-half-mile square—in some cases even a mile square—with six-, eight-, and ten-lane streets between them.[1] Buildings went up along the edges of these huge blocks but the deep interiors of the blocks did not necessarily ever develop. Where they did, it was more often than not with housing subdivisions or apartment complexes composed, at best, of incoherent mazes of poorly connected residential lanes and, at worst, a dendritic layout of nonconnecting cul-de-sacs.

There was a strange analog for this system in the specialized casino culture of the town, which infected other layers of the Las Vegas mentality. Casinos are deliberately designed to be as disorienting as possible so as to induce the wagering public to forget where they are, perhaps even who they are, how long they've been there, where else they might be obliged to go, and to what else their lives are connected (family, profession, value system, and ethical code) beyond the riveting hysteria of the wagering moment. There was always a legible entrance into the casinos, like any animal trap, but it was often very difficult to find your way out, amid the din of gleeping slots and the pulsing riot of lights, which were calibrated to the same numbing level not only throughout a given casino, but in all casinos. The very people who worked in that environment lived in the disorienting housing complexes east and west of the Strip. For them this state of disorientation was *normal!* They were accustomed to spatial confusion. Most had learned to navigate their way around the workplace by means of gerbil-like dead reckoning—*take a right at the "batter up" slot machine, hang a left at the "winners' circle bar," hang a right at the second crap table, go fifty feet straight down the aisle to pit number 14. . . .* They used the same method to find their way home at seven o'clock in the morning—*take a right at the Taco Bell on Flamingo Road, hang a left at the Jiffy Lube, go straight through the gate at "Hacienda Gardens," hook a Louie at the last beige apartment building, go past the pool complex to number 14. . . .*

These fiascoes of civic organization were typical of any suburban place, of course, but here they were refined to a distinct regional aesthetic: *The more confusing the better.* Also, the distances between things in Las Vegas were so vast, the scale so exaggerated (even by West Coast standards), and the heat so punishing, that the automobile became an indespensable prosthetic organ, without which no simple task of living could be accomplished. For instance, it was just five blocks from the Tropicana Hotel to the Liberace Museum. It didn't look like much on the rent-a-car map. But in reality it was a trip of nearly three miles down a ten-lane boulevard without continuous sidewalks, past innumerable strip-mall parking lagoons, gigantic vacant lots, apartment complex fortifications, chain-link fences, berms, hydrological earthworks, filling stations, and other unimaginably tedious landforms, in blaring sunlight that could elevate the ground temperature above 125 degrees. Lawrence of Arabia would not undertake such a trek.

In the face of these daunting conditions and the established culture, planning officials have quixotically attempted to make the Strip itself walkable. Or, rather, the Strip has evolved in such a manner during the 1990s as to make walking seem like something more than a theoretical possibility. It hasn't worked very well, despite considerable investment. The problem, again, is one of scale. With the renovations and innovations of the 1990s, the Strip hotels grew to outlandish proportions. They didn't move closer together, they just swelled to occupy more of the space between them—much of their vast frontage dedicated in one way or another to the coddling of automobiles, loading and unloading, limo stands, and parking. Caesar's Palace had a plaque on the front entrance declaring its cantilevered porte cochere to be the largest such structure in the world. It had the characteristics—and all the charm—of a freeway toll plaza. Where theme park attractions such as volcanoes and pirate battles had not been established on the hotels' front aprons, one generally encountered heroic vignettes in landscaping to conceal the drive-ups.

The idea with the landscaping, one city planning official told me, was to try to soften the hardscape of buildings with tropical foliage to give the illusion of being in a lush oasis rather than the merciless desert this really was, "the illusion of being comfortable," the official put it with self-conscious irony. In July and August, with the mercury well over a hundred for days at a time, merely being outside was exhausting. However, Las Vegas was also far enough north that periodic killing frosts occurred in winter, every three years or so. After the most recent freeze, the Mirage Hotel alone had "changed out" over a hundred palm trees.[2] It cost from one to three thousand dollars a tree to replace them. The northern half of the Strip itself had been embellished with a planted median to further tropicalize the ambience, at the cost of two lanes of traffic and $14 million. There were ten active lanes left.

"It's still all about cars," the planning official told me. "The policy is still to move as many cars as possible, only now you get to sit next to a palm tree at the light."

Sidewalk had been installed along the street-edge of the Strip during the 1990s, but at many stretches it was barely five feet wide, with no parking lane to cushion you from the travel lane right off the curb, so altogether the pedestrian experience was as psychologically gratifying as a stroll along the shoulder of the Santa Monica Freeway. For all the trouble they'd gone to, the ensemble of the Strip still only worked for those cruising in a car. It was nearly five miles from one end of the Strip to the other, from the Mandalay Bay Resort to the seedy old heart of downtown, Fremont Street, "Glitter Gulch." You could walk it in segments, but even then it was a grim assignment, trudging from one bloated attraction to the next. And things turned out to be much farther away than they seemed. To the casual observer the MGM Grand appeared practically catty-corner to Caesar's Palace. But actually getting from one to the other proved to be a half-day hike. The hotels didn't *look* that far away, standing out there on the Strip. But it was a kind of optical illusion, because they were relatively so huge, like the illusion that various peaks in a mountain range seem close together viewed from a distance—again, a question of scale.

Mixed in between the new megahotels were a few remants of an older Vegas—one-story strip malls tenented by the dreariest bottom-feeding establishments of Nevada tourist retail: wig boutiques, tattoo studios, sadomasochistic leather emporiums, fried-food take-out joints, pawn shops, psychic parlors, and instant divorce offices. Anyway, these outfits were set back far enough behind their own parking aprons so that one couldn't even enjoy the low-rent window-shopping for its kitsch value. At some stretches of the Strip, there was virtually nothing—sun-baked vacant lots, parcels never developed for mysterious reasons having to do, perhaps, with title disputes or shadowy owners who have not yet turned up missing.

For a touch of nostalgia, I even came across the abandoned carcass of the Aladdin Hotel, a quarter mile of cyclone fence guarding it against winos. What once must have seemed the embodiment of midcentury ultramodernity in its voluptuous, curvy precast concrete splendor now seemed as pitiful as a 1950s showgirl in a county nursing home. It would be demolished the following month in the kind of choreographed "implosion" that had become a theatrical extravaganza all its own in the town.

Of course, there were plenty of slick, high-tech gimmicks designed to distract you from the melancholy tedium of the Strip pedestrian experience: gigantic outdoor television screens playing colorful ads for nightclub acts, and a new generation of glitzy computerized electric casino signs. But the scale of things on the Strip ultimately defeated these lame attempts to make up for fundamentally bad design. You'd see packs of tourists, many of them elderly, wearing the childish souvenir T-shirts, polyester sports caps, and boatlike high-tech sneakers that unfortunately have become the demeaning uniform of their age cohort, dragging themselves across the moonscapelike expanse of the Caesar's Palace frontage—where the view from the sidewalk afforded glimpses down into a huge, craterlike sunken parking pit—the oldsters humping through the heat and the suffocating automobile emissions with expressions of nauseated wonder on their pink sunburned faces as though they had been snookered, by the Devil's own entertainment director, into a reenactment of the Bataan Death March.

It was even more appalling to watch them cross a major intersection, such as Tropicana Avenue and the Strip. The hotels on the four corners—Excalibur; New York, New York; MGM Grand; and the Tropicana—contained all together more hotel rooms than the entire city of San Francisco. From an engineering standpoint, it was the Godzilla of all suburban sprawl interchanges: eight travel lanes each way, times four, plus triple-left-turn lanes to mitigate the "stacking ratios." Here was a road 150 feet wide, half the length of a football field, not including the bonus territory added by immense curb ratios. Since the New York, New York, hotel and casino had opened in 1996, filling in the northwest corner of Trop and the Strip, huge mobs were now ricocheting back and forth among the four gigantic casinos. This new foot traffic queered all the equations of the highway engineers. Their beloved stacking ratios became meaningless as grandmothers from Fresno, toting king-size carboard cups of silver dollars, limped arthritically from corner to corner, halting traffic even after the lights had changed. Between the hours of four and seven P.M. it could take as much as forty minutes for a vehicle to get through this mess. With the opening of New York, New York, the number of car–pedestrian fatalities mounted to shocking levels—along with insurance losses and terrible public relations—until the Clark County authorites threw in the towel and ordered sky-bridges built over the streets to convey these valuable units of tourist revenue out of harm's way.

When I was there in the spring of 1998, the southern two corners had been bridged, but the northern half hadn't, and the tourists still crossed from the MGM to New York, New York, on the surface. A great mob would assemble at the corner beneath the looming gold statue of the MGM lion during the quarter of an hour or so that it took for all the turning lanes to clear in sequence. Finally, the light would change and the mob would start moving in a big blob across the strip. Invariably some elderly individuals would tire and and begin to straggle two-thirds of the way across as the signal light changed from green to flashing yellow. When the light turned red, the motorists stacked up there—who had been stuck at the corner of Trop and the Strip for perhaps half an hour already—would commence leaning on their horns. This would prompt the elderly stragglers to attempt to hurry the remainder of the way, many of them in raptures of angina pectoris and emphysema. So one saw this fantastic vignette of pathetic and unseemly behavior. It was a perfect microcosm of our sadistic national ethos.

Wet Dreams

The future development of Las Vegas is certain to run up against limits. One that will present itself soonest has to do with economies of scale in the operation of Las Vegas's chief business: the hotel-casinos. These monuments to a culture of avarice have been renovated at regular intervals, not just because of the opportunity to increase profits with ever-larger facilities, but because circumstances required it. Hotel decor wears out very quickly. Hotel guests do things to a room they'd never dream of doing at home. They spill coffee, beer, and bodily fluids over the furnishings without a second thought. They tramp around on the carpets dripping wet from the shower. They leave the TV on around the clock to deter interlopers. They smoke things. Carpets, draperies, beds, and suchlike all have to be replaced frequently at great expense.

The hotel buildings themselves could be described as relatively worthless throwaway containers for the decor. Therefore, the logic has gone, why not just demolish the whole package, along with the stinking carpets and tired box-springs, take the tax loss, get more rooms with new stuff in a bigger building to bring more players into a larger casino with more slot machines for ever-greater profits? Plus, get the cachet of having a brand-new establishment in a town were newness and bigness are the biggest draw? Well, sure. From a cost-accounting point of view, the hotel-casino business has had extremely short payback cycles—as little as six months. In other businesses a payback period of five to ten years on investment is *normal* and three to five *extremely successful*. Up to this point, then, the cycle of putting up and casually tearing down relatively large buildings after a short period of use has been economically rational—consistent with a particular period of American economic history: the age of national economy as Ponzi scheme. And that is how, over the last fifty years, a collection of fairly ordinary low-rise highway strip motels with attached casinos mutated into towering multithousand-room giants with attached theme parks.

The current generation of hotels, however, has reached such an inordinate size and scale of operation that it is unlikely this system can be continued, even if other economic factors—cheap petroleum, junk-bond financing, and entertainment tourism, to name a few—remain constant. The hotels may have reached that terminal stage of evolution where the organism can neither undergo further hypertrophy, nor sustain itself at the current scale of metabolism. For instance, the Bellagio, with its three thousand rooms, and all their furnishings, and the tremendous plumbing infrastructure and personnel (including fountain operators on rotating workshifts and maintenance scuba divers) for an artificial lake, represents an investment of more than a billion dollars. Yet, for all its enormity, it employs the same cheap construction methods as any taco stand—spray-on plastic foam fake stucco. The *culture* of the Las Vegas construction industry has not adjusted to the new needs of a monumental megahotel—namely, the need to endure for longer periods of time than has been customary in order to justify the new massive scale of investment. They are still using materials and means of assembly that are certain to disintegrate at a rate too fast to justify a duplication of effort and expense in replacing them. What's more, the capital expense of completely refurbishing these monsters at frequent intervals may prove excessive relative to the rapid depreciation of the cheesy buildings containing the thousands of beds, miles of carpeting, and tons of draperies. The upshot would be hotels that can neither be refurbished nor replaced, with a self-evidently bleak destiny.

Another questionable factor in the equation of Las Vegas's future is the water supply. Las Vegas occupies the driest region in North America with the greatest extremes of temperature. Las Vegas gets four inches of natural rain a year. Tucson, Arizona, in the Sonoran Desert, gets twelve inches. The springs that watered the ancient meadows Las Vegas was named after served as the city's water supply until the 1950s. Since then, the city has had to make do with the state of Nevada's allotment from the Colorado River. Since 1922, the Law of the Colorado River, a compact among seven western states, has ruled western water allocation, under formulae drawn up by the U.S. Bureau of Reclamation. The law was fashioned years before the bloated hallucination of contemporary Las Vegas was even conceived, and the allocations can only be revised on the basis of an absolute consensus by all seven states, with ratification by each state's legislature—an extremely cumbersome procedure.

Under the compact, California has long received the lion's share of the water from the Colorado River (since 1935 impounded behind Hoover Dam in Lake Mead, with a little dribble released to its original destination, the ancient delta at the top of the Bay of California in Mexico). California's annual allocation is 4.4 million acre-feet. An acre-foot is the amount of water needed to fill an acre 12 inches deep, or 325,851 gallons, or enough to theoretically supply two American familes for a year. A clause in the federal act stipulates that California has absolute priority over the Colorado River's water and is entitled to its 4.4 million acre-feet before other states can receive their first drop. This was the price that California politicians exacted for their support of the enormous federal projects the compact entailed—including the Glen Canyon Dam as well as the Hoover Dam, and various pipelines, canals, and aqueducts associated with the Central Arizona Project.[3] Nevada's annual allocation is a measly three hundred thousand acre-feet. (In 1922, Nevada had only eighty-one thousand inhabitants.) California is usually characterized as the bad guy in the picture. The head of the Southern Nevada Water Authority, Pat Mulroy, told me, "They've developed an attitude. They believe that they were there first. The Colorado River belongs to them. In size, they're more than equal. They try to con their way rather than entering into partnerships. Six states could solve these problems, but California makes it difficult."[4]

California uses the bulk of its allocation in agriculture, mainly in the Imperial Valley, growing not only winter fruit and vegetables but also "water-sucking" crops such as alfalfa, cotton, and sedan grass. The Imperial Valley corporate farmers—called "feudal oligarchs" by Nevada water officials—boast that they get a $1 billion annual gross product out of three million acre-feet of water. Hotel owner Steve Wynn boasts in counterpoint that he gets a $1 billion gross annual revenue out of 250 acre-feet watering the palms, pools, fountains, bathtubs, and bar wells of his Mirage Hotel. However, the residents of Las Vegas average 325 gallons per day of water, a per-capita consumption greater than that of any other city in the world. The casinos use about 8 percent of the city's water. Golf courses, of which there are three dozen, use another eight percent—and the water they use is pure drinking water. Homeowners account for 64 percent of the city's water use, two-thirds of that on their lawns. The remainder is used by small business and public service.

An effort has been made over recent years to conserve water. It has been difficult to persuade newcomers from more verdant parts of the United States to quit trying to grow grass lawns in Las Vegas and instead decorate their property with desert botanicals and gravel, called *xeriscaping*. The program tends to be at odds with one of the main reasons that Americans choose houses on large lots in the first place, which is, theoretically, so that children will have a patch of lawn to play on. Games of flies-up and snatch the flag don't work too well in a yard full of cactus, sagebrush, woolly butterfly bush, creosote bush, and mesquite, which are characteristic of xeriscaping. For a substantial part of the year daytime outdoor temperatures exceed one hundred degrees, which drives people of all ages inside, and children are more likely to be training on video games for their adult careers as casino *players*. Anyway, the plain truth is that the single-family detached house is an inappropriate building typology for the Las Vegas climate. It handles temperature extremes poorly. The attached courtyard house, of the type found in Latin America and North Africa, would make a lot more sense, would take up a lot less space, would regulate heat and cold better with less artificial air-conditioning, and, built at high densities with integral shopping, would require a lot less compulsory motoring—but, alas, the so-called stand-alone California ranchburger in a pod subdivision of identical ranchburgers, detached from the shopping and office pods, is what the builders are used to supplying to a market that doesn't want to consider anything else.

To compensate for the enormous costs entailed by running water pipes vast distances to, for instance, the twenty-two-thousand-acre Summerlin housing subdivision northwest of the city, the Southern Nevada Water Authority has begun charging hefty connection fees of up to thirty thousand dollars per house.[5] Adding to the cost is the nature of the desert soil in many parts of the valley, a concretelike hardpan called *caliche* so tough that a machine designed like a giant chainsaw is required to break it up for laying pipe. Yet, paradoxically, the actual water usage rates in Las Vegas are among the cheapest in the nation. The wish to keep the hyper–growth engine going trumps the fear of the rational limits to growth. An estimated six thousand newcomers arrive in Las Vegas every month looking for employment in a seemingly inexhaustible wonderland of relatively high-paying casino service jobs that are the only remaining equivalent in America of the high-paying blue-collar assembly-line work of the mid–twentieth century.

Amid this relentless expansion of mostly suburban fabric, the Southern Nevada Water Authority grows increasingly desperate to find a way around the wall of limits. It is estimated, based on present rates of growth, that the city will reach that absolute limit on its water supplies between 2007 and 2013. Trial balloons for various water schemes have been floated and dropped in recent years. One was to run a pipeline from northern Nevada to take a share of ground water used by the few agricultural producers there. This was shot down in state politics. Another plan, described by a former state Sierra Club officer as "a cocka-mamie scheme," involved capturing a tributary of the Colorado called the Virgin River, putting the whole thing in a pipe as soon as it crossed over the Utah/Nevada state line, and diverting it to Las Vegas. This was abandoned as impractical. Another idea, called "wheeling," would have allowed withdrawals of water from Lake Mead based on the amount that flowed into the lake from the Virgin. The compact wouldn't allow it. There was an idea to buy water out of western Colorado that Coloradans objected to. Finally, the last resort has been to make deals of dubious legality that would allow Nevada to simply purchase in cash part of Arizona's federal allocation (willing seller meets willing buyer), with the expectation that cotton and alfafa production in Arizona would have to be reduced in the years ahead—evaporation rates alone in fields irrigated above 110 degrees are just out of this world—and that the creeping urbanism of Phoenix and Tucson, however ominous, would require a lot less water than desert agriculture. In the last ten years, the explosive growth of the San Diego metro area has added an additional factor to the equation, as that city competes both with the Los Angeles Metro basin and the Imperial Valley for California's fixed allocation of Colorado River water. California is now greedily eyeing rivers as far north as British Columbia to solve its chronic water problems. Meanwhile, the Southern Nevada Water Authority resorts to desperate conservation measures—mailing out free low-usage shower heads and toilet-tank adapters to fifty thousand households, a ban on future artificial lakes, switching to "gray" water for golf course irrigation—to try holding the line against the future, but these are mere gestures in the face of that inexorable wall of limits.

There are some additional questions about the safety and quality of the water coming into Las Vegas. An outbreak of potentially deadly *cryptosporidium* bacteria occurred in 1994. A few years later, California notified Nevada that a chemical called perchlorate was showing up in the Colorado River water. Perchlorate is a highly specialized chemical used as solid rocket fuel. It can adversely affect thyroid function and metabolism in humans. Sampling led to two primary manufacturers of the rocket fuel in nearby Henderson, Nevada, just west of the Hoover Dam. Ground water and soil were both found to be contaminated there. The use of bottled water in Las Vegas is the highest in the nation.

Fast Forward

It is really impossible anymore to imagine a happy future for this dubious urbanoid organism. To the casual observer, Las Vegas has used up its future like the profligate young heir to a fantastic fortune. Its whole, short history has been dedicated to the extravagant idea that it is possible to get something for nothing, or, at least, to get all the goodies of life easily: wealth, sex, fame, a great meal, a good mood, lodging at once luxurious and cheap, and a lifetime's free parking. These wishes are present in all other quarters of the nation, and throughout our history as well, but in Las Vegas they were refined to their purest essences of avarice and venality. The pretensions of the kitsch-lovers aside, there was never anything innocent about Las Vegas. It has always been a product of the purest cynicism, real gangster cynicism, headless-corpse-in-the-desert cynicism. The city's current condition might be viewed more empirically as also the end product of an unprecedented half-century bonanza of a cheap petroleum economy, and the circumstances of relative world peace that left North America unmolested by major international struggles during that period. The result in Las Vegas is a world capital of foolish and absolutely incorrect notions about what it takes to reconcile human nature with the project of civilization.

Anyway, we are about to leave the cheap-oil era behind, and all the wishful thinking from sea to shining sea will not summon up a plausible reason to think that we comprehend the territory ahead. To me, the most plausible future for Las Vegas is as a ghost town, an atomic-age Teotihuacán, viewed, say, two hundred years from now, a scene of silent desolation, the ancient Strip empty of cars, the once-lush medians devoid of palm trees, the Bellagio's fabled lake a cracked concrete shell with the plumbing long stripped by salvage scavengers, the great hotels concrete skeletons, their spray-on stucco and foam insulation panels long since granulated under the relentless ultraviolet rays, the casinos gutted, here and there a tarantula, a buzzard, a rat . . . the excitement . . . over.

Rome

In Search of the Classical

The stillness on the Palatine Hill is like the weird aural void following the final crashing chords of a great symphony—an echo seems to roar in your head, but there's no sound there anymore. On the Palatine Hill, time's remorseless power is revealed in the silence that shrouds the enormity of a civilization's destruction and the palpable shock waves that still emanate from its physical residue. Silent and invisible as they are, the shock waves can still be felt on the Palatine Hill.

Of the city's fabled seven hills, this one is the most thoroughly encrusted with myth and history, the site where Romulus founded his fortified village of Latins around 750 B.C., where the republic (*respublica,* the public thing) was formed and endured far longer than our American emulation of it has so far, the place where the emperors Augustus, Nero, Tiberius, Domitian, and many others had their homes. Now, all is gone, and amid the rank spray of live acanthus weeds little but the foundations remain atop the hill, with the brick remnants of a few barrel vaults, retaining walls, and some stone garden path pavings that may have been laid only a century before yesterday, say some time after Lord Byron and before Henry James, who can tell?

Since the fall of the empire and the many incursions, sackings, and takeovers that ensued, Rome has been divided into two basic geographical entities: the *abitato,* where people live, and the *disabitato,* the empty quarters. At the height of the Renaissance the *disabitato* comprised most of the eastern half of the city within the ancient Aurelian Wall, the area that had been the civic heart of the empire, the layered fora of the Caesars, Hadrian's market, the temple of Jupiter, the arches of Titus and Septimius Severus', and so on, as well as the residential quarters composed of *insulae,* multistory apartment buildings, much like today's, where the Roman masses lived. For centuries, the ruins of antiquity functioned as the world's greatest salvage yard. The supply of free bricks seemed endless. All the metal hardware, grilles, railings, doorknobs, and statuary were mined away year by year. The dressed and carved marble façades of the great monuments were carried off by the Farneses, Nardinis, Ossolis, Borgheses, and other rich families and incorporated in their villas. By Napoleon's time, cattle grazed over the partly buried ruins and up the slope of the Palatine, and farms operated in once intensely urban areas. Since around 1900 the *disabitato* has become a protected architectural zone. Still, it's eerie to find so much empty stillness at the geographical center of a modern city.

The hills of Rome are baby hills in topographical terms, no more than fifty meters high. They are charming in scale, as though formed deliberately for human pleasure, easy to climb, and they afford views that are splendid but not dizzying. They have all worn away some since the height of the empire. In fact, the dirt and brick dust and bone particles and marble grains and every other shred of age-old debris, natural or man-made, had washed, blown, or shaken off the Palatine over the centuries and buried the little that is left of the ruins in the modest valley below it under many meters of loess so that the architectural treasures not previously salvaged had to be dug out laboriously in the modern era.

Around the backside of the Palatine Hill, in another little valley between it and the Aventine Hill, lies the massive oval of the Circus Maximus. The shape of the valley lent itself to the staging of chariot races, triumphal spectacles, and mock battles, and it evolved into a formally designed stadium over many centuries. Around 40 B.C., Julius Caesar (the transitional figure who refused to be named king but was more than a president) greatly enlarged the grandstands, which eventually accommodated three hundred thousand spectators. The succeeding emperors enjoyed casual views of the action from the loggias of their palaces on the Palatine above. Today, the Circus is a gigantic unadorned grassy oval field, often empty of human activity, except for a jogger here and there. A fraction of the old grandstand structure slumps in mute ruin at the east end of the oval, and a pentimento of the *spina,* the eleven-hundred-foot-long structure that the charioteers raced around, is marked by a slight earthen mound decorated by a few sparse cypress trees. The spectacles that went on here, greater in scale and wilder in content than our Super Bowls, are forgotten, the names of so many champions lost to history.

Down the road a quarter mile stand the ruins of the baths of Caracalla in similar desolation. These were the inspiration for Charles F. McKim's Pennsylvania Station in New York City—a monument that has now vanished more completely than its ancient model. The bath complex incorporated devices of architecture so complex and amazing that the industrial technocrats of nineteenth-century America stood in awe of its ingenuity. The baths operated for nearly three hundred years until the Goths wrecked the plumbing. Pennsylvania Station lasted a mere sixty years and was thrown away like a cellophane snack wrapper. Only a shell of the baths' thick rubble-filled brick and concrete walls remain. They look more like geological rock formations now, the edges rounded by weather, and woody shrubs growing out of the tops as brick and rubble slowly dissolve back into soil. On a sunny November afternoon hardly another soul was around and these ruins might have been as remote from any modern civilized center as the stones of Machu Picchu.

The sublime agony of the empire's long rise and fall is hard to conceive for those of us who measure our lives by presidential elections and cycles of popular music—a thousand years from the Romans' humbling of the Etruscans to the overthrow in 476 of the last western Roman emperor, named Romulus Augustulus in a nice bit of ironic symmetry. The city's population at the height of empire is estimated to have been greater than one million. Yet Rome came close to abandonment when the papacy fled the city for Avignon during the fourteenth century. In economic ruin and civil chaos, its population shrank to an estimated low of ten thousand. The medieval city was a ghost town. Rome remained a provincial backwater for a long time afterward. After the papacy returned from France in 1378, the church struggled for centuries to make Rome something more than an urban embarrassment. The pope's authority may have reached the farthest corners of Europe with great coercive power, but the point of emanation was a dump, and the recovery project we call the Renaissance included a desperate attempt to spruce Rome up for an increasing number of religious pilgrims and even tourists flooding in from the newly rich precincts of northern Europe, who needed to be suitably awed by the home of the Holy See.

The post-empire city shifted from the rugged area around the Palatine, Aventine, and Esquiline hills to what had been a flat swampy quarter upstream nestled in a bend of the Tiber: the Campus Martius, originally the old imperial military grounds. Now called the Campo Marzo, this is the Rome of Christian pilgrims, popes, and tourists, the city of the Spanish Steps, the Corso, the Trevi Fountain, and all the rest. There are several imperial monuments extant in this part of town and two cases are most interesting for the way they became incorporated in the latter-day city. The Piazza Navona, one of the world's great public gathering places, began its history as the Circus of the emperor Domitian (c. A.D. 87). Over two millennia, its grandstands were incrementally replaced by buildings, while the racetrack at center became the public space and the spina was replaced by an axis of three fountains (the central fontana dei fiumi being the work of Bernini, the sculptor/architect also responsible for St. Peter's Square). The physical presence of the old Circus persists ghostlike in the layout of the present piazza and with it the spirit of the empire. (The Vatican, a ten-minute walk across the Tiber, is built over the ruins of another great arena, the Circus of Nero, of which no trace remains.)

The second enduring ancient monument of the Campo Marzo (a few scant blocks away from Piazza Navona) is the Pantheon, the best-preserved of any building from the empire, a tremendous engineering feat of a domed temple with a columned portico in front. It was built first as an ordinary gable-roofed temple by Augustus's son-in-law, the tribune Marcus Agrippa, in the reign of Tiberius (around A.D. 37), substantially redesigned with a remarkable dome by Hadrian around 120 after a damaging fire, renovated again by Caracalla ninety years later, and finally consecrated as a Christian church in 609. Modifications by various popes followed (for example, Bernini's bell towers, removed from the pediment in 1883), but the building we find today is remarkably original, in particular the enduring dome (larger than St. Peter's), which was constructed all in concrete, a material that the ancient Romans innovated, and which would not be used again with such skill until the twentieth century.[1]

Much as we exalt them, the works of the Renaissance seem kind of paltry in scope and technical achievement next to what had been created a millennium and then some earlier—especially when you consider there was no precedent in scale, and few in kind, for the works of empire. Compared to the earlier majestic works of the emperors, Michelangelo's Campidoglio is a handball court between three tenements. What's more, the works of the Renaissance have now all joined in the inexorable march toward disintegration, already trodden by the ancients. The great churches and fountains of Boromini, Bernini, and the rest of the gang, so startlingly fresh in the age of Pope Alexander VII, are themselves now crumbling into dust. The time will come when they, too, will exist only in memory, and then another time will come when even the memory fades. We flatter ourselves to think of our era as the crowning destination of history—as though another thousand years won't eventually overheap us, too, and countless thousands more after that, and then more thousands still, until everything remembered is forgotten.

Standing on top of the Palatine Hill it is hard to avoid a tragic view of history, and yet every inch of living Rome today is enlivened with layers of decoration in the poignant assertion that the human spirit matters, that we-the-living matter. Faith has its uses and beauty arrests entropy. These extant artifacts of Rome add up to a detailed memorandum on the value of being human. Turn a corner onto an obscure byway, and there, lodged in a meter of wall, you will encounter a niche with the statue of an angel; up the street there is a door carved with profiles of obscure cardinals; the doorknob is the likeness of the merchant-owner of the building who died in 1712; over here the terra-cotta swags and bossage on the façade of a palazzo act like a human costume on the body of a building; over there on another exterior wall beams a painted likeness of woman who was somebody's beloved, who served as model for one of a hundred portraits of the Virgin. All this is woven into the vernacular architecture, which, at its most ordinary, strives for grace and meaning in the teeth of time's overwhelming indifference. Something unites these persistent strivings and resolves them through the cacophony of cultural change. On the Palatine Hill, the only things left in their pure states are the weeds and the silence, and it is in that silence that the spirit of the classical still dwells.

Classical Is Not a Style

I will concern myself here with what is generally considered Western or European-based classicism. There are Chinese, Persian, Mayan, and other classicisms. They may have striking formal differences, but they derive from identical human cognitive and perceptual processes. The important elements of classicism transcend the ways that they are mediated by local conditions and culture.

The classical idea came into Roman culture as the need to recognize that the things of this world existed in categories of order. The term *classical orders* is therefore a quaint redundancy.[2]

The Romans were prepared for all this by the Greeks, and really Plato and Aristotle were contemporaneous with the beginnings of the Roman *Republic* in the fourth century B.C. But while Plato and Aristotle concerned themselves with the *essences* of knowledge, and were greatly agitated to understand the nature of nature—an utter novelty to emergent human consciousness—the Romans appear to have been more content to understand the *uses* of knowledge. There are no philosophical texts in Roman history comparable to those of Plato and Aristotle. For the Romans, philosophy had already been thoroughly explored and settled. So, too, all metaphysical questions, which they bundled into their secondhand religion, with its diverting cast of mythological characters and their soap opera hijinks.

Mathematics was a fascinating alternative language to the Greeks, as it possessed qualities equally practical and mystical. Math enabled you to construct a lyre or a temple, but the magical harmonies and ratios also seemed to hold a key to many hidden mysteries of the universe. Pythagoras, the Greek mathematician who preceded Plato and Aristotle by more than a century, had discovered patterns and relations in numbers, especially in music, that led him straight to cosmology. The whole universe, he theorized, ran according to "the music of the spheres," an idea that persisted beyond the age of Sir Isaac Newton. About Euclid (who came less than a hundred years after Aristotle), as an historical personality, almost nothing is known. But he left behind comprehensive texts on geometry, optics, and other remarkable innovations in the language of numbers. The Romans did not substantially add to the Greeks' discoveries, but they went much further in applying them. The question was what to *do* with knowledge—and the Romans were much greater doers than the Greeks.

To the Romans, the classical was a means for ordering the ways of doing things, especially in building, which was the art above all other arts and the summation of applied technique (*architecture:* Latin from Greek, *archi,* the first, chief, or original; and *techne,* art). The Romans took Greek architecture, like their religion, as a received package, so for practical purposes it came into their culture already set into order.[3] The architectural treatises of ancient Greece are simply lost. We don't know how they viewed their system of architecture apart from the actual buildings they left behind. The sole surviving treatise of ancient architectural method and theory came from Vitruvius (Marcus Vitruvius Pollio, c. 90 B.C. to c. 20 B.C.), an engineer in the army under Julius Caesar, who in later life, under Emperor Augustus, compiled an encyclopedic work, *The Ten Books on Architecture.* This covered the Greek orders, methods for designing temples and private houses, city planning, building materials (including recipes for concrete), aqueducts, construction machinery, military machinery, and even interior decoration.[4] Apart from his treatment of civil-engineering matters, Vitruvius is believed to represent a very conservative view of architecture even in his own time, reflecting Augustus's preference for the traditional Greek system of trabeated construction— that is, buildings based on vertical columns holding up horizontal entablatures. While Augustus is renowned for the claim that he *found Rome a city of brick and left it a city of marble,* he was not so keen on the innovations that truly distinguished later Roman building from Greek, namely the arch and the vault (a sequence of interlocking arches) executed in that suspicious new material, cement.

Augustus was never actually called emperor, anyway, but rather *princeps,* something like "first citizen"—a savvy political move considering that the Roman people must have had mixed feelings about the loss of their republican form of government.[5] In keeping with his image of humility, Augustus's imperial dwelling on the Palatine was little more than a common upper-class villa. He slept on the same simple bed for forty years and wore homespun clothing made by his wife, Livia. However, as he matured in office, Augustus undertook many great public building schemes, including a new forum. He set up municipal police and fire forces, and made huge investments in the empire's road system, which he correctly viewed as essential to Rome's economic power and the military control of Italy.[6]

Augustus's essential conservatism in architecture might be attributed to his awareness that the Hellenic Greek system produced a public realm of great decorum and dignity—a very valuable quality in a politically turbulent time for reinforcing civil behavior and a sense of public order. The familiar building forms also promised the Roman people continuity, despite the fundamental shift in government structure from republic to autocracy. Indeed, this architectural language has been used repeatedly in the two thousand years since then to invoke a sense of permanence and continuity in many cultures under many different political systems.

Vitruvius established a context for understanding the classical orders that resonates to the present day. The fundamental idea is that our buildings reflect the human qualities of having a base, a middle, and a top, equivalent to the feet, torso, and head of a human figure. We stand erect, we address the world vertically, and perceive it visually that way. Our buildings express a like verticality and reflect it back at us, completing a feedback loop that reinforces the sense of our humanity in the things we make. Everything in traditional architecture—that is, all architecture before the schism of twentieth-century modernism—proceeds from this idea. It also instructs the method for establishing our spiritual position in the world, our *sense of place*. The fixed dwelling with its feet (its base) on the ground becomes the particular place we call home.

Vitruvius was straightforward (if fanciful) in describing an evolution of buildings from assemblages of natural materials—tree trunks and crossbeams—into the columned stone temples that the Greeks erected around the Mediterranean. How this comports with archeological reality of building types is something else. Vitruvius would have us believe that the primitive house evolved into the temple. This leaves a lot out, such as the epochal change in material from wood to stone, but is true enough to pass over. We are given to understand how the various parts of Vitruvius's primeval house evolved into the familiar devices of the classical vocabulary: The vertical tree trunk becomes the fluted column, the wooden rafter-tail becomes the Doric *tryglyph,* the space between rafter tails becomes the *metope,* and so on. All of this is pretty self-evident, if schematic. The important issues are, first, how the parts relate to the whole, and second, how transitions are made between the parts, and there is where so much of the difficulty lies.

In the Greek system, the whole building has a base, a main body, and a roof. Each of these parts is subdivided into three more parts. The column is made up of a base, a shaft, and a capital. The entablature is divided into the architrave, frieze, and cornice. These pieces, too, are subdivided, but not necessarily in threes. In these details—the moldings, the rhythmic decorations, and the ornaments—we are now at the scale of inches. The purpose of the moldings is to allow graceful transitions between the larger parts (for example, between base and shaft of a column), using curves, folds, and lips to resolve what would otherwise be visually interpreted as sharp edges and harsh, abrupt changes from one piece to the next. The moldings accomplish this by directing the fall of natural light into shadows that visually soften the transitions and give them figurative depth. This allows our eyes to move comfortably between the parts, to discern or "read" the parts as distinct, and make the whole legible.

These devices also convey tectonic meaning, that is, they give us an idea of the physical forces involved in a building as it relates to gravity and the role that each part plays in supporting the whole. For instance, the concave and convex moldings in the base of a column depict compression as the weight of the building meets the ground. The volutes at the top of an Ionic capital can be read as cushions between the columns and the weighty entablature they bear. The egg-and-dart, leaf, and dentil patterns on an entablature use rhythm to complete the transitions between architrave, frieze, and cornice, and are composed of familiar forms found in nature. A decorative figure such as the Greek key might appear pictorially abstract, but is actually a complex wave-form, representing one of the most fundamental dynamic processes found throughout nature. Anyway, these details, at the scale of inches, can only be made out from very close up, and are discerned not as individual figures but as patterns. Such rhythmic design elements in the classical orders are almost always found on the horizontal elements, not the vertical.[7] As a matter of human cognition, our brains may process visual information differently when the eyes scan horizontally. The inscribed rhythmic patterns may be an ocular trick to make the horizontal loads appear lighter and less daunting. Another subtle gimmick, called *entasis,* of giving the columns a slight outward bulge, was routinely used to correct optical distortions in the vertical elements of the building. Without employing entasis, the ancients realized, straight columns tended to be perceived as concave.

The great virtue of vertical organization in any order is that it is designed to be extended sideways by repetition. Sets of columns and entablatures repeated will compose a wall. Each section of an exterior wall retains the strong element of vertical composition, no matter how long the entire wall is, so that even monumental buildings composed in this way are able to reflect the human condition back to us.

This method of design is also highly versatile. It can both define an exterior and enclose an interior, using colonnades to create, for instance, the Greek agora or the Roman courtyard, forum, and basilica. In the early part of the twentieth century, the orders were used very imaginatively to lend coherence to a building type that the world had never seen before: the skyscraper. Great examples like the Metropolitan Life Tower (1909, Napoleon Le Brun & Sons) and the wonderful New York Municipal Building (1913, McKim, Mead and White) were exuberantly endowed with the classical qualities of base, shaft, and crown and they became beloved characters in the cityscape—unlike the modernist boxes that followed, which displayed no human qualities and were so widely disdained as to earn disparaging nicknames (for example, "Black Rock," the CBS tower on Sixth Avenue, from the fifties film-noir movie *Bad Day at Black Rock*).[8]

The orders therefore have long served as an instruction manual in pictorial shorthand for designing buildings according to the principles of vertical organization. Knowledge of the classical orders would theoretically enable a person to design any type of building in a way that dignified the public realm (and indeed the Beaux-Arts school produced typologies ranging from courthouses to electric power stations). The system is clear and succinct enough to be transmitted orally among people of greater or lesser skill, so that everyone from the architect down to the stonemason would understand the task at hand.

The three main orders that Vitruvius described and that come down to us canonically are the Doric, the Ionic, and the Corinthian. I propose that we think of them as *motifs* rather than *styles,* since the word *style* implies that things go in and out of fashion and these motifs are distinguished by their durability in the Western imagination. Vitruvius also includes a Composite order made up of both Ionic and Corinthian elements, and an Etruscan order that is a kind of crude Doric. The different motifs are not particularly significant in and of themselves, except that they afford an infinite range of combinations and possibilities of design elements, figures, details, and proportions within the formal syntax of the classical vocabulary. The Doric tended to emphasize massiveness and simplicity, the Corinthian was more elongated, delicate, and sumptuous in decoration, and the Ionic was somewhere in between. The Romans came to organize and employ them hierarchically: In the Coliseum, for example, they used the Doric order on the bottom, the Ionic in the middle, and the Corinthian in the upper story. So, as they rise vertically on the great stadium's outer walls, the orders become lighter and more elaborately decorated—a convention that keeps the most weight near the ground and blooms at the top (which expresses another quality of living, growing things: flowering).

Vitruvius describes a proportioning system for each of the orders that bases all measurements on the diameter of a column at its bottom. Each so-called *module* could be subdivided into sixty minutes of geometric measurement. The columns would be so many modules high. They would be spaced so many modules apart, and so on. This was particularly handy in a world where there was disagreement about standards of measurement and was among the features that gave the classical system so much technical durability in later centuries when standards were even more contested than in Roman times. The module system has the virtue of great simplicity. However, the mathematical formulae for determining other elements—for example, the spiral of a volute—seem as complex as the equations that put men on the moon in 1969. Anyway, in Vitruvius there are plenty of inconsistencies in proportioning and descriptive terminology, while actual buildings from classical antiquity exhibit pronounced deviations and errors that startled later academicians.

The Fall of Empire and the
Thousand-Year Train Wreck of Civilization

The Romans were the original Flintstones. They created an advanced urban culture without any of the technical wonders that we would consider indispensable two millennia later. They had no electricity, no motorized machinery or tools for lifting, hauling, and cutting, primitive metallurgy, no explosives, no printing, no telephones. Everything they built was handmade by large numbers of artisans and craftsmen of tremendous collective skill. Many of these people were, of course, slaves.

Up until the dawn of the Industrial Age in the mid-1700s, everything that had followed the Roman Empire seemed like an elongated and tragic anticlimax to the history of classical civilization. To the Enlightenment "moderns" who undertook the first systematic archeological excavations of the ruins, the Romans seemed like a race of supermen. It still amazes us that they managed to build the things they did—not just the grand scale of projects like the immense baths of Diocletian and Caracalla, the forum of Trajan, or Nero's stupendous palace, the Domus Aurea, with its mile-long colonnade overlooking an artificial lake on a site later occupied by the Coliseum—but the fact that every column, every carved acanthus leaf had to be wrought by hand and replicated by hand hundreds, thousands, of times. It is especially hard to imagine this mode of operation in an age when virtually all our building components are machine-made using powerful engine-driven tools. The technology of the empire entirely resided in human bodies and minds and was transmitted across time as an act of living culture.

The Romans had to work out systems that integrated the column with the arch, vault, and dome, and they accomplished this largely through their masterful use of concrete. As the lights went out in Rome, so to speak, the Eastern Empire in Asia Minor preserved some (but not all) of the culture's technical virtuosity. The center of Roman life and imperial administration moved east across the Mediterranean in order to get away from the disorderly Germanic peoples who were making life in Italy so difficult. The new center at Constantinople was a different Rome, peopled largely by Romanized Greeks, where Latin was the language of government and Greek was spoken in the streets. The Eastern emperors were Christians, in some cases exceedingly preoccupied with matters of theology and doctrine. It was a Rome that would eventually cease to be Roman.

In monumental building, they adapted the basilica from the familiar Roman hall of civil administration and added a dome to it to house the ceremonies of the Christian church—an apt reflection of the transfer of moral authority that occurred. Though none of these domes ever exceeded the scale of the Pantheon, the Eastern Empire innovated the technique of supporting a dome on pendentive piers rather than walls, enabling a very lofty interior with more windows. The result was their one extant great work, the Hagia Sofia (Church of Saint Sofia) built around A.D. 535.[9] Pendentive construction was their sole advance, a new way of organizing a longitudinal space with a dome, but the forces and thrusts required tremendous buttressing that in turn created ambiguous and superfluous spaces within. The exterior is startlingly plain. As a rule, in what we would come to call Byzantine architecture, embellishment is turned inward. The classical orders appear only in the inside—suggesting the correspondent inward-turning of the Eastern Roman Empire's political culture, which would increasingly be based on court intrigue and treachery with the cultural memory of the *res publica* fading away to nothing. The church, after all, was an explicit rival to the pagan classical legacy. There are no successors to the Hagia Sofia, and indeed the urban world of the Byzantines would become more and more an orientalized maze of passageways and chambers dedicated to Christian mysticism or palace conspiracies, with the public realm drained of civic meaning and reduced to the marketplace.

After A.D. 476, Constantinople could not control Western Europe politically or culturally. (Ravenna became the East's administrative outpost in the West, a pretense, really.) From Italy to Britain and Spain to Germany, life grew increasingly chaotic and impoverished. Skills were forgotten, especially technical skills in construction that required an enormous scale of social organization in an urban setting. People inhabited the shells of a civilization that seemed ever more lost and remote. We call this period the Dark Ages.

With the West in such disarray, Constantinople by default faced east, and mutated into a Byzantine Empire that made fine arts of despotism, violence, and cruelty. The city itself, strategically positioned on the strait between the Black Sea and the Mediterranean, became a rich cosmopolitan center estimated at times to contain more than a million souls. But it enjoyed material wealth with a steady erosion of political capital in a world undergoing drastic reorganization. An early blow to the city (and empire) was the first western appearance of bubonic plague (541–43), which reduced Constantinople's (or Byzantium's) population by as much as half, and recurred. Ethnologically, the Byzantine Empire was increasingly caught between contested territories and restless movements of ambitious tribal peoples. In the 630s, Islam pushed aggressively up from Arabia into what are now Israel, Syria, and Iraq. The Balkan peninsula to the north was an incessant battleground. The empire's one colonial frontier opened to the backward immensity of Russia, where the Byzantines went to spread Christianity and get raw materials. Otherwise, they were surrounded by water and fractious enemies. Finally, an obscure tribe of nomads called the Seljuk Turks ventured from the far east to what was then Persia and now Iran, became Islamicized and, with superb cavalry, swept westward around 1071 to overwhelm the peninsula of Asia Minor, a military tour de force down a geographic cul-de-sac.[10] The Byzantine Empire was reduced to little more than the fortified city on the Bosporus, which was almost continually besieged afterward by one group or another.

Meanwhile, in the late 700s, Charlemagne had emerged as the preeminent figure in a chaotic Western Europe, now dominated by Germanic and Celtic peoples. The population of the whole region shrank to half its number from Roman times because of political anarchy—and the ensuing difficulties in organizing food production. The architecture of what are today northern England, France, Germany, and Poland had been based on timber construction, while the urbanism (where it existed at all) had been based on the colonial *castrum* of Rome, a conventional grid plan of blocks centered on the intersection of two axial streets.[11]

Charlemagne traveled extensively, including, in 789, to the former Byzantine outpost of Ravenna, Italy, which he had taken from the Lombards who had snatched it from the Byzantines. He was so impressed by Justinian's Church of San Vitale (c. 547), a modest dome-within-an-octagon, that he constructed a smaller imitation for his own chapel at the Frankish capital of Aachen.[12] This is the beginning of the so-called Romanesque, which is really a process in Northern Europe of replacing timber with masonry. It was especially necessary because the periodic maraudings of one group after another virtually always included setting fire to the victims' settlement (and church), and the more Christianized people, such as Charlemagne's Franks, now desired a more permanent, settled way of life not subject to easy destruction.[13] The Romanesque is therefore the project of northern Europeans learning how to use masonry, and especially in vaulting methods that would create large interior spaces. The difference now, however, is that the Roman recipes for concrete had been lost, along with the technical knowledge for working with it on the scale of the great Roman projects. Cement still existed—the original plan for the monastery at St. Gall, Switzerland (c. 819), indicates an outbuilding used for lime kilns—but cement would only be used to "glue" stone blocks or bricks together, not as a structural material itself as the Romans had used it. True structural concrete in that sense would not reappear until as far forward as the nineteenth century.

The Romanesque (named as such in the nineteenth century) was masonry construction dedicated to the most stable institution of the medieval period: the monastery and its associated church, which had taken the place of civil government. In an age of freewheeling group violence, monasteries were defensible, self-sufficient islands of civilization. The public realm during this period would have been characterized by a lack of decorum, and the chief attribute of the architecture would have been sturdiness. Symbolic decoration would not count for much in a public realm that was essentially an uncivil no-man's-land. Canonical proportioning had lost its meaning, and the business of learning (or relearning) masonry technique in a world without an inexhaustible supply of highly skilled slave labor became an arduous matter of trial and error.

There is clear relation, though, between the increasing complexity of forms in the Romanesque and the lessening of chronic danger and violence in the West, especially after the first millennium, when Christians breathed a sigh of relief that their world hadn't been destroyed as widely prophesied. This era also marks the rise of feudalism, a new hierarchical social arrangement in which a growing peasant population gave up a degree of freedom in exchange for protection by a local political chieftain or lord who in turn owed services and loyalty to a greater chief or king.

The dominant role of religion in these feudal kingdoms had prompted a deep interest in the Holy Land where Christ's story had taken place, while the penitential aspect of medieval Christianity had provoked the zealous to make pilgrimage there. In connection with increased travel to the Holy Land, several momentous events occurred between 1050 and 1100. First, the eastern and western Christian churches divided in a formal schism in 1054, challenging the authority of the pope. Next, in 1071, the Seljuk Turks swept south from Asia Minor, captured Jerusalem, and began abusing the few Christian pilgrims who had made it there. Word got back to the West, and in 1095, Pope Urban II exhorted the knights and lords of Western Europe to embark on a great militant pilgrimage to take back the city of Christ from ascendant, infidel Islam—and, while they were at it, to try to bring the Eastern Orthodox Church back under papal control.

The Crusades could be regarded as a tremendous waste of time, capital, and human life by people who didn't have much to begin with, but it had some salutary cultural side effects. Because Saracen corsairs (Islamic pirates) made sea travel perilous, it became the custom for crusaders to make the journey to the the Holy Land overland as much as possible through Constantinople, with stopovers in Venice, the rising maritime rival to beleaguered Byzantium. In these cities westerners experienced urban life unlike anything in the feudal backwaters of France, Germany, and Britain. They became reacquainted with the residue of Greco-Roman culture that lived on in the eastern Mediterranean, they were exposed to levels of artistry beyond the crudities of their home places, and in their inevitable encounters with vigorous Islam, they discovered sophisticated mathematics on a level that had not been so far advanced since the Greeks.

The central problem of Romanesque architecture was that it did not admit much light to an interior. Lacking concrete, which could be poured into forms to solidify across generous vaults and domes, medieval masons were preoccupied with getting the walls to hold up ceilings of cut stone, and the walls themselves had to be so massive to stand up that windows could not be very large. The classical orders made their presence felt, if not necessarily visible, in the rediscovery of the replicable vertical bay of arches and columns as the basic element for composing large buildings. Classical details, such as a Corinthian capital, might be used in the interiors of major churches, but the workmanship was a crude approximation of ruins still lying on the ground, and the syntax was lost in the sheer difficulty of getting the stones to stand up. More and more, the artisans who labored on these buildings used carved human figures, deities, animals, and devils to tell the story of Christianity in the walls, ceilings, doors, and windows of the church, so that the church itself became something like a cartoon book of religious instruction that you walked into. Architectural decorum, order, and even beauty for their own sakes were subordinated to religious storytelling.

The First Crusade was short and sweet. Jerusalem was retaken in 1099. The crusaders who managed to return from a trip that was the equivalent of going from New York to Idaho brought back oriental motifs: lobed and pointed arches, ogees, lancet windows, mandalas, rosettes, and the polychrome geometric traceries of their Islamic adversaries, all of which would soon find their way into Western churches and cathedrals. The nine-or-so Crusades that followed into the 1270s ranged from the pathetic (the Children's Crusade of 1212, in which most of the participants either were sold into slavery or died of disease) to the several ridiculous instances when Crusaders turned on their hosts in Constantinople and wrecked the city. In some cases, such as the Fourth Crusade, they never got to the Holy Land at all.

The monumental architecture of the gothic, as exemplified by the great cathedrals at Chartres, Notre Dame de Paris, Salisbury, Cologne, and so on, was about performing miraculous building stunts for the glory of Christ and the Virgin Mary. How high can you make the nave of the cathedral? How skeletal can you make a building of glued-together stones? And how much colored light can you get into it? The rib vault and the pointed arch made cathedrals possible. The tremendous upward thrust of the gothic is verticality gone slightly mad. They were spectacular gestures in the service of a theocratic authority, but not necessarily of civilization. The system of labor required to build them was organized by that authority (the Catholic Church) and marshaled most of the creative energy of a given place—at the expense of other cultural activities. The cathedrals are awesomely beautiful but outrageous in scale, meant to terrify. As a practical matter, the gothic manner of building did not lend itself to nonmonumental typologies or scales, and as an ordering system it was extremely limited. Typically, all the buildings around a cathedral were dwarfed by it and composed in much cruder vernaculars. The other great buildings of the period, the castle homes of the kings and lords, remained preoccupied with fortification, even after towns and cities grew up around them. The impulse to build the cathedrals grew out of reconsolidated civil order following many centuries of frightful anarchy. It was a product of the rebirth of towns and cities in Europe. The Black Death would be another product.

The Black Death depopulated Northern Europe so severely that the lights went out again for a while. England lost a thousand villages; its population in 1400 fell to half of what it had been a century earlier. The total population of continental Europe may have fallen by as much as one-third. So many peasants died that tillage fell drastically—there were few left to produce food. But the plague would have beneficial consequences, too. Society began reorganizing itself again. The reduction of the number of serfs began to make feudalism obsolete, and new exchanges had to be forged between the classes. Labor of all kinds became more valuable. Wages for artisans rose, along with their status. Guilds of such artisans began to acquire political muscle in the cities, and to form the basis of something that had barely been seen since the Roman Empire: a middle class. This set the stage for the rediscovery of classicism and the launching of the true modern condition.

The Rescue of the Classical

In Italy of the thirteenth and fourteenth centuries, the human spirit finally escaped the collective depression that had followed the train wreck of Roman civilization. The Renaissance represents the end, in the West, of a long episode of preoccupation with mankind's failings and its relations with the supernatural powers that governed its destiny, and the beginning of an age of great collective self-confidence in human free will, of interest in the real world, and the thrilling discovery of ordering systems underlying the perceived real world, henceforward called *science* and understood to be distinct from (perhaps even superior to) the supernatural.

If the fall of Rome led to a nervous breakdown for the Western world, with analogous hallucinated doubts and fears given form in the compelling narrative of Christ, the Renaissance was a wonderful recovery, with reality returning to focus, hope in mankind's future restored, and the doom-laden Christ obsession steadily retreating into the realm of myth, increasingly subordinated to the more fruitful issue of relations between living people.

Classical knowledge and tradition had not completely vanished, or been forgotten, but simply lay around here and there, picked away at for a millennium the way that the marble and metal fabric of Rome itself had been used as a scrapyard, otherwise ignored. Aristotle's ideas were remembered, indeed recorded, but for centuries had only been used to embellish Christian dogma—which is to say, to support a world-view in which hope itself was a thing not of this world. What could be more depressing? The beginning of the rescue of classicism, and secular life, was therefore literary, in the recognition that old ideas added up to something more than the people in charge could previously admit, or even comprehend, and that, of course, provoked the tremendous sense of rediscovery.

ROME

The rescue of classicism may be said to start with Petrarch, Boccaccio, and Dante, given huge assistance by Greek-speaking scholars who fled the meltdown of the Byzantine Empire for a West that was looking comparably less chaotic at the time. It took many generations, but once it got going, once the collective hallucination of hopelessness was punctured, and men could agree that there was something of value in real life and take courage from their mutual agreement, the project of recovery—like the bubonic plague that shocked it into existence and periodically revisited it—became highly infectious. The search for order and meaning in nature became respectable, admirable, joyful!

As much as anyone, the spirit of the Renaissance was embodied by the figure of Leon Battista Alberti (1404–72). The illegitimate but well-loved son of a rich Florentine banker exiled in Venice, Alberti received an education in classical Latin that, with a gift for mathematics, defined all his later endeavors. Disinherited by family intrigues following his father's death, he went off to study law at Bologna, and seven years later moved to Rome to work as a classical scholar in the papal bureaucracy. There he produced a treatise on moral philosophy, *Della Famiglia,* drawn from classical literary sources, but written in vernacular Italian, which advanced a view of human virtue in accord with reason and personal accomplishment that was quite a radical departure from the passive Christian fatalism of previous centuries. Perhaps in an attempt to compensate for putting out these daring ideas, he also wrote a comprehensive hagiography of the Christian saints and martyrs and was rewarded with holy orders and offices.

When Pope Eugenius IV was driven out of Rome by a mob in 1434 (for quarreling with the family of his predecessor, Martin V), Alberti followed along as part of the papal retinue seeking refuge in Florence. The decade of the 1430s was a tumultuous one for that city, particularly for the Medici family (who ran it, and who also ran a vast banking empire with branch offices all over Europe). In the spirit of a time when cities were self-governing, Florence considered itself an independent republic, presided over by a ruling council or Signoria. However, as the leading banker in Europe, Cosimo de' Medici (1389–1464) exercised a supreme if subtle authority in his home town. He was all but duke in title, though he fastidiously avoided holding any official post for fear of ostentation—a justified fear as events turned out. Several of the other rich and powerful families resented Cosimo's pretensions as much as his power and wealth, and in the fall of 1433, they ganged up against him and declared him banished.[14]

Cosimo's exile, it turned out, lasted only one year. From Venice, he staged a remote-control coup d'etat that ousted the old Signoria. The new one lifted his banishment and he was able to return to the Florence in the fall of 1434. This was convenient for young Leon Battista Alberti, because in the aftermath of the power struggle, Cosimo's rivals were in turn banished, while his allies, including members of the Alberti family, had their exiles lifted, too. Pope Eugenius had been among Cosimo's friends in the contest for power in Florence, and it is likely that the talented young Latin scholar in the pope's train came to his attention. Cosimo was a collector of many things—books, antiquities, objects of art—but especially of talented people.

Now, quite a few years earlier, 1420 to be exact, Cosimo had sent his agent, the scholar Poggio Bracciolini, to the Swiss monastery of St. Gall to buy whatever ancient manuscripts he could lay his hands on.[15] Cosimo was the greatest book collector of his time. One of the manuscripts Poggio found was the only extant version of Vitruvius's *Ten Books of Architecture,* which had been utterly forgotten for centuries.

It also happened that a matter of months after Cosimo de' Medici returned from exile, the dome of the great cathedral of Florence—the Duomo—was completed after a fifteen-year ordeal of construction. The architect, the irascible Filippo Brunelleschi, had designed it to exceed the Pantheon in height and volume, and built it ingeniously without scaffolding or buttresses—to the amazement of the masons' guild. The Duomo was essentially a gothic structure, made of a double shell of bricks "glued" together with cement designed around ogival rib sections (pointed arches). There is no question that Brunelleschi was a long-time intimate of the Medici family. He had been involved with many family-sponsored public works, including the *Ospedale degli Innocenti* (the orphan's asylum). He considered himself a great student of ancient Roman construction methods, and, in fact, he spent considerable time in

Rome examining the ruins. We have no way of knowing for certain, but it is likely that he became acquainted with the manuscript of Vitruvius that was found by Poggio in 1420.

How much he absorbed from it is something else. The Corinthian column was Brunelleschi's favorite compositional element. But his mature works were based on an essentially medieval scheme of colonnades in which columns not incorporated into walls hold up a series of arches. Brunelleschi's proportioning methods were also fundamentally different from the modular system of the Romans. It was left to Alberti, a generation younger than Brunelleschi, to become the rescuer and interpreter of Vitruvius, and one of the chief methodological reforms he addressed was the incorporation of columns into true wall systems.

Alberti backed into architecture first by composing, in 1435, a treatise on perspective in painting, for which he was prepared by his knowledge of mathematics. His discoveries revolutionized the depiction of space on two-dimensional surfaces and were soon adopted in the studios of Florence and spread elsewhere. From here Alberti's restless intelligence shifted into mapping and surveying. It was a natural outgrowth at the next order of scale of the math involved in his previous project of rendering perspective. His writings on mapping were as influential as his book on perspective in painting. Around 1438, the Marchese Leonello del Este persuaded him to have a look at the Vitruvius manuscript in the Medici library. Alberti, with his relentless thoroughness, spent much of the next twenty years composing a *new and improved* version of the *Ten Books* of Vitruvius—whom he berated as a bad writer. The work was conceived not as a manual for the architects but as a handbook of standards for their patrons. Since Alberti's patrons were men of great intellectual distinction, he assumed that it would generally and always be the case that patrons would tell their architects exactly what they wanted and that the architects—obedient technicians that they were—would faithfully discharge their assignments, in the best circumstances with genius. He systematized the elements of architecture—the region, the site, walls, roofs, windows, and doors—and reintroduced the importance of the relation of parts to the whole, asserting that Beauty (capital B) was a result of the agreement between them. In the matter of fundamental criteria

for all architecture, Alberti reduced Vitruvius's vague and elusive terminology to the still-enduring triad of Function, Structure, and Beauty. Yet,
for all his tendency to formalize the principles, and his focus on classical
antiquity, Alberti strongly emphasized the need to move forward, to sur-
pass the achievements of history and use the imagination freely within
the governing unities he described. He viewed the act of building as directly analogous to the variety of organic patterns in nature, implying
necessarily growth, change, innovation, and evolution.

Alberti took up actual architectural practice while he worked on his
version of the Vitruvius, which he called *De Re Aedificatoria*. His first
commission was the base for the statue of his patron Leonello's father. He
soon graduated to more significant jobs. His design for the Palazzo Rucellai in Florence (c. 1450s) is in some respects a more cluttered attempt
at organizing a façade than Michelozzo di Bartolommeo's design of the
Palazzo Medici begun ten years earlier.[16] Michelozzo's treatment of
the base, middle, and top is much more clearly organized, using a scheme
that would become conventional for centuries afterward: rusticated
blocks on the ground floor with increasing refinement of finish going
up. A key difference, though, is the absence of engaged columns (pilasters) in Michelozzo's Palazzo Medici. Alberti incorporated pilasters in
the Palazzo Rucellai, though the effect was clumsy—the entablatures
they support are not much more than masonry string courses between
the stories. But however awkward the attempt, Alberti was struggling to
reintroduce the Greco-Roman classical syntax as well as vocabulary that
had not been used for a millennium. As a practitioner, he would be preoccupied with rearranging classical façade elements throughout his career, and he eventually became much better at it (for example, in the
church of Sant' Andrea in Mantua, 1470). Altogether, his contribution as
a theorist, writer, and teacher surpassed his own career as an architect.

The period in which Alberti worked on reinterpreting Vitruvius coincided exactly with the years during which Johann Gutenberg developed
the printing press.[17] The first printed edition of *De Re Aedificatoria*
(which was, indeed, the first printed book of any kind about architecture) appeared in Italy in 1485, thirteen years after Alberti's death. In the
years ahead, the line of authority passed directly from Brunelleschi and

Alberti to Leonardo da Vinci, Michelangelo, Bramante, Serlio, Sangallo the Younger,[18] and then on to another seminal figure, Palladio, through whose work and writings classicism became the architectural language of the Enlightenment across Europe. Alberti's rewriting of Vitruvius had filtered through Italian architectural practice for nearly a century when Andreas Palladio (1518–80) published his *I Quattro Libri Dell'Architettura,* the *Four Books on Architecture.* He had already made a comprehensive study of Rome, illustrated Daniele Barbaro's 1556 edition of the original Vitruvius, and taken his place as a leading practitioner. Palladio's *Four Books* had the virtue of tremendous clarity. He believed in the universality of the classical vocabulary and his straightforward, technically up-to-date manual established a set of norms for the Western world that lasted until World War One. A second edition of the *Four Books* was published in 1581. Palladio's influence appeared with great force in England with Inigo Jones (1573–1652). A complete English translation of Palladio appeared for the first time in 1715, and a second sponsored by Lord Burlington (1695–1753), both a patron and an architect himself, was published in 1738.

Meanwhile, Sebastiano Serlio (1475–1554) had established himself at the French court about 1541, bringing along his published glosses of Vitruvius and Alberti, and Serlio set a tone for the austere but incredibly durable character of French classicism in a line that would run through Lescot, Claude de Chastillon, François Blondel, Bruant, the Mansarts, Jacques François Blondel, and finally the institutionalization of classicism in the École des Beaux-Arts, which churned out competent classicists the way business schools today churn out competent actuaries. By this time, classicism had been fully rescued, restored, elaborated, and surpassed. The Americans got hold of it four times: first through the British Palladianism of the colonial period, then dynamically with the works of Thomas Jefferson, once again with Greek Revival movement of the 1850s, and finally—after a gothic interval—with the City Beautiful movement (also called the American Renaissance) of the period 1890–1930. It was the Americans who, in the late nineteenth century, finally equaled the ancient Romans' technical proficiency with reinforced concrete.

World War One, which I maintain was a nervous breakdown for

Western civilization, marks not so much the death of the classical idea in building, but the throwing away of all its hard-won principles, standards, and technical considerations into the dumpster of history—where they await retrieval. In America, which had not been physically battered by that war, the spirit of classicism lingered in architecture until the Great Depression, when all building stopped except for highways and dams. The First World War unhinged the Western world because it so cruelly dashed the optimistic expectations that the twentieth century would usher in a Golden Age of scientific progress. Instead, the scientifically proficient mass slaughter of the trenches destroyed faith both in the future and in the whole range of European institutions—from politics to education to art—that were the guardians of Western aspirations. Even in America, the decade following the war was drenched in cynicism. In came the modernists and out went twenty-five hundred years of cultural memory.

We know now the results of that break. I will not repeat the comprehensive description and criticism of modernism, which can found in Chapter Five ("Yesterday's Tomorrow") of my book *The Geography of Nowhere,* except to say that after nearly a century of its tortured, occult mystical practices and "formgiver," genius, celebrity personalities, we are still suffering the torture of its work.

Can the Classical Rescue Us?

The good news is that the twentieth century is over. We don't have to be modern anymore. We can be something else. Surely even educated people are tired of pretending to be on the *cutting edge* all the time, untethered from history or precedent, and weary of advocating that excellence exists only as a point of view. Human events appear to run in cycles. Perhaps we can now leave behind the age of anxious relativism and enter an era of confidence in established norms, and particularly in standards of excellence. The architectural establishment enters the new era in raw discredit, though its mandarins are fighting reform down to the last critical theory. As Leon Krier has said, buildings that get nicknames are buildings lacking in dignity, and every town in America has its Darth Vader Building, its Gumby Building, its Mistake-on-the-Lake. Architecture discredited itself by trafficking in the fake supernatural, and architecture will have to redeem itself by coming back to earth and making sense of the places we attempt to inhabit. The operations of modernism worked in perfect synergy with the automobile to drain the public realm of meaning and decorum, and the repair of the public realm is a crucial mission for people who care about the continuing project of civilization. The blank walls and concrete planters of the modernist office buildings, the industrial façades of the muffler shops, the jive-plastic signature parapets of the fry-pits, will someday have to be replaced by buildings that regard the public realm respectfully, that speak to us in comprehensible vocabularies, rhythms, and syntaxes—not just abstractions, and certainly not in cartoons and illuminated verbiage—and that respect the hierarchies of scale that compose the built environment from the smallest detail of window proportions all the way up to the coherence of the region.

Unlike the masters of the Renaissance, we do not have to hunt for obscure manuscripts in the dusty attics of far-off monasteries or sift among the ruins of history—at least not yet—to rediscover principles fallen into disuse. We don't have to reinvent the idea of beauty (or even Beauty), we just have to restore it to intellectual respectability. This will necessarily require a revolution in architectural education. The tortured crypto-metaphysical stratagems of a Peter Eisenman or a Rem Koolhaas (tenured professor at the Harvard Graduate School of Design) will have to give way to the cultivation of real skills (for instance, drawing) and to a respect for conventions of history (for example, the act of signifying the door to a public building so that one can gain entry without undertaking a field reconnaissance).

The project of restoration is already underway. The classical is on its way back not just to respectability but to practice. We've had half a century now to recover from the misuse of classicism by Hitler and Stalin and it is once again possible to believe that classicism does not stand for the glorification of the bureaucratic state, but rather for dignifying the human condition, which is sublime, tragic, and fraught with beauty. It offers us a comprehensive set of tools for resolving some of the practical problems of the human ecology, namely how buildings regard the public realm. A consensus on the vertical organization of building façades would be a good and simple start. Acknowledge and accept the convention that buildings have a base, a middle, and a top, and many great things will naturally flow from that condition without torture or strain. Ground floors can be organized for activities appropriate to the site—for instance, shopping in the center of town. And since America is now composed overwhelmingly of one-story buildings, the sheer concept of verticality may prompt us to allow more than one activity to take place within a building footprint—implying upper stories. This could lead to a solution for the "affordable housing" problem, which has been greatly exacerbated by our foolish disinclination to build mixed-use, multistory buildings the past half century.[19] My personal sense of things is that once we become reaccustomed to the vertical organization of buildings, decoration of the façade will follow naturally, too. One can even imagine a financial incentive to construct a more beautiful building than the next guy. It has happened before in history.

Necessity may prompt us to once again think of buildings as things that ought to last more than a couple of generations, and therefore *ought to be memorable because they are beautiful*. Roger Scruton writes: "A beautiful object is not beautiful in relation to this or that desire . . . [i]t pleases us because it points to a satisfaction that lies beyond desire, in life itself."[20] The whole ethos of the late twentieth century encouraged throwaway architecture. It is conceivable that we will look back at this practice in horror and bewilderment from a future in which the long-term view is taken more seriously along with the corollary value of the public realm, which by its nature must be a long-term project. This revolution in the way we construct our everyday world may or may not be the result of scarcities in materials, labor, or skill. Such an outcome might be culturally determined, say, by the human longing to a part of something greater and longer-lasting than the individual: a place worth caring about, a place worth living in, a city worth defending. For decades in America we have been attempting to compensate for the lack of these things with gadgetry and simulacra. Believe it or not, the day will come when all the *imagineered* fantasies of Disney will see their last paying customer, and the very idea of attempting to replace the authentic with the virtual will seem an out-of-date, twentieth-century sick joke—as ridiculous as the *galvanic cure* for tuberculosis from our great-grandparents' day now seems.

When this comes to pass, the classical will no longer seem an inert set of museum pieces or a bundle of outdated malicious notions once *hegemonistically wielded by dead European white males for the suppression of women and minorities.* We will once again recognize it as mankind's cultural transmission wire, our method for conveying models of excellence from the past to the present time and into the future. The classical germ will be self-evidently understood as the thing that makes it possible to live in a confident present suspended between memory and hope.

BOSTON

Overcoming History and Modernism

The city has become, in the American imagination, the place
where the foreigners live. It is the place where people have
funny accents, worship strange gods, and probably can't be entirely trusted.

ROBERT CAMPBELL

When friends and colleagues complain that someone is not treating them the way they would like, or the way they expected, or that some deal fell through, or that somebody failed to keep up his end of an agreement, or that someone broke her heart, or that someone did something absolutely bizarre and unexpected to them, or wantonly harmed them, or made an unreasonable demand, or insulted them, or misjudged them, or did anything else that implies the collision of two independent wills, I try to remind them, as untendentiously as possible, that human character is unfathomably mysterious and perverse. This ought to be the first law of politics, which is the art of managing human will in the aggregate by force of character.

Since the aggregate of humanity is often found aggregated in places called cities, politics achieves its most florid expression there, and produces colorful characters. Politics remains robust in Boston, Massachusetts, because these days, unlike the vast majority of other U.S. cities, Boston is still populated. People actually live there. What's more, it is populated by people of all social ranks, not just the intransigent poor, but a striving middle class and even a healthy clump of the rich. I say healthy because it is in the public interest for cities to include rich people, who are capable of supporting enough cultural infrastructure to keep us informed about who we are and how we are doing in carrying on the difficult enterprise of civilization. It is good, too, for politics to involve people of all social ranks in the city because the management of conflicts in human will is the business of all classes. It ought not to be left exclusively to the well-off, or to those vexed by a struggle to survive, or those in between.

In other American regions, these days, the well-off banish themselves to suburbs far outside the city, an arrangement that has been catastrophic for our national civic life.[1] Boston has problems, including its own vampire suburbs, but it is entering the twenty-first century way ahead of Cleveland, Baltimore, Philadelphia, Chicago, and other comparably big, old U.S. cities. It has clear, bright prospects for the future, not just vague hopes for survival in a Hobbesian global economy. Over the past quarter century, its politicians have made a lot of fortunate decisions—if sometimes dragged there kicking and screaming—that have positioned it for success in a rapidly changing economy. These decisions have roused the city to many bold actions, including the biggest urban public works project of our time. To some degree, Boston could be accused of peculiar dumb luck—it was a leading intellectual center at the dawn of the Information Age, when brains started to matter again as a form of capital.

Lest I'm accused of a snooty northeastern bias, I pause to remark that Boston is my hard-luck city and Massachusetts is my hard-luck state. I'm not a fan of occult theory, but I can't help feeling that the place has got it in for me in some supernatural way. A few personal snapshots:

The year my parents got sick of each other and made new living arrangements, 1957, I was sent away to summer camp on an estuary north of Boston. It was a nice place, with an emphasis on sailboat instruction. I spent most of the summer in the infirmary after putting a sixteen-penny nail through my foot the first night there.

I had the worst summer of my college career on Cape Cod in 1969, year of the moon landing, Charlie Manson, Chappaquiddick, and Woodstock. I worked fourteen hours a day as a scullery slave and never got to the beach.

I spent my first year out of college working in Boston as a freelancer for a couple of hippie weekly newspapers and practically starved to death.

I married a girl from Boston and it didn't work out.

A couple of years ago, driving home from a lecture at MIT, I missed getting killed by a fraction of a second on the Massachusetts Turnpike when my car spun out on a patch of black ice, rammed the left-lane guardrail, bounced back across two traffic lanes, and nearly collided with an eighteen-wheel tractor-trailer.

So, I have no reason to shill for Boston. It was never especially nice to me. But I still believe it will be the best American big city to live in in the years directly ahead.

Age of Glory, Age of Blunders

Every schoolchild knows that Boston was the "cradle of liberty" and all. We'll pass over that material except to note that physically the early city was confined to a rugged fist of land, the Shawmut Peninsula, that stuck out into the cold Atlantic and was connected to the mainland by a slender sandy wrist.

From this fist of land rose a set of knuckly hills. Just east of the wrist stood a three-peaked ridge called the Trimountain: Beacon, Pemberton (also called Cotton), and Mt. Vernon hills.[2] (The name Tremont Street derives from Trimountain.) On the southern edge of the peninsula stood Fort Hill and on the northern rim Copps Hill. On each side of the wrist lay broad, shallow tidal mudflats and salt marshes. Over the years the Trimountain had been dug away and used to fill coves and low spots around the city until Pemberton and Mt. Vernon were substantially reduced and only Beacon Hill remained.

In the decades after the Revolution, Boston became the hub of America's first major industrial region and the town underwent a striking physical expansion. By the 1850s, a constellation of new factory towns hummed around the city, seven new railroads penetrated it, and a wave of impoverished Irish immigrants overwhelmed the available housing. Boston suddenly seemed as cramped as a sea chest. The North End, birthplace of Ben Franklin, composed of winding, medieval-scaled streets that Paul Revere knew, became a neighborhood of crowded tenements. Old Fort Hill (today the financial district)[3] gave way to business buildings and more immigrant rookeries. Beacon Hill remained the aerie of the old Yankee *brahmin* elite. The West End below the statehouse, back of Beacon Hill, was also still fashionable, but included a lively commercial district, Dock Square and Scollay Square, among other things headquarters of William Lloyd Garrison's abolitionist paper, *The Liberator.* The old South End was merging into the downtown business district, while, in the early 1800s, a whole new speculative residential South End addition rose on seventy-five acres of former salt marsh filled with Roxbury gravel. This new South End grew systematically like a coral reef, composed of sturdy and dignified, if monotonous, red brick bow-front rowhouses on neat geometric streets, some around squares that eventually grew to be shady. The promising neighborhood would soon be dramatically eclipsed by the much grander Back Bay development.

The creation of Boston's Back Bay district, from a stinking mud flat to the finest ensemble of urban homes in America of its time, was such a stupendous task that it is hard to imagine it being accomplished even in our own era of giant earth-moving machines and power tools, let alone in an age lacking these things. Except for a few rudimentary steam shovels and railroad hopper cars for distributing fill, the Back Bay was built by hand labor. What's more, it was furnished with a stock of buildings designed to standards of excellence so far beyond anything today's professional builders can produce that the casual observer goggles at it in astonishment, wondering if the human race has suffered some reverse evolutionary mutation since then. In our time we can fly to the moon, but even a billionaire cannot purchase a house worth looking at from an entire tenured faculty of architects. It is hard to believe that the people who built the Back Bay are related to us biologically or culturally.

The Back Bay was inspired in part by Haussmann's renovation of Paris in the 1850s and 1860s—as indeed Haussmann's work excited the envy of city people all over the civilized world then. The plan was a strict orthogonal grid, in contrast to the wandering cowpath pattern of old Boston. It comprised 450 acres, requiring an average twenty-foot depth of fill. The gravel came from Needham, nine miles away. The work was undertaken as a partnership between the state (or commonwealth) and the city, and its cost was recouped from the sale of valuable newly created city property. The new blocks were organized into individual building lots and sold off as such so that the Back Bay developed at a fine grain of small increments controlled by numerous different owners (in contrast to the ruinous method for organizing and redeveloping city land a hundred years later, where large parcels are controlled by one developer). Altogether, the project took about twenty-five years to complete, though the new blocks were quickly inhabited as they were created.

A rigorous architectural code established basic design controls—building height, setback, window bays—within which many different styles could be executed, while maintaining a general order of unity. The project's centerpiece, Commonwealth Avenue, was a monumental boulevard with a broad parklike promenade down the center. Eventually, it formed a green corridor connecting the Public Garden and the delta of Muddy Creek, which Frederick Law Olmsted, by another heroic act of civic design artistry and engineering, converted into the ornamental Back Bay Fens. Commonwealth Avenue retains much of its intended character today, apart from the depredations of automobile traffic, which, of course, was not part of the original design. A few blocks north, the water side of Beacon Street along the Charles River was turned into another landscaped public promenade.

Back Bay was a spectacular success. It came off exactly the way it was planned. There were no goofy surprises, no citizen uproars, no financial fiascoes, no transportation headaches, no political liabilities. It worked beautifully. It was the product of a confident and competent culture, of people who knew what they were doing and accomplished what they set out to. It was aesthetically rich and complex, yet urbanistically legible. It was densely populated, yet it afforded plenty of air, light, greenery, and water access. It provided sites for many churches and important cultural institutions as well as commercial establishments to service all the new households. It solidly connected the old Shawmut Peninsula with the growing communities of the mainland—some of which were eventually annexed as neighborhoods into metropolitan Boston. From its inception the Back Bay has been a place beloved and still is, retaining high economic and social value. It represents a quality of civic purpose that seems nearly incomprehensible today.

In comparison, the twentieth century was rather cruel to the city of Boston. The old anglo/brahmin establishment that came triumphantly out of the Revolution, and made the great commercial fortunes, and owned the mills, and built the Back Bay, and wrote all the books, and parsed the law, and created modern medicine, and ran Harvard—this group was swept out of power in the twentieth century and replaced by an Irish political mafia that rabidly hated the old Yankees and wanted to punish them. From the 1840s when the potato famine drove them to America, to the turn of the century when they seized power, the Irish had been limited in Boston society to roles as servants, laborers, jobbers, and barkeeps. They had been locked out, pushed around, patronized, overworked, underpaid, scorned, caricatured, and laughed at, and they were sore about it.

Their political rise coincided with two other events of consequence: the decline of the New England mill economy and the introduction of mass automobile ownership. The first left Boston in a more or less chronic state of economic malaise from just after the First World War until the 1980s. The second offered the new political establishment a technical means for exacting revenge on the old "codfish aristocracy" by mutilating the physical fabric of the city. The automobile turned out to be a perfect instrument of class warfare. It was widely portrayed in popular culture as a social, economic, and moral good. It was understood to be the basis of whatever *modern* economic activity the city was lucky enough to still have after the textile industry fled. Any public work carried out for the sake of the car could not be challenged. To be against it was to be against progress, against the very future. Curiously, in later decades, this campaign of class vengeance and civic mutilation was cheered on and abetted by the architectural intelligentsia across the river in Cambridge, specifically the Harvard faculty, the apostles of Walter Gropius, who had their own political axes to grind against the old oligarchy.[4]

The Boston city hall gang commenced its major blitz in the mid-1950s by flattening a neighborhood called the New York Streets, filled land developed in the 1830s whose streets were named in honor of then-burgeoning western New York: Oneida, Seneca, and so on. It had become, over the years, an ethnically diverse slum of blacks, Chinese, Filipinos, Greeks, and Lithuanians. Its postrenewal destiny was to become a waterside industrial wasteland. Next, the city hall gang bulldozed the historic West End of Charles Bullfinch and William Lloyd Garrison, including Scollay Square, the commercial heart of the old city, Bowdoin Square, and Pemberton Square. True, it had become a sad and seedy district of gin mills, strip joints, tattoo parlors, whorehouses, the haunt of sailors and Harvard undergrads. (A police commissioner of the time pronounced it "unfit to be a tenderloin anymore.") But the West End also happened to be another ethnically diverse residential neighborhood—Italians, Jews, Russians, Poles dominated, with the Irish composing the smallest fraction at 5 percent—containing twenty-seven hundred households in all. It had a rich stock of historic brick buildings and an armature of fine urban form. Under Mayor John B. Hynes, the city utterly obliterated it. Hardly anything was left standing except the Charles Street Jail and Massachusetts General Hospital. The federal government paid two-thirds of the cost of the demolition and compensation to property owners. *The Boston Globe* was all for it.

In short order, another gang of insider developers acquired the land at a bargain-basement price in a politically wired deal and hired the trailblazing suburban shopping mall architect Victor Gruen to design a scheme called Charles River Park that was touted as "five urban villages."[5] These ended up being sets of dreary high-rise "luxury" apartments, mechanistic glass boxes with no relation to the scale, history, or local building traditions of the city, deployed in no meaningful relation to the streets. In fact, an extraordinary percentage of the old streets simply disappeared from the West End, never to return.

Around the same time, the Massachusetts State Department of Public Works ran two freeways into the center of town, with city hall's blessing and the federal government's financial support. Boston had been left behind once before transportationwise, when Worcester, forty-five miles inland, was allowed to become New England's railroad center, and the Boston officials didn't want to lose out again in the age of the interstate highway.[6] Thus, the Massachusetts Turnpike extension was brought into town below grade in an open trench through Olmsted's Fenway—turning a formerly stylish neighborhood into a semislum and creating a huge noxious moat of traffic between the Back Bay and Roxbury (earlier the center of Jewish life in Boston; then transitioning into the new black ghetto).

Equally damaging was Interstate 93, also called the Central Artery or the John F. Fitzgerald Expressway (after President Kennedy's grandfather, a Boston mayor). This project had been on the drawing boards as far back as the 1920s, but depression, war, and postwar malaise had postponed it. In the 1950s, with the Interstate Highway Act suddenly providing 90 percent of the money, the project finally went forward. The new elevated artery sliced clear across the tip of the old Shawmut Peninsula, around the financial district, cutting off the historic North End from the rest of the city with a great wall of noise, perpetual darkness, and tailpipe emissions. The spaghetti wad of bridges, access ramps, and freeway connectors that accessorized the Central Artery had the added baleful effect of destroying what remained of City Hall Square in Charlestown, the neighborhood across the river at the foot of Bunker Hill.

These wholesale demolitions and fiendish public works of the postwar years made even the shameless city hall lifers look bad. They ended up stuck with a huge supply of as-yet-unrenewed urban renewal land on their hands. Downtown property taxes remained punitively high despite the city's decades-long economic malaise. Now, with the freeways in place, virtually every type of city activity—office, residential, department stores, movie theaters, restaurants—fled to the new suburbs, and the pols didn't have a clue how to proceed with any kind of downtown redevelopment that might compete under the circumstances. So, in 1960, the new mayor, John Collins, brought in a Robert Moses–style master builder named Edward J. Logue to run the Boston Redevelopment Authority.

Ed Logue was an Irish Catholic from Philadelphia and a Yale-trained lawyer. Previously he had been in charge of urban renewal for the city of New Haven, a wholesale blow-and-go project that left the downtown gutted like a Connecticut River sturgeon. He then filled it back up with a shopping mall (Chapel Square, now failed and partly demolished), a convention center (mostly unused and now partly demolished), a farrago of freeway connectors, and hectares of surface and structured parking—a real classic of its time. Logue himself was a classic postwar urban planner, a high-powered administrative whiz who excelled at *getting things done,* but who had no background in civic design as such. Logue's New Haven work had been showered with praise.

It happened that a few months after Logue came to Boston, Senator John F. Kennedy (D., Mass.) landed in the White House. Then, a short while later, Representative John McCormick (D., Mass.) became Speaker of the House, while another Kennedy (Ted) replaced his older brother in the U.S. Senate. The city of Boston suddenly found itself in a very favorable position after decades of stagnation and decline. A blizzard of federal funding indeed ensued.

Logue's flagship project was an ambitious "Government Center" to occupy the bulldozed vicinity of Scollay Square, featuring a brand-new city hall, federal office complex, state office building, and tons of parking. The site plan job was awarded to I. M. Pei, an MIT-trained architect then coming to national prominence, and his partner, Henry N. ("Harry") Cobb. Pei and Cobb devised a plan that reduced the number of streets in the area from twenty-two to six, creating a set of superblocks upon which they would deploy both vertical towers and horizontal "landscrapers" in the *Ville Radieuse* mode that had by then become the stock-in-trade of every ambitious architecture firm from sea to shining sea.

The design of City Hall was awarded, by a national competition, to an unknown firm out of New York called Kallman, McKinnell and Knowles. The winning design (completed in 1968) looks like the back office of Darth Vadar's Death Star, a *brutalist* trapezoidal heap of stained beige concrete on a despotic brick podium that meets the plaza with blank walls on the building's front, and, at rear, presents a two-hundred-foot-long blank wall to Congress Street—right across from that wonderful remnant of humane architecture, Faneuil Hall (original 1742; skin-job by Bullfinch, c. 1806). City Hall is a mere archetype of the period, but the plaza around it is a nonpareil: Windswept, cold, vacant, cruel, at the same time that it is petty and bland, it's an agoraphobe's nightmare of the uncomprehended space. It shows a fundamental misunderstanding of the nature of public space, particularly of how the edge needs to operate in order for people to feel comfortable and interested—to clearly define the space and provide destinations for people walking in the vicinity. Boston City Hall Plaza fails with the grandiose and narcissistic self-assurance characteristic of the period.

The other components of the Government Center turned out equally disappointing. The federal building, named for the assassinated president Kennedy, designed by Gropius's old firm over in Cambridge, the Architects' Collaborative, was a boring dual slab of glass and concrete that might have been a provincial headquarters for the Soviet ministry of mines. A major new office building on what had been one side of Scollay Square managed to follow the graceful curve of Cambridge Street and at the same time relate so poorly to it that it acted like a gigantic urban autoclave, sterilizing everything within range. By far the largest building of the whole set, naturally, was the parking garage.

Like many other architectural abortions of its time, Government Center won major awards. This was the architecture profession's technique for warding off criticism. The public tried to love it, really wanted desperately to love it, because they were stuck with it. But it remains unloved and unlovable. Kevin White, the first mayor able to occupy the new City Hall, spent most of his time instead in a suite on the fifth floor of the city-owned Parkman mansion several blocks away. Attempts over the years to do something about the abyss of City Hall Plaza have so far failed because they have focused on filling up all the empty space with doodads and programming rather than repairing the dead edges.

The disappointing outcome in Government Center came to mean something more profound than a mere overreach of civic ambition or the fault of a particular design ideology. It reinforced the unhealthy belief that we as a culture are incapable of creating new things as good as the old things. It was one of the signal events that set into motion the historic preservation frenzy of the last thirty years—the effort to save every scrap of old building because our new ones are so inept. Scollay Square was universally understood to be a slum by the 1950s, even by sentimental bohemians. But in decay it was a finer ensemble of buildings than the bombastic abstractions that replaced it. This should not be taken as a dismissal of historic preservation. It is tragic when a people recklessly erase their cultural memory. But is also tragic when a people have no confidence in their ability to generate a material future worth caring about. This was the biggest effect of Boston's Government Center. It made the city's future appear both obscene and ridiculous.

The failure of Government Center was underscored a few years later when the old Quincy Market and adjoining Faneuil Hall on the other side of Congress Street underwent a major renovation by the developer James Rouse and the Cambridge architect Ben Thompson. Ed Logue was gone by then, but to his credit he had managed to at least reverse an earlier decision to destroy these old buildings. Everything about the renovated Quincy Market was a rebuke to the ethos of Government Center. The market buildings integrated beautifully with their surrounding streets and plazas. Scores of shops and vendors along the ground floor opened to the outside and generated a flow of pedestrian activity. The buildings were humanly scaled with clearly signified entrances. The many restaurants sent out tantalizing aromas. The buildings spoke in a graceful architectural language that had a real connection to local history and culture.

Quincy Market was a tremendous success. People felt good there. It instantly became far and away the premier public gathering place in Boston, a major tourist attraction, and also the prototype *urban festival marketplace*—now, unfortunately, a cliché that has been imitated with mixed results in other cities that had lost much more critical infrastructure than Boston.[7] Quincy Market has remained a successful magnet for people and business for over twenty years now. The contrast between the abyss of City Hall Plaza and the comfortable tree-lined lanes between the old market pavilions is always striking.

The Wrecking Crew

Few architects have done as much wholesale damage to any city as the partners I. M. Pei and Harry Cobb did in Boston. Albert Speer actually accomplished much less in Berlin. After the Government Center site plan job, Pei's firm went on to design a pair of luxury apartment buildings at India Wharf. Ed Logue himself was so disturbed by the firm's drawings for the dull boxes called the Harbor Towers that he dared voice his misgivings to Pei. Pei responded by declaring enigmatically that, well . . . he'd "lost interest in housing."[8] Interested or not, the project was built as Pei's firm designed it. Apart from their sheer banality, the towers also selfishly blocked the view to the harbor from buildings behind them, and part of the waterfront that might eventually have been turned into a public esplanade ended up privatized.

At about the same time, the early 1970s, Cobb was finishing the design for the new John Hancock Tower in Back Bay. It had to compete for attention with the somewhat earlier Prudential Center (1965, by Charles Luckman & Associates) a few blocks west, a building that the architectural scholar Donlyn Lyndon describes as "an energetically ugly, square shaft that offends the Boston skyline more than any other structure."[9] The "Pru" was set off Boylston Street on a massive, sterile podium and accessorized on its back side with a set of Soviet-style apartment slabs placed on blank wall fortifications to protect the inhabitants from some imagined horror on the adjacent streets.

Anyway, the John Hancock Insurance Company felt obliged to compete against the Pru for architectural glory. Part of the Hancock's mission was to exceed the Pru's fifty-two-story height, so the Hancock topped out at sixty stories, a weirdly shaped parallelogram of mirrored greenish glass that addressed the street at an odd angle and bore no relation in scale, materials, or detailing to other buildings in the vicinity. The ground floor was a minimalist corporate vanity entrance offering nothing to pedestrians. As the building neared completion, a frightening problem developed: Windows started mysteriously popping out and falling to the sidewalks below, huge green-glass guillotines that might have sectioned a pedestrian longitudinally as neatly as a surgeon's scalpel might slice through a thymus gland. And it happened more than a few times, so the liability implications began to impress the John Hancock Insurance executives, who had commissioned the darn thing. The problem turned out to be a design flaw that caused winds to "Bernoulli" the panes out of their mullion gaskets.[10] Luckily no one got killed, sectioned, or maimed before the street barriers went up. But the solution required the replacement of the entire skin of the building at stupendous expense—truly one of the great architectural blunders of the century. For the next several years, the Hancock wore a temporary dressing gown of dowdy plywood sheets. Now, years later, the windows are secure and the Hancock is merely a mute despotic behemoth on the Back Bay skyline with its mate-for-life, the Pru.

Pei's next project for the city, in this masochistic phase of its history, was a major addition to the Boston Museum of Fine Arts. It took the form of a great blank-walled granite bunker accessorized by a surface parking lot. This eventually came to be used as the main entrance to the institution, since so many of its patrons were suburbanites on wheels. The old main entrance on Huntington Avenue through Guy Lowell's 1907 neoclassical portico was literally sealed shut. Whatever else the merits or shortcomings of Pei's addition, it destroyed the MFA's orientation to Huntington Avenue.

Pei was far from finished. His firm designed the huge Christian Science Center, wedged between the Back Bay and the South End, which managed to convert the site's former character of industrial railyard desolation into something nearly as desolate and not necessarily more interesting. Pei struck again with the pharaonic John F. Kennedy Library out at Columbia Point in Dorchester Bay. Cobb's last stand appears to be the new 760,000-square-foot federal courthouse, another architectural UFO on the grand scale, which landed on the South Boston waterfront at the old Fan Pier.

Heroes and Goats

When Massachusetts Governor John Volpe was tapped to become President Nixon's secretary of transportation in 1969, he was replaced in the statehouse by Lieutenant Governor Francis Sargent. Sargent had been the state commissioner of public works in the 1960s. He was considered a *highwayman,* sympathetic to those who saw the American future as a drive-in utopia. It was the absolute high tide of the interstate highway construction program. Volpe was expected to bring maximum benefit to his home state in his new cabinet role. The highway interests hoped especially that he would expedite the construction of an urban freeway project called the Boston Inner Belt, I-695. It was a howling super dog of a road. Among other features the design called for a five-story-high interchange with I-93 in the South End. It would have cut clear through the neighborhoods of Hyde Park, Roxbury, Brighton, Allston, and then across the Charles River through Cambridge and Somerville, taking out an estimated three thousand homes, with a lot of collateral property degradation along the right-of-way. In fact, some site work had already commenced. A mile-long swath of the route had been cleared by bull-dozers in Boston's most defenseless neighborhood, Roxbury.

To this point, opposition to the project had been flaccid and unfocused. There was some vague sense that the city was about to be gutted like a codfish. The momentum of the zeitgeist and the accumulation of body blows to the civic fabric over the years had left citizens of all ranks numb and apathetic. The election of the Democratic progressive Kevin White as mayor, along with the rise of an "environmental" consciousness in the late 1960s, changed that. Among other things, it marked the end of the willful mutilation of city fabric by the Boston pols. Joe Kennedy's boys had dragged the city Democrats out of the dark bogs of Irish xenophobia into the sunny vales of the forward-looking, culturally assimilated, liberal mainstream. Meanwhile, the Republican John Volpe's rise to secretary of transportation under Nixon, and its implications for the city, catalyzed the shift in public opinion. Suddenly the Republicans could be painted as antineighborhood, anticity, freeway-crazy maniacs. A coalition of forces now formed that ran across class, party, and ethnic lines from rich brahmins in Milton to poor working Irish constituents of Congressman Tip O'Neill in blue-collar Cambridge to "black power" militants in Roxbury, some of whom stood to lose their homes to I-695. The issues came into focus. They'd all had enough of urban freeways slicing and dicing the city. They wanted better streetcars, subways, and commuter rail. They wanted to rescue the historic city from the Highwaymen.

Three days after Frank Sargent moved into the governor's office on Beacon Hill, a civic group called the Greater Boston Committee staged a raucous protest march called "People Before Highways Day" on Boston Common, within shouting distance of the statehouse. Governor Sargent, who had earlier been one of the Inner Belt's biggest boosters, was persuaded to make an abrupt about-face. To the consternation of Secretary Volpe and the politically potent road-building interests, Governor Sargent declared a moratorium on *all* new highway construction in the metropolitan area. Months later, when Sargent had to run for his job against the popular mayor Kevin White, the two outdid each other in their opposition to the Inner Belt. Both were youthful, handsome, and energetic. But declaring the moratorium had made a hero of Sargent. He managed to beat White (who nevertheless remained mayor for three more terms). Two years after the election, and the deliberations of an elite transportation review commission, Sargent canceled the Inner Belt altogether and that was the end of it.

With the highway dead, the state's powerful Democratic delegation to Congress, namely Tip O'Neill and Ted Kennedy, moved in 1973 to pass important legislation called the Interstate Transfer Option, which, for the first time, allowed states to use federal highway funds for public transit. Sargent's successor, Governor Michael Dukakis, was the first real beneficiary of it. In Dukakis, public transit had a true friend. While he was governor, Dukakis commuted from his home in nearby Brookline every day on the old Green Line electric trolley car, like any other Boston executive heading "inbound" to work. It wasn't a stunt, either, but just a continuation of his normal life, and he got tremendous friendly press out of it.

Dukakis had been around the block a few times in state government. He'd been a state representative and run for lieutenant governor on White's ticket. He had been an early opponent of the urban freeways. His only criticism of Frank Sargent was that it had taken Sargent too long to make up his mind that the Inner Belt was a mistake. In any case, he beat Sargent in the 1974 election.

Under Dukakis, major reconstruction and extension of the transit system began. Aside from the few cities that were building subways from scratch at that time (San Francisco and Washington, D.C.), Boston was the only U.S. city engaged in serious rehabilitation of existing lines. Dukakis also made a major effort to restore regular-gauge commuter rail. The state bought the decrepit and bankrupt Boston & Maine line, poured millions into track repair and new rolling stock, and then contracted with the B&M to run the service. The Boston & Maine carried commuters to the towns of the North Shore: Lynn, Beverley, and Salem. The restored Old Colony line carried them south to Plymouth. South Station was sparklingly restored.

BOSTON

During the Dukakis years, the city of Boston finally emerged from a half-century economic coma. A robust computer industry, primed by fat contracts from the Defense Department, spun out of the region's elite universities to fill the empty role vacated by the long-departed textile mills and factories. A demand for offices spurred a real estate boom, and a score of new high-rise glass boxes—many of them architectural abortions in the spirit of the times—rose up in the heart of the old Shawmut Peninsula. Computerization also allowed Boston to develop a corporate finance and banking center second in America only to Wall Street. Many old factories were converted into loft apartments and house prices soared. Gourmet restaurants sprouted like shiitake mushrooms. The media dubbed this ebullient period the "Massachusetts miracle." Like all booms, it came to an end. The end of this one unfortunately coincided with Michael Dukakis's embarrassing defeat in the presidential election against George Bush. The national economy went into recession and the "Massachusetts miracle" tanked especially hard, taking a couple of major New England banks with it. Of course, Dukakis was blamed and deprived of the credit he deserved for making tremendous material improvements in Boston's infrastructure.

The greatest effect of the Dukakis years, though, was that the city was reestablished as a desirable place for well-off people to live. Most other old American cities had completely lost their gainfully employed middle classes and had no realistic prospect of enticing them back. Baltimore suffered from a form of urban gangrene. Cleveland was shutting down like a geriatric patient in the final throes of life support. Detroit was an empty parking lot. St. Louis looked like the bombed-out capital of a former Soviet republic. Philadelphia and Washington, D.C. were officially bankrupt. Hartford had turned into a set for a road-company production of *Blade Runner*. Buffalo was a basketcase. Wilmington was closed until further notice. And Newark had become a morgue. This was the old industrial North, of course, but the Sunbelt cities were just as bad in a completely different way that equally devalued the essential nature of the traditional city and rendered their cores uninhabitable. And midwestern cities like Chicago, Minneapolis, and Kansas City were adopting the worst development habits of the Sunbelt. In Boston a civic revival was truly underway, supported by the presence of live bodies, especially of the middle class and even the rich.

The Big Dig and the Future

Another legacy of the Dukakis era was the enormous infrastructure project that would be called the Big Dig. It had started with Fred Salvucci, Dukakis's secretary of transportation, when an older department colleague casually remarked to him that the elevated Fitzgerald expressway that cut across the old North End should have been buried in a tunnel underground from the get-go. The idea stayed with Salvucci and began to inflame him. *Bury the highway!* The expressway had been carrying more than twice the daily number of vehicles it was engineered for. Traffic jams commonly lasted ten hours a day, and the accident rate was four times the national average for urban freeways. By the early 1980s it was clear that the Fitzgerald Expressway was falling apart in any case. Four times while Salvucci was secretary, huge chunks of concrete had fallen out of the roadway to the city surface below. Nobody had been underneath when it happened, luckily. They had the whole structure X-rayed and discovered that the steel reinforcing rods holding the concrete together had all but dissolved in a little more than twenty-five years. They blamed it on slipshod work by mob-connected construction companies.

The Big Dig would indeed bury the old Fitzgerald Freeway in a very complicated tunnel that had to snake up and down and around a snarl of subway lines and subterranean water, sewer, electric, gas, and phone lines. The new underground highway would increase the total lanes of traffic from the present six to ten, while reducing the number of access and exit ramps from twenty-seven to fourteen. An important part of the scheme was to carry out all the work without shutting down the old Fitzgerald Expressway so that some semblance of normal business could continue in the financial district through the years of construction. Two big add-ons to the project were a new, second tunnel to Logan Airport and a new bridge over the Charles River to replace the decrepit Tobin Bridge. The

Big Dig was viewed by many in the state public works bureaucracy as primarily a transportation improvement project, with beneficial civic byproducts. Nobody questioned whether American life in the twenty-first century would even entail car and truck use on the outlandish scale that had been achieved in the last decades of the twentieth. It was assumed that the future would be just like the recent past, only more so.

The Big Dig would require the removal of 541,000 truckloads of dirt. Much of it was being barged out to Spectacle Island in Boston Harbor, a former city dump, and heaped on top to create part of a new Harbor Islands State Park (with twenty-six other islands). Some excavated clay would be sold to towns elsewhere as the necessary material for capping their old decommissioned landfills. The immense excavation would then be replaced with 3.8 million cubic yards of concrete, enough to build a three-foot-wide sidewalk from Faneuil Hall to San Francisco. The amount of reinforcing steel used in the project would make a one-inch-thick steel bar long enough to girdle the earth at its equator. The project employed four thousand construction workers at its peak in 1999 and the cost for the whole thing was estimated first at $8 billion in the early 1990s and then $14 billion at the time of writing.[11]

While the project was hideously complex and gigantic in scale, in a way that perhaps frighteningly evoked earlier "urban renewal" boondoggles, it was designed specifically to undo the damage of those previous blunders. The most obvious civic benefit would be the removal of the grotesque obstruction presented by the elevated freeway and the knitting back together of the North End with the rest of the historic city. A problematic aspect of the project was the question of what would replace the old freeway up on the surface once the last rotten concrete trestle abutments were hauled away. The vacated corridor through the financial district and the West End would amount to twenty-seven acres. It was characteristic of the times that the only consensus arrived at was to turn those acres into "green space" or "open space."

In the context of contemporary cultural confusion, "green space" or "open space" essentially means build nothing. It is a rhetorical device for putting city land in cold storage in *the only currently acceptable form,* that is, covered by grass and shrubs, aka *nature.* This happens because we have lost confidence in our ability to produce buildings worthy of our spirits and aspirations. So many twentieth-century buildings are failures in one way or another—looks, relation to the public realm, attitude toward the pedestrian, quality of workmanship—that we assume any new building is liable to be at least unrewarding and at worst another horror. The aggregate failures of all the glass boxes, like the Hancock and the Pru and the dreary slabs of Government Center, of all the public place botches like City Hall Plaza, have taken their toll on the public imagination. Citizens are now thoroughly conditioned to expect the worst. A large fraction of the public has actually taken this attitude a neurotic step further and decided categorically that urbanism is a menace to the human spirit and therefore that the only acceptable use of vacant city land is for installation of the putative antidote to the city: nature.

I hasten to insert that a decent human ecology must contain *nature* integrally deployed in the form of parks, squares, planting strips with street trees, gardens, even windowboxes, and other formal elements of traditional civic design, and the more liberally these are furnished the happier we are apt to be in the urban setting. The contemporary city is as troubled as it is in large part because it has been systematically *de*natured. We *crave* the sight of plants growing and flowering, the sound of birds, the sight, sound, and smell of water, sunlight, a glimpse of stars, the feel of weather. We need desperately to be connected to the greater organism of our biosphere to remind us who and what we are. However, this being true, the city cannot be simultaneously urban and a wilderness. These two things really are mutually exclusive. Unfortunately, though, this is the wish of many who want to repair or improve the city by replacing pieces of it, whenever possible, with the city's supposed opposite: "green space," to have city be both the city and not-the-city at the same time.

This wish has become the default position for citizens' action groups. It is also the logic of suburbia, but it has infected all levels of society, including people who ought to know better, namely, the well-educated, politically progressive, "environmental" activists. To make matters worse, "green space" and "open space" in this context are always presented as abstractions—and if you ask for an abstraction, that is exactly what you will get. You'll get a . . . berm! But a berm is not a park. A bark mulch bed has no civic meaning. This is "nature" in cartoon form. Unfortunately this is the current recipe for the twenty-seven acres of valuable downtown land that will be available when the Fitzgerald Expressway is gone: "green space." The term "green space" should be a tip-off that we're thinking too abstractly.

Something else that contributes to this outcome is Boston's legacy of linear parks designed by Olmsted—the Emerald Necklace—and the reverence in which their designer is held. (He lived and worked in nearby Brookline.) The Olmsted type of park was a wonderful artistic creation. But the Olmsted park can't be the only answer to all problems of urban design, any more than bypass surgery can be the cure for all diseases. Olmsted only worked at the large scale. Smaller urban squares and parks require a formality that is rarely used in Olmsted schemes, and then only as a counterpoint to the dominant informal romanticism.

The recaptured lands from the Big Dig require something else: the reestablishment of a compelling street pattern and good buildings designed to become part of tomorrow's cherished history. It might be appropriate to lay aside a few of the twenty-seven acres for the creation of two small formal parks or squares within this district. But it is silly to leave it all unbuilt. Boston Commons and the Public Garden are a five-minute walk from the Old State House. The waterfront is five minutes in the other direction. The Quincy Market complex is a major public outdoor gathering place in its own right. The North End contains several appropriately scaled pockets of tranquility. Post Office Square occupies the center of the financial district. Twenty-seven acres is a lot of land in the urban setting. It could be composed to contain tremendous civic amenity, activity, and value, *without skyscrapers.* Indeed, if the old city is to be truly knitted back together, this land must be built upon.

Politics Rules

Another major element of the Big Dig is the proposed Boston Seaport redevelopment plan. The Seaport is a roughly one-thousand-acre area of filled lands lying between the old Shawmut Peninsula and South Boston separated by a finger of water called the Fort Point Channel. Formerly it was a district of factories and warehouses, but as manufacturing eloped to the low-wage South after the 1920s, the buildings came down until, by the 1970s, much of the district was devoted to surface parking lots for the adjacent financial district. Technically, the seaport lies within the election district of South Boston, a political problem.

Of the thousand acres, over two hundred acres, an area about four times the size of Beacon Hill, was slated for development into new neighborhoods at the outset of the Big Dig. The industrial seaport proper occupied the rest and would remain a working port, not a mere nostalgic theme park devoted to the history of shipping, with a few chowder joints thrown in for *ambience.* In addition to the freight tonnage, it also contained a major fish-processing center and a growing cruise ship terminal business. The BRA saw the district as a huge opportunity to do the kind of true urban *renewal* that never actually happened in the sixties and seventies, because of the intrusions of abstract modernist methods. The BRA wanted to create five or six distinct neighborhoods in the two hundred acres and pack each one with a rich mix of activities, including a lot of apartments and townhouses (meaning traditional urban buildings, not suburban-style garden apartments), plus offices, light industrial spaces, artisans' ateliers, theaters, cafés, civic amenities such as libraries, athletic centers, and an allotment of "green space," loosely specified. It was a good wish list but a rather vague manual of assembly. Also on the program, as a political necessity, was a new convention center. Boston already had a 1960s-vintage convention center, the hulking Hynes Auditorium on Boylston Street at the edge of Back Bay, but huge as it was, it was deemed insufficient for the Roman circus–style trade shows of the present day and age. So a full forty acres (equal to the entire financial district) was given over to a massive new convention facility in the seaport district.

The BRA's initial plan, cooked up in-house, was deemed to be inadequate by everybody who had a say in it. Evidently, the city planners lacked design expertise, particularly in the technical details of creating a street and block plan and the regulating codes to enforce them. So, after a period of fumbling and recrimination, the BRA hired the firm of Cooper, Robertson & Partners out of New York. Jaquelin T. Robertson had been dean of the University of Virginia School of Architecture and Alexander Cooper had been dean at Columbia University, as well as chief of the New York City Planning Department. Among the firm's many accomplishments was the regulating plan for Battery Park City in New York and, more recently, the master plan for the Disney Corporation's new town of Celebration, Florida, a massive job of over a thousand acres.

The "concept" plan they came up with for the Boston Seaport district was an elegant scheme of several small, distinct neighborhoods, small-scale blocks, intimate streets, dramatic vistas to the harbor, and a rich network of small parks, waterside esplanades, and tree-shaded avenues, creating a physical armature for all the mixed-use goodies off the BRA's wish list. Buildings would be based on existing Boston typologies, with a 150-foot height restriction, and sloped back from the water to avoid the obstruction of vistas that had occurred with Pei and Cobb's Harbor Towers.

To mitigate the presence of the colossal convention center, Cooper, Robertson stipulated liner buildings to occupy the front one hundred feet of the facility's street frontage, and programmed them for mixed-use ground-floor retail with residential and office above to activate what would otherwise certainly be a set of dead streets along the edge of the behemoth. It was a sound, refined, ambitious, and attractive plan. It went a long way toward reestablishing urban design norms that had been lost to several generations of the city-planning officialdom. It would have added terrific value to the city.

Then it ran into a wall of politics.

For starters, the Cooper, Robertson plan called for up to eight thousand apartments and houses ("dwelling units," in the jargon). "Over our dead bodies," replied the politicians of South Boston. They set an absolute maximum at four thousand. Why? Because they feared that such a huge influx of middle-class newcomers (probably educated and apt to be politically progressive) would result in machine political hacks like themselves being voted out of office. South Boston, known affectionately as "Southie," has long been almost a separate nation within the city— though it was annexed into Boston as long ago as 1804. Traditionally, it had been the capital of the Irish working poor, which, up until the 1920s, ·

meant most of the city's ethnically Irish citizens. It was insular and xeno-phobic. South Boston had, accordingly, been the city's epicenter of smol-dering Irish grievances—resentment against those descendants of the hated Yankee brahmins, who made them urban serfs in the New World; resentment against the other striving immigrant groups such as the Ital-ians and the Jews; and most explosively in the 1970s against the Boston School Committee and the federal courts over the issue of school inte-gration. Since then, paradoxically, the vaunted familycentric social fabric of South Boston had started to unravel in exactly the same way that the fabric of black Roxbury had decades earlier with the rise of the welfare life. By the 1990s, drug use, teenage pregnancy rates, and street crime in-volving South Boston male youths were as high statistically as in any other urban ghetto in the nation, and for pretty obvious reasons, mainly the accelerating loss of blue-collar jobs that paid decent wages, so that South Boston was less and less a neighborhood of poor working people and more and more a neighborhood of economic losers spiraling down a behavioral sink. This only made their politicians more atavistically hostile toward anything that represented the encroachment of people doing bet-ter in life.

The Seaport redevelopment plan by Cooper, Robertson was that in spades. Homes for yuppies. Boutiques (that is, stores selling status totems to life's winners). Restaurants where the waiters told you their first names and rattled off every ingredient in that evening's specials. Outdoor cafés (for wine- and coffee-sipping snobs) that were the polar opposite of the typical dark Irish bar where real men steadfastly drank themselves into cirrhosis. Walkable streets . . . ! This last one was especially galling because it was construed as a moral put-down to Southie's car culture. The automobile, which had been both a marvelous instrument of ag-gression against the old brahmin establishment and a workingman's status symbol, was a sacred thing there. None of the city's many subway lines came anywhere near Southie, and its denizens had become as car-dependent as any suburbanites. Cars remained a symbol of modernity, upward mobility, and progress. That automobile traffic degraded Southie's streets was not an issue in a place where aluminum siding was considered aesthetically superior to materials found in nature.

In fact, the rather perverse result of all this friction over "walkable streets" was a protest against any further restrictions on truck traffic within South Boston generally and through the Seaport redevelopment area in particular. Most residential neighborhoods in urban America are at odds with truck traffic one way or another. The politicians of Southie declared themselves in favor of trucks, loudly and emphatically, the more the better. It came down to a jobs issue, they said. Trucks were a lifeline to the port facilities, indispensable to the operation of containerized shipping, in which whole eighteen-wheeler loads in giant aluminum boxes were shipped halfway across the world, hoisted straight out of the cargo hold, and plopped onto a tractor-trailer—a further irony of this being that containerized shipping had eliminated longshoremen from the picture, and therefore a substantial number of high-paying blue-collar jobs once held by the residents of Southie. In any case, the Southie pols stirred the pot of this controversy—knowing that traffic management was the most technically challenging problem in the whole Seaport redevelopment—in order to impede the project.

What they surely feared as much as the loss of their elected positions was the very survival of Southie itself, and in this respect they were no doubt correct in their apprehensions. If four or five new neighborhoods were successfully developed in the Seaport district, then it was logical to infer that adjoining Southie would be the next target of a yuppie invasion. The neighborhood was loaded with classic triple-decker houses and other excellent wooden building types made long ago when lumber was still good and carpenters knew what they were doing. Beneath all that aluminum and vinyl cladding were thousands of fixer-upper gems. As the yuppie feeding frenzy commenced, property values would rise, assessments and taxes would go up, and families who had resided in Southie since time immemorial would be driven out. It was only a matter of time. In short, they feared the specter of *gentrification*.

It was a legitimate fear, but as a moral matter the debate over gentrification had become rather insane, especially when taken up as a cause by members of the old politically progressive intellectual elite, those crusaders for social justice, heirs to many past crusades in a direct line from abolition and women's suffrage through ban-the-bomb, civil rights, the antiwar movement, feminism, school busing, and saving the whales. (That all these noble causes had led the same intellectual elite into the swamps of political correctness is another of life's ironies.) Gentrification, to their minds, was a low-grade form of *class genocide*. To drive the poor from their homes so the better-off could live in them was, to them, an act of unmitigated wickedness. Court cases had been fought over it.

The point had a certain obvious emotional appeal, but if one applied even a moment's further reflection, it no longer looked quite so cut and dried. For instance, if gentrification was flat-out wicked, how would any city neighborhood escape the fate of an ultimate slide into slumdom? How could the city as a whole expect to regenerate itself over time? Were some run-down neighborhoods okay to fix up and others not? And on what grounds?

As a philosophical matter, the argument against gentrification soon foundered on the shoals of logic. If it were morally unacceptable for the better-off to revive devalued city property and live in it, then where should they be *allowed* to live? A process of elimination left either a) the neighborhoods already occupied, b) the suburbs, or c) the rural hinterlands. Under this logic, the number of middle-class city dwellers would be forever fixed at the current level. And what would be the fate of these neighborhoods already occupied by the middle class when, after a period of time, they inevitably became run-down? Would it not be okay for the property to be sold and fixed up by new, hopeful owners?

It seems to me that following the logic of the antigentrification forces would lead us to precisely the predicament in which America finds itself today: massive disinvestment in our cities, many of them in ruins, and the well-off relegated to making their homes in the suburbs and the exurbs.

The question of where the poor go when they have been gentrified out of their neighborhoods is a legitimate one. But it is worth considering that the character and behavior of the poorer classes has changed over time and will probably continue to change. In the early years of the twentieth century, for instance, fully 10 percent of *all* wage-earners in America were employed as domestic servants. Their relations with the more affluent classes were far different from relations between the poor and everybody else today. For one thing, they *were* employed. Their wages might have been low, but they were busy, and in the plainest way: making themselves useful to other people. Their hours were filled with tasks, duties, and obligations. This is not true for many of today's poor, whose unstructured, chaotic lives reinforce their own hopelessness and transmit it to the next generation. (Some of today's supposed poor—the drug dealers and criminals—are not even poor in the money sense.) Many among this enormous class of servants were housed by their employers, and many households were run as institutions, with very clearly defined divisions of labor, authority, responsibilities, and benefits. Among the benefits (besides a place to sleep) was a complex family social structure that often supported a poor person's aspirations to become a better-off person. It is also true, of course, that many of the urban poor in that period lived in desperate and awful conditions—as documented by Jacob Riis—but even the denizens of the worst slums in America had access to a public realm that was furnished with institutions of self-improvement that included good free schools, free libraries, and settlement houses that taught useful social skills. One of the reasons that there is even a debate about displacing today's poor is that we are now encouraged to perceive the condition of poverty itself as being utterly static and intractable. In a way, those fighting gentrification have internalized the hopelessness of the very people they supposedly want to help. The battle against gentrification ends up being a quixotic effort to keep the poor literally in their physical place.

In the normal course of things throughout history, affordable housing has been found in the buildings that are older and less desirable. Traditionally, these buildings have been more or less mixed into the civic fabric at a fine grain. There have always been better city neighborhoods and better streets than others, but even the best ones, such as Back Bay or Beacon Hill, have had a good supply of apartments for the less well-off, including the working poor (who may take the demographically non-ethnic form of young people right out of college working entry-level jobs for little money). The traditional city also has been composed of buildings suitable for adaptive reuse. In our time, the overwhelming majority of new buildings have been put up outside the city, in suburbia, and in single-use forms that do not lend themselves to adaptation over time. Most U.S. cities have missed two or three generations of residential building, and in the meantime, the older stuff has been so poorly cared for that it is beyond repair. Due to this predicament we have had to invent an artificial commodity called "affordable housing."

My guess is that the suburbs are destined to become the slums of the future, moving outward from the center, ring by ring, and that as the reconstructed fabric of the city becomes more desirable for those who are doing well, the poor will, for a time, be relegated to asteroid belts of aging subdivisions. They may even come to unhappily inhabit the bankrupt strip malls for a while. It will take a generation or more for the natural cycles of decay and regeneration to reassert themselves in cities like Boston. But not all the neighborhoods of Boston will regenerate at the same time or the same rate. Some will remain less desirable and be places that the poor will live. The question remains whether these poor will aspire to become something other than poor, and whether our culture will support those aspirations.

The antigentrification forces overlook the salient characteristic of cities: that they are dynamic organisms continually undergoing cycles of change, of decay and renewal. To demand an end to these processes would result in the death of the city. The antigentrification movement, therefore, is against the well-being and the future of the city.

The Future

It will be interesting to see what happens in Boston. Despite its status as the capital of political correctness, the educated classes are gentrifying it at a faster rate than anyplace else in America, including San Francisco, Chicago, and Brooklyn, the runners-up. Neighborhoods that were the dreariest slums when I lived in Boston almost thirty years ago are now taking on a nearly European vibrancy, for instance the old South End (not to be confused with South Boston). Back in 1972, I had to go down there to take a tuberculosis test at the old Boston City Hospital in order to qualify for substitute teaching assignments. The neighborhood was only a ten-minute walk from Symphony Hall, but it had never recovered from being eclipsed by the more spectacular development of Back Bay in the 1860s. By the early twentieth century it had become a district of rooming houses, growing steadily shabbier every decade until, by the 1970s, it was a frightening slum. I went back in the spring of 1999 and it was the hottest real estate market in the city. The South End's physical form of small gridded blocks and red brick row houses had proved sturdy, durable, and resilient. Four-story bow-front brick row buildings that had been worth less than ten thousand dollars in the seventies were now going for half a million or more. The owner could live there like a Venetian duke in a spacious high-ceilinged flat and collect substantial rents from half a dozen apartments. The most desirable houses were the ones lining the several leafy squares that were part of the neighborhood's original design. It was a five-minute transit hop from the South End to the financial district, Fenway Park, Quincy Market, and Newberry Street, the Back Bay's art gallery and café district. The South End's main arteries, Columbus Avenue and Washington Street, once desolate, were now lined with new bistros and shops. It was a revelation to see what a difference investment and hope make, to see the contractors' trucks and the construction dumpsters and the painters' scaffolds at every turn. It just wasn't the kind of thing you're used to seeing in an American city.

The same scene is being played out in other former slum neighborhoods in Boston and in Cambridge across the Charles River. The North End, Charlestown, Jamaica Plain, Somerville are all getting fixed up by gainfully employed middle-class strivers who believe in city life and want to be part of the dynamic organism. No doubt other run-down neighborhoods are next: Southie, Dorchester, Mattapan, and Roxbury. All are showing some signs of stirring to life. Roxbury was so far gone a decade ago that angry, despairing local politicians sought to secede from the city and become a separate municipality called Mandela, after the president of South Africa. Today, Roxbury is a hotbed of new small businesses as a mixed group of Asian, Caribbean, and Spanish-speaking immigrants move in and initiate another cycle of urban regeneration.

My own prediction is that Boston will be America's most habitable big city in the first quarter of the new century. It is way ahead of almost all the others. In Boston, there seems to be a new and clear consensus that city life can be wonderfully rewarding, and that we possess the means to make it so. That kind of civic self-confidence and self-consciousness is exactly what is missing in so many other cities across America.

LONDON

Landscape as the Cure for Cities

The English are a rural-minded people on the whole, which perhaps explains why our rural domestic architecture is so much better than our urban. Our cities, generally speaking, are deplorable. There is a lack of design which must make the French smile.

VITA SACKVILLE-WEST

It is probably a good thing that the mistress of Sissinghurst did not live to see the likes of millennial Las Vegas, with its lugubrious eight-lane motor vistas of the mega hotel-casinos and the imperial median strips of embalmed tropical foliage, but she illustrates an interesting point of Anglo-American culture, namely, that we have very ambivalent feelings about city life as a general proposition and view rural landscape as the sovereign antidote to the baneful necessity of urbanism.

We Americans, of course, being the naive, prideful, narcissistic extremists we are, have taken these ideas to ridiculous new frontiers. We have devised a new kind of city perhaps more repulsive than the archetypal English industrial Coketown (a name coined by Dickens) and tried to mitigate it with expropriations of landscape symbolism, and the entire system is a goddammed mess both materially as a thing made for our daily use, and as a way of thinking, as expressed in a range of mentalities from the venal dreams of the most swinish Sunbelt land developers to the noble agendas of the "environmental" elite. Nature is sacred and everything else is hopelessly profane, and that's the end of it. This limited view of the human condition has prevented us from doing anything about the aforementioned goddammed mess that America has become, and it is worth tracing some of its origins if we are going to ever get past this predicament and find a way to construct civic surroundings that are worth living in.

London's Great Fire of 1666 is a good starting point for our consideration of these paradoxes, because London then was already an old city and the New World enterprise in North America was by then also well underway. The fire that started in Pudding Lane on Sunday night, September 1, 1666, burned until Tuesday night, September 3, and reduced 395 acres of the central city to cinders. (This, by the way, followed on the heels of London's Great Plague of 1665.) Most of the city's—of the English nation's—leading business headquarters went up in smoke. The chief cathedral, St. Paul's, and eighty-seven other churches burned down, and more than thirteen thousand house were destroyed. The fire occurred six years after the defeat of Cromwell's puritan dictatorship and the restoration of the British monarchy. Despite decades of acute political disturbance, England had been transforming itself into a great maritime trading colossus and was soon to be the world's first industrial empire. At the time of the fire, the population of London stood at 350,000. It would double by 1700. Terrible though it was, the fire presented London with a tremendous opportunity to reorder urban life on a scale suited to what its future demanded. This opportunity was botched. Bold personality that he was, Charles II could not overcome the legacy of the Civil War, which had shifted power to the secular authorities—Parliament, the corporation of the city, and the rising business interests—and these bodies could not overcome their conflicting interests for the greater good of London's future.

The fire left an enormous heap of stinking, smoldering debris that took months to clear away. The destruction was so complete in places that old property lines couldn't be reestablished and many of those prepared to rebuild immediately were stymied. At the same time, the authorities worried that burnt-out businesspeople and householders might abandon London permanently and altogether. As winter approached, the king appointed a royal commission for rebuilding. It included a thirty-three-year-old astronomy lecturer turned architect, Christopher Wren, who had responded quickly to the disaster with a proposal to completely redesign the street-and-block plan for the city center. It took the form of a grid of orthogonal blocks with widened, straightened streets modified by diagonal connecting arteries, and civic institutions strategically sited on new public squares and terminal vistas. Wren's scheme, much admired by architects and civic designers for its baroque clarity, would have transformed the city from an overgrown medieval termite mound of narrow passages and miserable transport routes into the sort of spacious capital that Paris would become two centuries later under the regime of Louis-Napoleon and his prefect, Haussmann.

The king liked Wren's plan because it was devised in the spirit of André Lenôtre, designer of Louis XIV's gardens at Versailles, and also of the Champs-Élysées, the monumental and as-yet-unbuilt-upon new boulevard leading west out of the Tuileries in Paris. In exile before the restoration of his crown, Charles II had become a great admirer of Lenôtre and of the French design manner in general. But neither the king nor his commission could impose Wren's plan on the other bickering parties, and except for two new thoroughfares, King and Queen streets, Londoners eventually rebuilt the heart of the city along its old medieval lanes. Meanwhile, the royal treasury was strained from carrying on a war with The Netherlands, so even the sensible proposal to construct a stone embankment along the noisome Thames had to be put off. In the Great Fire's aftermath, the crown managed only to introduce a set of building codes regulating materials (brick or masonry, not wood), number of stories, overhangs, shopfronts, and signs. But the old central district, ever after called "the City," did change permanently after all. Many merchants and prosperous professionals indeed took up residence elsewhere, relocating in the country towns beyond the fortifications left over from the recent civil wars, or in new houses sprouting in the fields beyond Westminster, both upstream and upwind from the City. These would become, and remain to this day, the most desirable residential neighborhoods of London. In any case, a potent counterforce to the civic ideal was flourishing in the countryside well beyond the outskirts of London town.

Arcadia

The religious (and political) crisis Henry VIII had set off when the Pope refused to grant him a divorce from the barren Catherine of Aragon smoldered like a root fire for a hundred years and finally burst out above ground in the Civil War between Protestant parliamentary factions and the Catholic Stuart kings.[1] Parliament had brought to trial and beheaded the intransigent Charles I in 1649. Cromwell's parliamentary "protectorate," a disorderly dictatorship really, succeeded hardly better in holding together the new commonwealth than Charles I had his kingdom, and by little more than the force of personality. Cromwell's fractious government achieved little. A Council of State under Parliament managed to abolish the House of Lords (though not aristocracy itself).

This aristocracy derived its wealth largely in land rents from large estates and in the political commotion of the mid-1600s many aristocrats fled London to lie low in their country seats. Some royalists were banished outright from the capital. Thus a generation of English aristocrats made a virtue of necessity and developed a way of life quite different from, say, the contemporary French court at Versailles, where the entire aristocracy resided under one roof in a kind of theme park with their domineering king. Apart from the most obvious advantage of being removed from the political quarrels of the day, the English country lords found tremendous solace and pleasure in their rural surroundings. They ruled little realms of their own. They developed a rich culture of country pastimes, in particular hunting, riding, and gardening. They became very intimate with their lands and the other people and things that lived there. They applied their wealth to the improvement of their homes and of the terrain that surrounded them.

In the aftermath of the regicide, there was a consciousness among these landed lords that they were living through a time similar to the period of political chaos in classical Rome that followed the assassination of Julius Caesar, when many Roman nobles had retreated to their farms and country villas to stay out of trouble. Virgil's *Georgics,* extolling the delights of rural retirement, became a popular text among the wealthy rural English, who sought meaning in many other classical themes, especially the Greek myth of Arcadia, the ideal place, where nature and civilization existed in perfect balance, and the landscape was beautiful, familiar, always interesting, but never a menace to existence—in short, heaven on Earth.

The country seats became worlds unto themselves, and their squires had the means to fashion them to suit their fantasies. This became a principal preoccupation for many of them, and an elaborate new culture of landscape garden design evolved to serve their aspirations. The movement involved many hundreds of great estates, some comprising thousands of acres, and coincided in the 1700s with the Enclosure Acts that altered the social organization as well as the landscape of agricultural production. In many cases, the private estate parks were created out of the less desirable lands left over from the enclosures, and the only thing that could be done with them in the absence of good tillage or pasturage was to make them beautiful.

The geometric formality of pleasure gardens modeled on the example of Versailles, itself based on Renaissance Italian and medieval ideas—or a little later on Dutch gardens when William of Orange was installed on the throne in 1688 by a Parliament desperate to be rid of Stuarts forever—gave way in England to an irregular, informal, "natural" style that was no less entirely an artifice. There are rumblings of this in the writings of John Evelyn and William Temple, whose own Moor Park was executed strictly in the Dutch manner, and the landscape sketches of Stephen Switzer.[2] But the first true practitioner of the informal and irregular style was William Kent, who came as a house guest to Lord Burlington's Palladian villa at Chiswick in 1725 and stayed for twenty years as its landscape gardener. It was Kent, with the very active Burlington, who began to formalize the vocabulary of the English landscape "park" with its lawns gently meeting placid water in serpentine shapes, strategically deployed clumps of oak and beech, the insertion of little classical buildings—just as in the idealized canvases of the new school of landscape painters: Claude Lorrain, Nicolas Poussin, and Salvator Rosa. Kent himself had begun his career as a landscape painter, and had met Burlington first while painting in Italy. In fact, the arts of landscape painting and landscape gardening became so mutually reinforcing that their character as essentially abstract exercises lay open to ridicule, as a character in Tom Stoppard's play *Arcadia* (1993) suggests:

English landscape was invented by gardeners imitating foreign painters who were evoking classical authors. The whole thing

was brought home in luggage from the grand tour. Here, look—
Capability Brown doing Claude [Lorrain], who was doing Virgil.

Lancelot Brown (1715–83), Kent's successor, was called Capability not
because he was conceited, but for his habit of exclaiming, when inspect-
ing a client's property for the first time, "It has capability!" (that is, of being composed by Brown into an Arcadian landscape). Brown called
himself "a placemaker," not a gardener He was renowned for destroying
extant formal gardens in order to install his lawns and serpentine pools—
achieved by damming natural streams and brooks. Stoppard, again, cap-
tures it nicely:

The whole Romantic sham. . . . It's what happened to the Enlightenment, isn't it? A century of intellectual rigor turned in on
itself. . . . There's an engraving of Sidley Park in 1730 that makes
you want to weep. Paradise in the age of reason. By 1760 everything had gone—the topiary, pools and terraces, fountains, an avenue of limes—the whole sublime geometry was ploughed
under by Capability Brown. The grass went from the doorstep to
the horizon and the best box hedge in Derbyshire was dug up for
the ha-ha so that fools could pretend they were living in God's
countryside.[3]

Stoppard is perhaps a little harsh. Most striking, though, is his observation that a severe reaction to the Enlightenment set in so early, really
while all the great figures of the age were hitting their stride—Voltaire,
Burke, Jefferson, Frederick the Great, Catherine of Russia, and her gifted
prime-minister-and-boyfriend-in-chief Potemkin—while Diderot had
barely gotten started on the *Encyclopédie*. The world already was growing
tired of reason, perhaps had been overly dazzled by it in the first place,
and began to feel twinges of regret when it began to undermine the institutions that held civilized society together. One of the principal characters of the age, the odious Rousseau (1712–78), fomented diligently
against reason and civilized institutions his whole career. In fact, it *was* his

career—when not mistreating his family, dodging his imagined enemies, and welshing on his debts. Harold Nicolson writes of Rousseau:

> The fact remains that Rousseau and his doctrine of "natural" emotion and the equality of man succeeded in destroying the age of reason and in substituting a universe of fantasies that introduced much confusion, much unhappiness, much cruelty, and many illusions into the civilized and even into the uncivilized world.[4]

All this is curiously anticipated in English landscape as carried on by Capability Brown, Sir Humphrey Repton, and Henry Hoare, master of the exemplary Stourhead estate in Wiltshire. There came to be, as Nicolson put it, "a growing preference for the element of surprise over the element of expectation." And then absolutely coincident with the French Revolution—that triumph of inflamed popular emotion over reason—the English turned even further to an even more wild and spooky form of landscape composition, as though everyday life should be lived like a ghost story, full of delicious morbidity and plangent melancholia. Of course, it too was artifice, what we today would consider a form of showbiz. This was the landscape of William Gilpin, Richard Payne Knight, Uvedale Price, J. C. Loudon, and eventually, by association if not practice, John Ruskin, all gothic ghoulishness, sceneographic melodrama, the awesome and the sublime, emotion rampant—a world ready for Sigmund Freud. It was England trying hard to be someplace other than England.

Now, it is necessary to pause in this elaborate argument—and you shall see by and by that it *is* an argument—to graze in a couple of related pastures. One rumination is that whatever fine artistic point any of the landscapists might have made about naturalism or wildness, the English landscape of the eighteenth century was, in reality, thoroughly domesticated, tamed, housebroken—much more so even than that of France, where wolves still roamed, and certainly in stark distinction to America, which to a great extent remained unexplored in 1800. England was settled, comfortable, and familiar. A second point worth chewing on is that

throughout the eighteenth century, roughly the period of the Enlightenment, the English upper classes continued to elaborate a form of social
organization markedly different from that of France, the leading continental power and the intellectual hot-spot of the Enlightenment. The
English aristocracy had succeeded in becoming detached from the life of
their cities, principally London, and could exist in a realm beyond politics, while the French aristocracy, penned up in the fantasy camp of Versailles, had nowhere to go when the mob rose, and were rounded up like
so many spring pullets—and lost their heads like them, too. A few lucky
ones got out of France early and had to stay out for quite a while. In the
meantime France imploded institutionally while Paris became a *grand
guignol,* a theater of blood. It took the exceptionally forceful personality
of Napoleon Bonaparte, barely thirty years old and barely French, to
smack the French nation upside its head and get it to stop the hysterical
nonsense of the permanent revolution—and then, of course, Napoleon
embarked on twenty years of his own nonsense on a continental scale.
The upshot of all this mischief was that it kept Europe too preoccupied
with the Napoleonic Wars to do what England and the new United
States of America had set about doing by the early 1800s, namely, indus-
trialize.

The picturesque romantic landscape, therefore, is a kind of precogni-
tive metaphor, expressed in painting and real property, for the massive
disruptions about to come about through industrialization and the raw
emotion it aroused in a new age where emotion would have to take a
backseat to science, technology, and a society ever more strictly and rationally organized for production.

By the early 1800s, Capability Brown's leading professional descen-
dant, the Scotsman John Claudius Loudon, sneered at Brown's design
method as "one uniform system of smoothing, leveling, and clumping of
the most tiresome monotony joined to the most disgusting formality."[5]
He could have been describing the new type of city about to be built.
Let's consider the industrial leviathan that London was becoming.

"Hell Is a Place Like London"

So the poet Percy Bysshe Shelley said.

Ruskin called it "the Great Foul City of London . . . rattling, growling, smoking, stinking—a ghastly heap of fermenting brickwork, pouring out poison at every pore."

By 1820, when the Prince Regent succeeded his long-ailing father as George IV, London's population had swollen above one million. It was by far the greatest city of Europe. The political and religious inflammations of the Stuart era were long extinguished. England had settled comfortably into constitutional monarchy and it had gotten over the humiliating loss of the American colonies by vanquishing Bonaparte's war machine. Commercial trade over the eighteenth century had multiplied fivefold and the British merchant fleet and navy ruled the seas absolutely.

England's nobility had gotten used to country life, and many made their main residences there, coming "to town" for a brief social "season." Country living had become more or less emblematic of the group, a separate and exclusive subculture. Meanwhile, though, a new wealthy commercial and manufacturing class had risen up to take the nobility's place in the city—the aristocracy regarded careers in "trade" as indecently beneath them. The Enclosure Acts, paralleling the increased need for industrial labor, kept the city flooded with uprooted country people looking for work. Then, after 1834, the railroads came and altered life in the city like nothing before. By 1840 London's population reached 1.5 million, and every decade thereafter for the rest of the century it steadily increased another half million, the majority of these newcomers laborers, clerks, wage slaves, the worker ants in the antheap of the new industrial urban scene.

The pace of change and growth must have been frightening for many (and exhilarating, too, for others). A journey in one of the first railroad cars at fifteen miles per hour was like riding a lightning bolt for people used to seeing the world go by no faster than a trotting horse. It is worthwhile to recall again that the world had never experienced anything like the industrial city before. Classical Rome, with a population around one million, and with its immense rancid quarters of tenement *insulae,* came closest, though Rome was handmade and run by the power of human slaves. But the new industrial city of machines, factories, steel, and slums produced overwhelmingly worse living conditions for far greater numbers of people than any kind of city ever seen before, and it established a shocking new base level of urban squalor for all ranks of society. For instance, the Rome of Hadrian was a city of great public baths. In the London of Victoria public baths barely existed, except as exotic entertainment spots, and until the nineteenth century, the vast monotonous blocks of worker barracks housing almost never included so much as running cold water. The supply of labor was so bottomless, and the pay so minuscule, that standards in housing virtually disappeared. Landlords could rent anything with a roof and walls. Typhus, cholera, and other diseases of bad sanitation burned through the city, killing rich and poor indiscriminately. Tuberculosis especially thrived in the dark, dirty, moist, overcrowded conditions of the slums, where one room per family remained the rule for decades among the working poor, and perhaps 10 percent of the population lived in lightless basements.

Living conditions that would have seemed less than human two centuries earlier became absolutely normative in the new industrial London, as did the din, stench, and dirt of the factory. Oily coal dust got into everything. Black coats became the predominant male costume of the managerial classes and upward because the soot didn't show. Smogs of coal smoke persisted all winter long and killed thousands. The technical innovation of industry and the degradation of urban life advanced at a steady inverse ratio.

Lewis Mumford became a mad dog in his writings on the subject of nineteenth-century urban life.[6] "In these new warrens," he wrote of the London slums in *The Culture of Cities*, "a race of defectives was created." He went on:

> There have been periods in the past that exhibited greater animal ferocity, gashing or burning the flesh of people who had sinned against the prevailing moral code or theological beliefs. But the nineteenth century, smugly conscious of its new humanitarian principles, converted such outright brutalities into a slow quiet process of attrition and inanition. A minimum of schooling: a

minimum of rest: a minimum of cleanliness; a minimum of shelter. A gray pall of negative virtue hung over the urban improvements of the period, and its highest boast was the expansion of these minimum conditions and these negative gains. . . . [N]ever was human blight so wide-spread; never before had it so universally been accepted as normal—normal and inevitable . . . not only the absolute unfitness of this environment, but its extraordinary quantitative multiplication.[7]

The development of neighborhoods for the middle class and the rich occurred, too, of course. With the growth of enormous business bureaucracies, the multiplication of huge hierarchies of middlemen, managers, and merchants, a particular system of housing development evolved. It was exemplified in London by the hereditary owners of large tracts of urban land, for instance the duke of Bedford, who converted his estates of Bloomsbury into an urban quarter of row houses for the better-off, typically arranged around little green squares that brought light and putatively better air into buildings that otherwise differed not much typologically from the tenements of the poor—except that fewer people inhabited them. Almost all the housing of this kind was built under leaseholdings of as long as ninety-nine years, an arrangement unknown in America. Its other salient characteristic was its remarkable monotony. Not only did the buildings possess a numbing uniformity—even the austere townhouses of the very rich in blocks like the Wilton Crescent—but in the "better" streets' shops and services were kept away from their ground floors (an extension of the aristocratic bias against "trade"), diminishing convenience, amenity, and variety for pedestrians. The English showed, too, an extreme bias against apartment living (as opposed to the French, who would make an art of it). In London toward the end of the nineteenth century, even the row house typology would be abandoned in favor of single-family detached houses on tiny lots, in endless insectile agglomerations that spread far out into what had not long before been the distant countryside of "green England"—now turning coal-black, smoke-gray, and hardscaped.

The great torment of the nineteenth-century city, apart from its sheer shocking hypertrophic growth, was "congestion." And apart from the efforts of housing reform—which often backfired in unanticipated economic consequences—and the use of zoning to segregate obnoxious industrial land uses, the main response was the movement to try to ruralize the city. Hyde Park in London had been given to the public by Charles I. At the time, it lay on the western edge of the city proper and lay farthest from what would become the East End slums. It was at first essentially a promenading and equestrian park for the hangers-on to the Court of St. James. The adjoining Kensington Gardens were the grounds of Kensington Palace and not open to the public until 1790 and then only on Sundays (until the reign of Victoria, when it was opened year-round). Both Hyde Park and the grounds of Kensington were infested with thieves. Hibbert writes that George II was robbed personally of his purse, watch, and shoe buckles by a bandit who boldly climbed over the Kensington Garden wall, and Horace Walpole, aesthete son of Prime Minister Robert Walpole, was robbed and shot at—the bullet missed—in Hyde Park.[8] Fairs were held at Hyde Park, gentleman skaters enjoyed its Serpentine lake in winter (note the cooler climate of "the little ice age" in the 1700s), and it was a popular place for duels. Both nearby Green Park and St. James's Park composed the formal public approaches to Buckingham Palace along the axis of the Mall—the original Buckingham House having become the favored royal abode of George III. It was greatly enlarged by George IV and is now *the* main royal residence in London. St. James's Park became, with development of the West End and the concentration of government offices in adjacent Whitehall, the notorious haunt of prostitutes, as recorded many times, for instance, by Boswell.

Regent's Park, roughly a half mile north of Hyde Park, was conceived as a real estate development by the Prince Regent and his architect John Nash on what was in 1810 still open land. By creating a landscape park frontage for substantial numbers of up-market row or "terrace" houses, Nash was, in effect, creating a communal manor park for the rich within the context of the city. There would be a lake and clumps of trees, à la Capability Brown, Repton, and Company, to look out upon from the urban drawing room as though surveying one's country domain. In addition, Nash expected a few very exclusive freestanding villas deployed within the park itself, giving it an additional flavor of the domesticated countryside. The animating idea behind the project, never explicitly articulated by Nash or the prince, was the ruralization of urban life for the well-born, so that the city might conform to the terms and norms of country living that the aristocracy has grown used to. The lords were happiest on their own rural estates. The fouler and bigger industrial London became, the less inclined they were to visit or remain there. Nash's Regent's Park project surely must have been a way for the convivial prince to entice this class to spend more time in the city, with him, where duty constrained the head of state to remain much of the year. But by the time Regent's Park really started coming together as a real estate venture, the industrialization of London had accelerated shockingly, with new railroad lines radiating all around the new development, and even fresher suburbs leapfrogging far beyond it, and in a few decades Regent's Park would no longer be the edge of town but near the center of a completely unanticipated, suddenly gargantuan urban organism. "In this new environment," Mumford wrote, "only machines could be quite at home; for they express order, purpose, regularity, without the mechanically irrelevant need for love, or sympathy, or beauty."

Meanwhile in America

The purpose of this chapter has been to describe the origins of the conflict between urban and rural life, to show how this conflict manifested itself in the practical living arrangements of Industrial Age people, using London as the prime case in point, and to discuss how these ideas about rural and urban life evolved and mutated over time to leave Americans of the twenty-first century in a special predicament where the quality of our everyday environment is concerned. The argument now shifts ground, so to speak, to America, where we find ourselves stuck with the consequences of these attitudes and ideas in an increasingly debilitiating condition of permanent placelessness—where the urban and the rural have cruelly canceled each other out and left only a void of abstraction that fails to add up to any places worth living in.

New York City in the 1840s and 1850s was growing as relentlessly as London was then, and under the same remorseless regime of industrialization. Only the pattern of growth was a little different. Under a plan drawn up as early as 1811, the entire eleven-mile-long island of Manhattan was platted into a gigantic mechanistic grid of rectangular blocks unresponsive to the rugged topography and unrelieved by a single device of urbanistic scenographic diversity, no squares, no round-points, no terminated vistas. Just a checkerboard of streets off into the horizon. Where London's explosive growth was both monotonous *and* incoherent, New Yorkers settled for unadulterated monotony. Besides, extreme regularity of lot size and shape was better suited to our land tenure traditions and speculative real estate practices.

Manhattan therefore presented a special predicament in the relation of urban people with their surroundings. As an island between rivers then considered unbridgeable, its full development according to the municipal plan would leave its inhabitants cut off absolutely from access to any countryside whatsoever. What's more, the development of the island was occurring at such a furious rate that adults living, say, in 1857, could realistically expect the whole island to be filled up with buildings and pavements within their lifetimes. The prospect was dreadfully bleak, especially within the forms dictated by industrial urbanism: block after block of walk-up row buildings for hundreds of blocks, all deficient in air and light, and no relief except by taking a boat off the island city. Even at the time, when building was just pushing north of Thirty-fourth Street, New York was shamefully devoid of public parks for a city of its size. There were no royal gardens to be given over to public use, only a tiny residue of lands that speculators had been unable to seize and sell—the Battery, which had been a fortification for so many years, the Bowling Green (a drinking and gambling spot, really), and the scruffy parade ground enfronting City Hall, all gone to weeds and horse droppings. Gramercy Park, then as now, required a key to get in. The social and aesthetic need for relief was only taken seriously after the repeated cholera epidemics of the 1840s brought the public health shortcomings of the industrial city to public attention, and then the argument could be made to the land speculators that parks not only improved the public health, but increased the value of real estate on park frontages—which happened to be true.

I have told the story of Central Park and Frederick Law Olmsted in my previous book, *Home From Nowhere,* and will not repeat it here except to emphasize for the purpose of this argument that the great park was the particular product of a very special set of circumstances. While Olmsted is revered in American urban history and in the practice of landscape architecture, and Central Park considered the foremost model of an urban park, his work presented new problems of urbanism that we have still not overcome 150 years later, and that are reflected in the increasingly abstract and peculiar thinking in our own time about the relation between city and country.

Olmsted's conception of Central Park sprang from several sources. First from the long tradition of English landscape practices already discussed, as modified in America by the different kinds of terrain and social relations in the New World. Olmsted's methods arose from the problems of urban development specific to New York City in the mid-nineteenth century. He was influenced by developments in American landscape painting and its wilderness-worship branch called the Hudson River School (itself an outgrowth of Old World landscape painting). Olmsted was familiar with the preaching of Andrew Jackson Downing, the first self-consciously professional "landscape gardener" America produced, and an originator of American-style suburbia as a distinct idea (Downing drowned in a Hudson River steamboat explosion, 1850). Olmsted took further cues from the cemetery landscaping movement as exemplified by Mt. Auburn Cemetery in Cambridge, Massachusetts. All of these influences came together for Olmsted and synthesized into a new vision when he visited Birkenhead Park in Liverpool, England, in 1850.

Birkenhead Park's 120 acres in a Liverpool suburb were laid out in 1844 by Joseph Paxton, who would go on to design London's Crystal Palace for the Great Exhibition of 1851, the first modern world's fair. Witold Rybczynski tells us that Olmsted discovered Birkenhead by accident days after his arrival in Liverpool, when he had set out for a hike in the new precincts across the Mersey.[9] Rybczynski also says that what most impressed Olmsted was that Birkenhead was entirely man-made, engineered from nothing. It had been little more than a clay pit that Paxton had ingeniously drained, sculpted, and planted—and voilà, the solution to the oppressiveness of this new abomination, the industrial city! A picturesque vignette of a "natural" rural landscape! Birkenhead lit a fire in Olmsted, who had thus far in life dabbled in many occupations—sailor, journalist, "scientific" farmer—but had not acted as a professional landscape gardener in the tradition of Brown et al., or even of Downing, whom he admired and corresponded with.

The Central Park project was a municipal design competition, and it is likely that Olmsted won the job in 1858 because he had chosen the perfect partner in Calvert Vaux, the young Englishman who had been induced to come to America some years earlier to be Downing's assistant. Vaux had brought to that partnership a comprehensive knowledge of English landscape history and certainly now applied it in the detailed "Greensward" plan with which he and Olmsted won the park competition. Eighteen months later, in the midst of the grading and road-building operations in the new park, Olmsted took a six-week leave of absence from the job and sailed for Europe, where he visited some of the great English estates, the London parks, and met in Paris with Haussmann's redoubtable chief engineer Alphand, who was then converting the Bois de Boulogne from a long-neglected royal woods to a public park twice the size of Central Park. Olmsted also revisited his beloved Birkenhead Park in Liverpool. Everything he saw reinforced his own landscape design instincts—his use of elements from across the English tradition: the stately lawns of Brown, the lakes of Repton, the irregularities of Uvedale Price, the narrative vignette-making of Loudon, with incidents of formality like Nash's mall in St. James's, and even a little bit of Lenôtre thrown in (Bethesda Fountain).

Olmsted also returned to New York with a vision for the general salvation of society from this new monster, the industrial city—the idea of a comprehensive system of connected parks, greenbelts, stream corridors, and vehicular "parkways" that would insert large tracts of rural landscape around American cities at their current stage of development, with the expectation that when the cities expanded beyond these ruralesque insertions, as Olmsted knew they would, the great park networks would be in place and would make urban life at least tolerable and perhaps splendid. He was also filled with ideas about how the future suburbs would develop, as a new type of place with all the benefits of both the country and the city, and none of the drawbacks of either. His vision was complete, and he would see significant aspects of it built out in his lifetime. But he got a couple of things wrong, and he certainly never imagined the mess that the twentieth century would make of both the city and the country (including some of his signature works), leaving both nearly unlivable. We will return to this issue after a glance back at England.

Garden Cities of Tomorrow: Utopia not Arcadia

Ebenezer Howard (1850–1928) was the quintessential eccentric British progressive reformer of the industrial zenith. He came from a humble background. At twenty-one, he ventured to America—the Nebraska prairie, of all places—where he idealistically tried farming with two partners, ended up miserably in the employ of one of them, and eventually gave up the enterprise in despair. Having learned shorthand, he got a job as a court reporter in Chicago, eventually returned to England, and worked at that vocation the rest of his active life while he campaigned for urban-planning reform on the side.

Howard's imagination was inflamed especially by the utopian novel *Looking Backward* by the American Edward Bellamy, published in 1887, which sought to depict the way life would be lived in 1950. To the reader today, Bellamy's book is laughable. For instance, he predicted that the entire city (in this case, Boston) would be rigged with speaking tubes connected to a central symphony hall that would broadcast music into every home—completely overlooking the future role of sound recording technology that Edison had already pioneered ten years earlier, not to mention the telephone, patented in 1876. Bellamy also imagined that the entire city population would gather for meals in great central refectories. In fact, his vision exemplifies the particular kind of myopia found in utopian visions: the tendency to project linear extrapolations of current conditions into the future, in Bellamy's case the centripetal and centralizing tendencies of the industrial city as it operated in the late 1800s.

Howard, who was a kind of highly intellectual tinkerer rather than a philosopher or technocrat, viewed the ghastly mess of expanding industrial London at its height and devised a hypothetical unit of new and improved development, which he called the Garden City. His instinct was probably correct at least in these respects: that ideally a city should grow by the replication of organically integral neighborhoods, rather than incoherent sprawl of monocultures, that the neighborhood unit should come complete with workplaces, homes, and shopping strategically deployed for health, convenience, and the reward of the human spirit, *and* that the lands beyond the urban edge ought to be maintained in rural condition, ideally for farming, that is, for the production of food for local consumption. He called this the "greenbelt," a term that still reverberates in our despair-laden public debates today, a century later.

Two elements of Howard's Garden City were a little screwy. One was the elaborate system of public ownership and finance that he must have spent far more hours working out than the actual design aspects of his utopia. They smacked of the kind of naïveté about human nature that would eventually lead Fabian socialism down the road to Lenin and Stalin. Howard's economics were based also on a calculus about the price of things, such as skilled labor, that are not necessarily constant over long periods of time. In short, Howard wasted a lot of energy on these financing details—as though the design of a new house in the year 2015 might be based on the hourly wage of sheetrock hangers and the cost of home heating oil in 1965.

The other screwy element of Howard's scheme was that his actual drawn plan of the proposed Garden City was completely diagrammatic, little more than a series of compass scribes transected by ruler lines with labels attached: "houses and gardens," "Boot factory," "Grand Avenue," "farm for epileptics." It made no more sense than the notorious "bubble diagrams" used with such profligacy by the suburban-planning officials of our day. Yet Howard's schematic idea was taken seriously and, miraculous to relate, brought to life in two actual new towns: the Letchworth and Welwyn Garden suburbs outside London. Howard even got to live for several years in each of them. He was a persuasive public speaker and a sedulous civic organizer.

Neither Letchworth nor Welwyn would have been possible without the work of the great civic designer Raymond Unwin and his partner Barry Parker, who were hired to translate Howard's crude schemata into actual street-and-block plans based on what was then state-of-the-art town-planning technique associated with streetcar and railroad suburb design, united with comprehensive plumbing, electric, and telephone service, and with provision for yet another new marvel, the automobile. Unwin and Parker's work was very similar in kind and execution to the suburban design work that could be seen all over the United States during the same period in new streetcar suburbs such as Shaker Heights, Ohio; Country Club Plaza in Kansas City; and Pasadena, California—an inevitable product of its time and circumstances. Howard succeeded in getting the suburban London municipalities to acquire the necessary land for Letchworth and Welwyn because there was a growing consensus in England by the turn of the twentieth century that industrialism might utterly ruin the little country if something was not tried to modify its effects on the landscape. Howard, therefore, eccentric dreamer that he was, came off as a brilliant prophet and successful innovator. He, personally, had not even anticipated the motorcar in his writings. In the original 1898 edition of *Garden Cities of To-morrow* (sic), he didn't mention the automobile once. Ebenezer Howard was knighted the year before his death.

A more complex actor in these issues was Howard's contemporary, the Scotsman Patrick Geddes (1854–1932), less concerned with experimental housing policy than with attempting to describe and comprehend the urban fiasco that industrialism had produced and prescribing future therapies. Both Howard and Geddes were in thrall to the terminology and methodologies of *science*—Howard with statistics and Geddes with charts—making them characteristic personalities of their age but also captives of its conventional thinking, a little too infatuated with the simple nostrums of *efficiency* and economic rationality that reflect ultimately the worst excesses of Taylorism and the assembly line.[10] This was particularly a loud and ironic chord in the work of Geddes, who understood how problematic industrialism had been, but still looked to scientific advance and technical solutions to mitigate the mess that had been made of the human habitat by previous technical advance. Both Howard and Geddes represent the still-keen faith in scientific progress tied to inevitable social progress that would be smashed by the industrial slaughter of a whole generation in the trenches of World War One.

Among other things, Geddes coined the useful pejorative terms "conurbation" and "megalopolis" to describe the urban condition at the turn of the twentieth century. He identified the previous two-hundred-odd years of industrialization as "paleotechnic" and the age just dawning around 1900 as "neotechnic." In this he was also visibly a captive of current intellectual fashion, as his terms obviously parallel the evolving argots of anthropology and sociology and remain in thrall to the notion of inevitable scientific progress. Geddes viewed town planning, too, as a scientific discipline that would evolve in the *neotech* "Eutopia"—and, seeking to make itself more "scientific" and hence respectable, the planning profession did indeed lose itself in the abstract wilderness of statistical analysis, where it has remained mired since Geddes's time. Geddes approved of the Garden City ideas of Ebenezer Howard, and of the work of Raymond Unwin. He gave very little attention to the effect that the automobile was having on the physical organization of life in Europe or America—though he lived until 1928, when cars had already become a nuisance. He made three trips to the United States in his life, the last in 1923 to lecture at the New School for Social Research, where he made a dazzling impression on twenty-three-year-old Lewis Mumford, who would elaborate Geddes's ideas about the history and meaning of *techne* in several books, while he absorbed and attempted to transform Geddes's town-planning theories (along with Howard's) for practical application in the period following the debacle of World War One. (Mumford would name his son "Geddes," and the boy would be killed in World War Two.)

The Olmsted Legacy and Its Strange Repercussions

Central Park settled Frederick Law Olmsted's career uncertainties and he spent the rest of his long life as America's leading landscape designer. Though he designed his park and parkway systems in some of America's great cities I do not think he can be called an "urbanist" in the sense Rybczynski would have us believe. In fact, I would consider him an unwitting antiurbanist because he established several ideas that made city life worse in general and exacerbated the public's confusion about the nature of place and the place of nature in the everyday environment. In trying to bring the country into the city, Olmsted to an unfortunate degree devalued the idea of the city per se, a condition that lingers in the goofy debates of our own time.

As I have said, Central Park, Prospect Park, the Emerald Necklace of Boston, and other major Olmsted landscape parks are all true works of art, and there is much about them that remains wonderful. But they must be understood as products of a period in history when the familiar countryside—and traditional ways of life associated with it—seemed to be vanishing under the urban industrial juggernaut. Olmsted's work was an attempt to preserve an artifact remnant of that beloved rural landscape within the city. This had at least two unfortunate repercussions. First, the Olmsted park, a large, rambling, picturesque construction, became the predominant, really the *sole,* model for park-making in America, the problem being that Olmsted's methods—indeed the methods and tradition of the rural English landscape park—cannot be used for other urban park typologies, *especially at small scale.* A neighborhood square cannot be composed of rambling vales and rocky defiles. The paved plaza is obviously unsuited to the vocabulary of picturesque earthworks decorated with botanical plantings. Olmsted's methods omit the one device that can avail on the small scale, and that is conscious rigorous formality of the kind that the French use so well to make trees, shrubs, flower beds, fountains, paths, pavements, and statuary integral with the surrounding urban hardscape of buildings. This kind of fine-grained formality is absent in American landscape design, and hence our dearth of small parks, squares, and small urban gardens. The only other element commonly present in American urban park design is sports facilities—ballfields, swimming pools, running tracks, and so forth.

The second unfortunate consequence of Olmstedism is partly a consequence of the first. Having left us with no tradition for creating the small urban park, or square, or modest green intercession in the hardscape at the scale of the block, the street, or the neighborhood, and combined with some of our other national proclivities, such as our monotonous use of the grid, and our zeal for real estate money-grubbing unchecked by aesthetic concerns, American cities compare very unfavorably with other American environments, namely the noncity, the rural and wild lands. We have a tradition since Olmsted of venerating the places of "nature" and holding in contempt the abode of human beings, loving the wilderness and hating the city. This is as deeply ingrained in American culture as the idea of free speech.

The Garden City movement in England was an attempt to mitigate huge, overwhelming forces of technology and explosive population growth by imposing something like the traditional neighborhood or village pattern out of England's own tradition against a background of runaway urban incoherence.[11] The Garden City movement was plucky, quaint, and a bit pathetic in a way that reflected perfectly Britain's national situation at the time—being on the verge of losing her empire, of becoming decadent, of being stuck with a vast, hideous landscape of obsolete industrial urban infrastructure, and of falling into the backwash of history. America, on the other hand, entering its high imperial moment after 1900, chose instead to ride the technological juggernaut.

Having established, through Olmsted and his disciples (including his son and nephew, who carried on the family business), the superiority of composed ruralesque landscapes and the hopelessness of urbanism proper, America embarked on the project of wholesale suburbanization, a process that still continues—really forming the basis of our millennial economy. I have described its perversities and shortcomings and will not rehearse even the aftertones except to make the point that the current reaction to suburban sprawl by politically progressive so-called "environmentalists" grows more abstract and futile every day.

This reaction proceeds in a direct line from Ebenezer Howard's Garden City movement, through Geddes, Mumford, and Benton MacKaye, the forester, "regional planner" (if there is such a thing), and godfather of "environmental conservation," through Ian McHarg's *Design With Nature* movement of the 1960s (which might have just as well been called the *Design Without Towns and Cities* movement), to the "environmental" policy victories over air and water pollution of the 1980s, to the current generation of "green space" and "open space" advocates, who are all deeply concerned about the unbuilt, rural, and wild places but show no interest in the subject of urbanism, of the design of the place where the people ought to live, namely the town, the city, the neighborhood, or the village.

Open Space, Green Space, and
Other Fatuous Abstractions

I was in Missoula, Montana, a few years ago to give an illustrated talk called "Can America Survive Suburbia," and, having come in early the night before, was invited to attend a meeting of the city council the day of my spiel. There, in the kind of typically ignoble municipal meeting room that could as easily have been a wholesale beverage warehouse, the citizens and officials divided into two factions, Pro-Growth and Anti-Growth, and sat or stood hollering at each other about the issue of the day, which, naturally enough, had to do with a new proposed "development."

The Pro-Growthers predictably ranted about "property rights" because in the American West the idea that there is plenty of space to be left alone in has been extended to include the incongruent notion that land ownership therefore entails no duties, obligations, or responsibilities whatsoever to the public interest. It is enough to simply state that this argument is without merit or precedent in U.S. history. Anyway, the opponents of the development at issue, the Anti-Growthers, one by one got up and made impassioned speeches about "open space." The problem with Missoula, they contended, was that it did not "have" enough "open space."

This was very funny because Missoula happened to be located in a part of the country where you could walk five minutes out of town in any direction and find yourself facing the greatest contiguous wilderness in the lower forty-eight states, including man-eating bears, cougars, and other bioregional incunabula. The problem as I saw it from a civic design point of view was that Missoula had too much "open space" *right there in the center of town.* As in many towns of the American West, Missoula's streets were uniformly too wide and its buildings too low and too spread out with too many parking lots between them. Civic space in Missoula was poorly defined, the building façades were of a uniformly dreary, artless quality, on the whole poorly maintained, too, and there was no systematic planting of street trees. The only dedicated park was located in the flood plain of the Blackfoot River, and its only design feature, besides an absence of houses and stores, was a lonely carousel standing in the slush-covered hardpan. The edge of the city—indeed much of the land along its main traffic arteries, too—contained the usual horrific clusterfuck of chain stores, franchise fry-pits, muffler shops, parking lagoons, and the rest of the typical nauseating furnishings of drive-in commerce found in every American town, big and small. The trouble with Missoula was not a lack of open space. The problem was that everything it contained was poorly made, not worth caring about, and unworthy of the condition of collective self-respect called civilization. But there was nothing special about it by American standards. They asked my opinion, of course, and I told them what I thought. I hasten to add that I did not change their minds. The Open Space fanatics complained that I was cracked in the head, and of course their opponents thought I was slandering the Land of the Free and the Home of the Brave.

Wherever I go in the United State these days, it's the same story. We want Open Space, that's all. We ask for an abstraction, and an abstraction is delivered—in the form of bark-mulch berms planted with juniper shrubs and other such landscape "buffers" between the Kmart and the apartment "complex." We get these little cartoons of the countryside deployed everywhere, and we are no better off for them. We want these "nature" Band-Aids because the wound to our urbanism cannot heal. We cannot even imagine it will heal: The scores of thousands of discount malls, and the subdivisions of vinyl doublewide manufactured "homes," and the tragic collector boulevards lined with "power centers," and the high schools with ample parking for the whole senior class, and all the rest of the cheap, ugly, provisional stuff that we've filled our world up with is too much with us. We gave up on the human habitat in America generations ago. Now we just grimly put up with what we're stuck with until the next annual trip to admire the scenery in a sacred "wilderness," such as Yosemite. Heaven, for Americans, is a landscape by Capability Brown with sand traps, numbered holes, and convenient free parking.

It's not hard to believe that we are hopeless.

In a Little Hampstead Wood

A few months after that depressing visit to Missoula, I found myself exploring London again, that immense stately pudding of a city, its plumbing and sanitation substantially improved since Queen Victoria's day, but its layout still completely disorienting—even to someone with a confident sense of direction. Its nineteenth-century neighborhoods of houses originally built for the likes of maritime mutual assurance clerks and tea company regional merchandise inventory managers are now occupied by internet hotshots and performance artists. Its Dickensian slums have been replaced by the infamous postwar council flats where the superfluous poor are now organized vertically instead of horizontally and have become accustomed to plumbing. England has enjoyed a twenty-year swim in North Sea oil profits. When those fields of petroleum pass peak production—and they are expected to do so after the year 2001—then we shall really see about the age of neotech and the global economic miracle.

I entered the great park called Hampstead Heath at the north end in the vicinity of Hampstead Lane and Bishops Avenue. I came shortly into an area called the North Wood. It had the character of a real woods, too, not like the bosky little rambles of Central Park where the understory is all worn away from the traffic of basketball shoes, but as though you were truly in an ancient natural landscape of mature forest. You could not see through it to the open meadows and verges on the other side. It was rather dim under its full July canopy of foliage. Though a little daunted by some residual primate fear of a dark and gloomy wood, I pressed forward down a little gully and into the thick of this pretend wilderness. Seconds later, I was surprised—a little shocked really—to see the shadowy figure of a man pop out from behind a stout tree. I quickly ascertained that he was dressed in a business suit, and a rather well-cut one at that, perhaps even Armani. I went on to surmise that he had been taking a leak behind a tree. I kept my eyes on him as I passed by. He returned my gaze intently in a way that left me less than entirely comfortable. Perhaps, I mused, he was some sort of park detective, and it was I who looked suspicious to him. Who knew? I was a foreigner in a strange land with different customs.

But I'd proceeded barely a few steps further along my way when out from behind another tree popped another man, this one dressed in the kind of banlon shirt and tight trousers of the working class. He at once started combing his ample head of hair in a rather strangely demonstrative way, as though he were giving a lesson in hair-combing. I passed him by, too. And then I saw a third man and a fourth, popping out of the greenery like characters in a penny-arcade shoot'-em-up game. Or like figures in one of those spooky George Tooker paintings that describe with such intense, cold-blooded perfection the loneliness of crowds in a metropolis. And that's when I finally understood: I had just passed through a pick-up glade.

It suddenly seemed fitting, here, in an anomalous interruption of the great city's dense fabric, in an archetypal place of gloom and mystery, to come upon a market for the more furtive, shadowy assertions of human desire. It seemed oddly logical to think that all the lofty Arcadian dreams of the English placemakers, through all the viccissitudes of landscape, had led finally to this somewhat sordid destination. The human spirit is a deep vessel and the human heart is a strange engine. Put them in a darkling wood and all the lights of the surrounding city may not avail to guide home the personality that has truly lost its way. The same is true of a culture in general.

Me, I came out of those woods and made my way through a series of lovely sunlit hay meadows, strangely unpeopled, and down a little dirt lane that might have been a farm-to-market road not much more than a century and a half before, which eventually opened onto the grand sweep of Parliament Hill, with the immense groaning city spread out in a gray haze below, and then past the groomed grounds of the cricket players and the soccer players and the bathing ponds surrounded by their lovely old trees swaying like women gathered at a sacred pool to wash their hair, and I burst out of this strange rural fragment of territory back into the streets of bustling London town and caught a bus back to the little hotel on Frith Street to meet my wife for whiskies in soft leather chairs by the bumpered fireplace and tell her all about my adventures.

Notes

Paris

1. In July 1830, Charles X was thrown out by the postrevolutionary rich who had inherited much of the wealth of the Ancien Régime and resented Charles's attempted to re-Bourbonize the nation. Louis-Philippe, duke of Orleans, was installed on the throne and remained there until 1848, when the widespread upheavals of bourgeoning industrialism sent him packing. Louis-Philippe's eighteen-year reign was ever after known as the July Monarchy.

2. Louis-Napoleon was the son of Napoleon I's brother Louis Bonaparte (king of Holland, 1806–10) and Hortense de Beauharnais Bonaparte, stepdaughter of Napoleon I. "I am my uncle's nephew," he liked to proclaim ironically about his fate.

3. *The City as a Work of Art,* by Donald J. Olsen (New Haven: Yale University Press, 1986).

4. They still reverberate in the shrill cries of suburban American NIMBYs in their quixotic war against "density," a curious testament to the persistence of cultural memory.

5. The masonry walls and bastions formed a thirty-five-kilometer ring around the city. They proved utterly ineffective during the Franco-Prussian War in 1870, when the Germans easily lobbed artillery shells over them into the city. The last of the fortifications was not entirely demolished until 1932.

6. Sebastiano Serlio (1475–1554), Italian architect and theorist who introduced the principles of classical architecture into France.

7. Charles X (b.1757, d. 1836), brother of Louis XVI, former Count d'Artois.

8. Olsen.

9. The second floor sometimes came in the vestigial form of the *entresol,* which in former times was a second-floor business loft or storage area for the ground-floor trade establishment.

NOTES

10. Charles Garnier's Opera House being the most extravagant and eclectic exception, with its orgasmic festoons, exuberant statuary, and deep relief—though it, too, featured plenty of classical elements.

11. *The Second French Empire,* Edward A. Crane, ed. (New York: Appleton and Co., 1905), p. 146.

Atlanta

1. The *Atlanta Constitution,* February 28, 2000, Section C, p. 8.

2. "Atlanta Megasprawl," by Robert D. Bullard, Glenn B. Johnson, and Angel O. Torres, Forum for Applied Research and Public Policy, Volume 14, Number 3, Fall 1999. Published jointly by the University of Tennessee's Energy, Environment, and Resources Center and TVA Rural Studies at the University of Kentucky.

3. "Suburban Comforts Thwart Atlanta's Plans to Limit Sprawl," by David Firestone, *The New York Times,* November 21, 1999, p. 1.

4. The thirteen-county region ruled noncompliant for air quality by the EPA, mentioned earlier in the chapter, includes three more counties beyond the ten within the jurisdiction of the Atlanta Regional Commission.

5. Harvested cotton acreage in Georgia declined 35 percent from 1914 to 1930, and total production fell 40 percent. Since then, the boll weevil has been controlled, but not eradicated, using a range of pesticides from calcium arsenate to DDT to Guthion and Malathion, which have themselves led to additional and consequential pollution problems. Figures from the University of Georgia College of Agriculture and Environmental Sciences, Research Bulletin Number 428, November 1998.

6. Willis H. Carrier is credited with the "air-washing" refinements that significantly controlled the humidity in artificially cooled air to make it really comfortable. He went on to become a major manufacturer of air-conditioning equipment.

7. The so-called OPEC (Organization of Petroleum Exporting Countries) oil embargo of 1973 and the OPEC price hike in 1979 were intense, acute events that had severe consequences for the national economy through the 1970s to the mid-1980s and caused extraordinary adjustments in government policy (such as a national fifty-five-mile-an-hour speed limit). But by the 1990s, these events were largely, and rather strangely, forgotten. The American public was paying less for gasoline in constant dollars than ever before, and it had gone back to sleepwalking through the issue of petroleum dependency.

8. *Atlanta Rising,* by Frederick Allen (Atlanta: Longstreet Press, 1996), p. 137.

9. Margaret Mitchell was struck by a taxicab on Peachtree Street August 11, 1949, and died five days later.

10. Probably the greatest victim was Detroit, whose Portman-designed Renais-

sance Center has been a white elephant for a quarter of a century, in the heart of a downtown whose utter desolation is now complete. The Ren-Cen possessed some additional elements of extreme fortification at street level that made it nearly impregnable to pedestrians. It was built by Henry Ford II, who, unable to find tenants for it, moved thousands of Ford employees in as economic window-dressing. In 1998, the megastructure was sold to General Motors.

11. Allen, p. 197.

12. Back in 1982, Atlanta Braves pitcher Pascual Perez gained renown for getting lost on the I-285 perimeter highway and missing his scheduled start in a night game. Driving the sixty-one-mile circumference for hours, Perez later said he could not find a downtown exit off the freeway.

13. *Physicians Weekly,* Volume XVII, Number 1, January 3, 2000, p. 1.

14. Andres Duany and Elizabeth Plater-Zyberk (born 1949, 1950), the principals of the town-planning firm DPZ. Their excellent book, *Suburban Nation: the Rise and Decline of the American Dream* (New York: Farrar, Straus & Giroux, 2000), written also with DPZ's project director Jeff Speck, is the most coherent discussion extant of the problem and its solution.

15. Andres Duany explained in a December 1999 interview with the author: "We tend to find lots of savings in infrastructure. We discovered that we could eliminate a road which had been the *grand gesture* of the local guy. His credibility was at stake. So, when our revised plan went back to them, they weakened it considerably. For instance, we had wanted to retain the great steel sheds [from the old steel works] to use for markets. They erased them. The plan will probably be built, but it will be diagrammatic."

16. The concept of peak oil production, a subject laden with political and economic implications, was first advanced by the geologist M. King Hubbert at the Colorado School of Mines in 1949. He predicted that the fossil fuel era would be of surprisingly short duration. His further prediction in 1956 that U.S. oil production would peak about 1970 and decline thereafter was scoffed at then, but his analysis has since proved to be remarkably accurate. He went on to predict that total world oil production would peak between 1995 and 2010. There is little disagreement about this among geologists today. In a response to Exxon Corporation's David Nissen in 1982, Hubbert famously remarked, "So long as oil is used as a source of energy, when the energy cost of recovering a barrel of oil becomes greater than the energy content of the oil, production will cease no matter what the monetary price may be." NBS Special Publication 631, pp. 140–41.

17. See *Home From Nowhere,* by the author of this book, Chapter One.

18. *The Collapse of Complex Societies,* Joseph A. Tainter (Cambridge, UK.: Cambridge University Press, 1988).

NOTES

Mexico City

1. Recorded by the priest Bernardino de Sahagun, prepared in Nahautl in 1555 from accounts of surviving native eyewitnesses, with emendations 1585, and collected in the Florentine Codex, the most complete indiginous account of the conquest of Mexico.

2. *The Origins of Consciousness in the Breakdown of the Bicameral Mind,"* by Julian Jaynes (Boston: Houghton-Mifflin, 1976).

3. Jaynes also observes that virtually all modern religions are based on the worship of gods who have, in one way or another, abandoned their subjects.

4. *The Biography of a City,* by Jonathan Kendell, p. 51

5. "An Ecological Basis for Aztec Sacrifice," by Michael J. Harner, *American Ethologist.* Volume IV, Number 1. pp. 117–35.

6. *Cannibals and Kings: The Origins of Cultures,* by Marvin Harris (New York: Random House. 1977). p. 99

7. Ibid., p. 105.

8. Ibid., p. 109.

9. *Cortes and Montezuma,* by Maurice Collis (New York: Harcourt, Brace and Company, 1954).

10. From *The Codex Florentino,* compiled by Fray Bernardino de Sahagun, c. 1555. Included in *The Broken Spears: The Aztec Account of the Conquest of Mexico,* Miguel Leon-Portilla, ed. Translated from Nahuatl by Angel Maria Garibay K. English translation by Lysander Kemp. (Boston: Beacon Press. 1962), p. 33

11. Ibid., p. 35.

12. *The Conquest of New Spain,* by Bernal Díaz, translation by J. M. Cohen (Harmondsworth, Middlesex, England, Penguin Books, 1963).

13. Ibid., p. 387.

14. For reasons that should be obvious, I cannot reveal the identity of my informant.

15. "In the first four months of 1998, more than 650 tourists were assaulted by Mexico City's taxi drivers" "Labyrinth of Solitude," by Paul Berman, *The New York Times Magazine,* August 2, 1998.

16. In the 1860s, it was so common for stagecoaches from Veracruz to be attacked by bandits en route to Mexico City that hotels kept blankets on hand to wrap up arriving guests who had been robbed of everything down to their underwear.

17. The system has 110 miles of track and 154 stations, roughly comparable to the Paris Métro. Though I was repeatedly warned against it, I took the subway all over, and found it to be dependable and easy to understand. No one bothered me there.

18. See note 14.

Notes

19. In August 1998, Swiss drug police rooted out the bank accounts of Raúl Salinas de Gortari, brother of former Mexican president Carlos Salinas de Gortari. The accounts contained a sum equal to $132 million. Raúl Salinas has been in a maximum-security Mexican prison on charges of ordering the assassination of a political enemy in the PRI, Mexico's long-dominant political party. He claimed that the money in the Swiss banks came from Mexican industrialists and were intended for "investment." His brother Carlos, the former president, stepped down a few months before the collapse of the national economy in 1994. He lives in exile in Ireland. Source: *The New York Times*, Tuesday, August 4, 1998, p. A8.

Berlin

1. *The Ghosts of Berlin*, by Brian Ladd (Chicago: University of Chicago Press, 1997), p. 18.
2. *Modern Times*, by Paul Johnson (New York: Harper and Row, 1983), p. 111.
3. *Hitler's State Architecture: The Impact of Classical Antiquity*, by Alex Scobie (University Park, Pa., and London: Pennsylvania University Press, 1990).
4. *Berlin, the Politics of Order*, by Alan Balfour (New York: Rizzoli, 1990), p. 86.
5. Ibid., p. 175.
6. Ladd, p. 98.
7. "The New Berlin: A Phoenix Rises From the Rubble of History," by Alan Riding, *The New York Times*, April 11, 1999, Arts & Leisure.
8. Not to be confused with Daniel Libeskind's Jewish Museum half a mile south in the Kreuzberg district. Upon visiting Libeskind's museum for the first time, ninety-three-year-old Phillip Johnson (Harvard, 1927), a fascist sympathizer in the 1930s, called it "the best Holocaust memorial I've ever seen."

Las Vegas

1. There was an additional problem with two major dry washes, named the Flamingo and the Tropicana, which crossed what is now the middle of the Strip at a perfect diagonal. These were classic desert arroyos that were dry 99 percent of the time, but that could, at unpredictable intervals, be subject to catastrophic flash flooding.
2. Palms have relatively small root balls. Mature trees can be plucked out, moved on a flatbed truck, and easily transplanted, giving the illusion of a tree that has been growing in place for a long time.
3. *Cadillac Desert*, by Marc Reisner (New York: Viking Penguin, 1986).
4. Author's interview, May 1998.

NOTES

5. Summerlin was originally started by the Hughes Corporation but was sold in 1998 to the Rouse Corporation.

Rome

1. The aggregate stone used in the concrete was ingeniously graded from the heaviest basalt, used around the base of the walls, to lighter volcanic tufa in the base of the dome, and finally ultralight pumice used in the highest reaches of the dome's coffered vaults.

2. The word *classic* "is closely related to the oldest Latin root, *classicus,* pertaining to a process of classification into groups by some sort of rank, or especially to the highest rank or quality, particularly as that quality was later identified by its durability as a useful standard of excellence. By classic we therefore mean an exemplar whose distinction is proven by a longstanding consensus of esteem." From "Who Put the 'Ism' in Classicism? A Theory of Authority," by John E. Hancock, *Classicist,* Number 1, 1994.

3. The Etruscans were already practicing a crude form of Greek architecture, having migrated to Italy from Asia Minor. Meanwhile, the Greeks had established colonies all over the Italian peninsula and Sicily, complete with monumental buildings, and the superiority of their architecture must have been self-evident to the larval Romans.

4. Vitruvius was an obscure figure in his own time and culture. There are no references to him in other Roman texts. Interest in him dates from Carolingian times, increasing in the High Middle Ages, and leading during the Renaissance to fame as his *Ten Books* were rescued by Alberti, Serlio, Vignola, Palladio and others. "In the history of architecture there is probably no other example of a systematic textbook aiming at contemporary influence, missing its target, and yet achieving such overwhelming success centuries after its appearance." Herbert Koch, 1951, *Vom Nachleben der Vitruvius.*

5. The time of Augustus (aka Caius Octavius or Octavian) was an age of political upheaval. The civil wars that followed Julius Caesar's assassination in 44 B.C. went on for a long time and the Romans must have been relieved when the turmoil finally ended with the defeat of Marc Antony (by Agrippa) at the Battle of Actium, 30 B.C. Henceforth, the prudent Augustus assumed extraordinary authority, but the Roman populace had no way of knowing that Augustus's reign would usher in nearly five hundred years of imperial rule. He eventually received other titles from the Senate besides *princeps,* including *imperator* (commander) and *pontifex maximus* (supreme priest). The summer month Sextilus was renamed Augustus in his honor. After death he was deified, establishing a dubious new tradition. During Augustus's lifetime,

Notes

however, empire and all its trapping were still a novelty for the Romans, who found themselves making up a new postrepublican political culture on the fly, as it were.

6. The aftermath of the great fire of A.D. 64, said to have been aggravated when the emperor Nero ordered the Roman fire companies to sit on their hands, allowed Nero to extensively rebuild the city. Scoundrel that he was (murderer of his mother and wife, among many others), Nero introduced an ambitious urban modernization program of broad new streets and new buildings based on all the architectural elements that Augustus had disdained: the arch, the vault, and reinforced concrete.

7. The exception being caryatids, columns carved to represent human figures, such as those on the Erechtheum in Athens. The only other examples from classical antiquity were found on two small treasury structures at Delphi.

8. The architect Leon Krier has a theory that buildings unworthy of affection and respect inevitably acquire nicknames.

9. The four familiar and prominent minarets associated with the Hagia Sofia were added after the Ottoman conquest of 1453 when the building became a mosque. It is a museum now.

10. The Mongols under Genghis Khan swept up the floor with the Seljuks around A.D. 1220. The Mongols did not occupy Turkey, and in the vacuum that followed the Ottoman Turkish dynasty established itself, eventually to become a major world power.

11. The Romans had used this template everywhere in their empire but Rome itself, which, due to its antiquity and hilly topography, remained a city of twisting, torturous streets.

12. The interior of Charlemagne's palatine chapel at Aachen employs sets of Corinthian columns more as decorative elements.

13. The Vikings and the Magyars were particularly adept at burning down churches.

14. There was talk of beheading or defenestrating Cosimo, but this was overridden by concern over the reaction of Cosimo's customers, including many heads of state who depended on him as a lender.

15. Poggio, as he is known to history, was born the son of a poor apothecary but became a leading scholar in the generation that preceded Alberti's. Like Alberti, he served as a papal functionary and studied law. "Resourceful, charming, cheerful, convivial, humorous . . . he was not above bribing monks . . . in seeking out manuscripts in Germany, France, and Switzerland." Among other volumes he unearthed were Lucretius's *De Rerum Natura,* a history by Ammianus Marcellinus, a work on education by Quintilian, and a cookbook by Apicius. Cosimo considered Poggio's personal handwriting a model for all his scribes, and early Italian printers based their

NOTES

typefaces on it. A shrewd businessman, he eventually became rich and was treated as a friend and intimate equal of Cosimo de' Medici. *The Rise and Fall of the House of the Medici,* by Christopher Hibbert (New York: Morrow, 1974).

16. Michelozzo (1396–1472), a colleague and collaborator of Donatello, was primarily a sculptor. There should be little question that he was familiar with the ideas contained in the Medici Vitruvius, if not with the text itself. The artistic and intellectual world of Florence in the age of Cosimo was a very tight circle.

17. Gutenberg (1397–1468) worked slowly, systematically, and secretly on his invention, taking on partners and investors along the way. He had intended to become rich mass-producing Bibles. His first was printed in 1455. A lawsuit brought by one investor, Johann Fust, a goldsmith, compelled Gutenberg to reveal in court exactly what he was working on. Fust was awarded Gutenberg's equipment in addition to cash and went on to print Bibles himself.

18. Antonio da Sangallo the Younger (1483–1546). The whole family was a development and architecture firm. His Farnese Palace in Rome, completed by Michelangelo, codified many of the conventions of the High Renaissance.

19. As seen in the chapter on Haussmann's renovation of Paris, residences for different income groups can be organized vertically to occupy the same building, too.

20. *The Classical Vernacular: Architectural Principles in Age of Nihilism,* by Roger Scruton (New York: St. Martin's Press, 1994).

Boston

1. See *Home From Nowhere* (1996) and *The Geography of Nowhere* (1993) for a full description of the catastrophe.

2. Beacon Hill was originally named Sentry Hill, while Mt. Vernon was sometimes called Mt. Hoardam or Whoredom on account of activities that took place there during the Revolutionary War.

3. There is a different Fort Hill in Roxbury today.

4. Walter Gropius (1883–1969). Seminal modernist guru. Director of the German Bauhaus (formerly Weimar School of Art), and from 1937 to 1952 head of the Department of Architecture at the Harvard Graduate School of Design. After that, an architect in private practice. His most visible work was New York's Pan Am Building (now called the Met Life Building).

5. The full gruesome story, with adumbrations both forward and back, is told in *Planning the City Upon a Hill,* by Laurence W. Kennedy (Amherst: University of Massachusetts Press, 1992).

6. This is the theory of John R. Stilgoe, author of *Borderlands* and other books on urban history and professor at Harvard.

NOTES

7. *Major tourist attraction* sounds hopeless, I suppose, but American cities, by and large, are so uninviting that any decent fragment of civic form is apt to be regarded as extra special.

8. Author's interview with Edward J. Logue, February 1999.

9. *The City Observed: Boston,* by Donlyn Lyndon (New York: Random House, 1982), p. 196.

10. When air moves over a surface, pressure decreases on one side, causing "lift" from the now relatively greater air pressure on the reverse side, as with the wing of an airplane.

11. Figures from the Central Artery/Tunnel Project (Mass. Turnpike Authority) http://www.bigdig.com, May 1999.

London

1. Charles II had agreed to support Presbyterianism when he accepted the throne of Scotland in 1651, but he married Catherine of Braganza, a Catholic, in 1662. He formally declared himself a Catholic in 1670 to pursue a third war against the Dutch.

2. *Upon the Gardens of Epicurus,* by William Temple (1685).

3. The ha-ha: a kind of ditch and bastion intended to contain livestock without disturbing an open field of view.

4. *The Age of Reason,* by Harold Nicolson (London: Constable and Company, 1960), p. 399.

5. *Country Residences,* by J. C. Loudon (1806).

6. Mumford was born in New York City in 1900, on the eve of the Progressive Era in politics, when the problems of the industrial city began to be recognized and addressed.

7. *The Culture of Cities,* by Lewis Mumford (New York: Harcourt, Brace and Company, 1938), pp. 179, 195, 198.

8. *London: the Biography of a City,* by Christopher Hibbert (London: Longmans, Green, and Co., 1969).

9. *A Clearing in the Distance: Frederick Law Olmsted and America in the Nineteenth Century,* by Witold Rybczynski (New York: Scribner, 1999).

10. Frederic Winslow Taylor (1856–1915), the father of "scientific management" in the industrial factory. 11. By "traditional neighborhood or village" I mean a unit of urban development based on a quarter-mile radius from the center, composed of a street-and-block pattern, with streets interconnecting, and ranging in transect from dense building at the center to sparser building at the edge. One traditional neighborhood of this type will make a hamlet or village, several a town, many (plus special-use districts) a city.

Index

INDEX

INDEX

JAMES HOWARD KUNSTLER is the author of two previous nonfiction books, *The Geography of Nowhere* and *Home from Nowhere,* and eight novels. His articles appear regularly in *The New York Times, Atlantic Monthly, Slate,* and *Metropolis.*